Understanding Schools and Schooling

Understanding Schools and Schooling explores the contemporary history of compulsory education, focusing particularly on the secondary sector. It provides an overview of educational policy and organisation through key issues, events and documents. Topics covered include:

- The administration of government policy since the 1944 Education Act
- The development and implementation of the National Curriculum
- Recent educational policy changes under New Labour
- The impact of changes on teachers and pupils
- Possibilities for the future of secondary education

Punctuated by questions, points for consideration and ideas for further reading, *Understanding Schools and Schooling* provides a comprehensive framework of educational history and theory within which readers can develop informed opinions on the nature of secondary education.

Clyde Chitty taught English and history in a number of London comprehensive schools for over a decade before moving to Leicestershire in 1977 to become Senior Vice-Principal and later Principal of a pioneering community college. Between 1985 and 1997, he taught in the Curriculum Studies Department at the Institute of Education, London University, and then in the School of Education at the University of Birmingham. He is currently Professor of Policy and Management in Education and Head of the Department of Educational Studies at Goldsmiths College. He is the author, co-author or editor of over thirty books and reports on education, and is co-editor of the campaigning educational journal *Forum*.

Key Issues In Teaching and Learning
Series Editor: Alex Moore

Key Issues in Teaching and Learning is aimed at student teachers, teacher trainers and in-service teachers. Each book will focus on the central issues around a particular topic supported by examples of good practice with suggestions for further reading. These accessible books will help students and teachers to explore and understand critical issues in ways that are challenging, that invite reappraisals of current practices and that provide appropriate links between theory and practice.

Teaching and Learning: Pedagogy, Curriculum and Culture
Alex Moore

Reading Educational Research and Policy
David Scott

Understanding Assessment: Purposes, Perceptions, Practice
David Lambert and David Lines

Understanding Schools and Schooling
Clyde Chitty

Understanding Schools and Schooling

Clyde Chitty

London and New York

First published 2002 by RoutledgeFalmer
11 New Fetter Lane, London EC4P 4EE

Simultaneously published in the USA and Canada
by RoutledgeFalmer
29 West 35th Street, New York, NY 10001

RoutledgeFalmer is an imprint of the Taylor & Francis Group

© 2002 Clyde Chitty

Typeset in Bembo by Keystroke, Jacaranda Lodge, Wolverhampton
Printed and bound in Great Britain by TJ International Ltd, Padstow, Cornwall

British Library Cataloguing in Publication Data
A catalogue record for this book is available from the British Library

Library of Congress Cataloging in Publication Data
Chitty, Clyde.
 Understanding schools and schooling / Clyde Chitty.
   p. cm. — (Key issues in teaching and learning)
 Includes bibliographical references (p.) and index.
 ISBN 0–415–23879–X
 1. Education, Secondary—Great Britain—History—20th century.
 2. Education and state—Great Britain—History—20th century.
 I. Title. II. Series.

LA634 .C47 2002
379.41—dc21

                                                        2001041604

ISBN 0–415–23879–X

For Hitesh

Contents

Tables

Acknowledgements

My thanks are due to all my students at Goldsmiths College, who have heard many of the ideas outlined in this book at lectures and seminars over the past three years and have never been reluctant to come forward with constructive criticism and advice. I also owe a special debt of gratitude to Margaret Brittain and Lesley Yorke, who have played such an active role in the preparation of the manuscript in its final form, and to the Series Editor Alex Moore for all his helpful suggestions with regard to layout, style and student activities.

Series Editor's Preface

THE KEY ISSUES IN TEACHING AND LEARNING SERIES

Understanding Schools and Schooling is one of five books in the series *Key Issues in Teaching and Learning*, each written by an acknowledged expert or experts in their field. Other volumes explore issues of *Teaching and Learning, Understanding Assessment*, and *Reading Educational Research and Policy*. The books are intended primarily for beginner and newly or recently qualified teachers but will also be of interest to more experienced teachers attending MA or Professional Development courses or simply interested in revisiting issues of theory and practice within an ever-changing educational context. *Understanding Schools and Schooling* will also prove an invaluable reference book for a wide range of professional and lay readers involved in compulsory education, including school governors and school inspectors.

TEACHING AND THEORISING

There is currently no shortage of books about teaching, offering what must sometimes seem a bewildering choice. Many of these books fall into the 'how-to' category, offering practical tips and advice for teachers on a range of matters such as planning for students' learning, managing classroom behaviour, and marking and assessing students' work. Such books have proved very successful over the years, providing beginner teachers in particular with much of the support and reassurance they need to help them through their early experiences of classroom life, as well as offering useful advice on how to make teaching maximally effective. Increasingly, such books focus on sets of teacher competences – more recently linked to sets of standards – laid down, in England and Wales, by the Office for Standards in Education (OFSTED) and the Teacher Training Agency (TTA) (see, for instance, OFSTED and TTA 1996). Other books have focused on the teacher's need to be reflective and reflexive (e.g. Schon 1983, 1987; Valli 1992; Elliott 1993; Loughran 1996). These books may still be described as 'advice books', but the advice is of a different kind, tending to encourage the teacher to think more about human relationships in the teaching–learning situation and on the ways in which teaching styles connect to models of learning and learning development.

More predominantly theoretical books about teaching for teachers are perhaps in shorter supply, and those that do exist often address issues in decontextualised ways or in very general terms that do not immediately speak to classroom practitioners or take account of their particular academic backgrounds. There is, furthermore, evidence that, partly through time constraints, some of the most profound works on sociological educational theory are very little read or discussed on teacher training courses (Moore and Edwards 2000), while the work of developmental psychologists, which used to feature very prominently on PGCE and BAEd courses, has become increasingly marginalised through a growing emphasis on issues of practical discipline, lesson planning and meeting National Curriculum requirements.

Understanding Schools and Schooling, like the other books in the *Key Issues in Teaching and Learning* series, seeks to address this imbalance by exploring with teachers a range of relevant educational theory and policy, rooting this in professional experience in a way that encourages understanding, interrogation and debate, and presenting it in language that is immediately accessible. None of the books in the series ignores or seeks to devalue current trends in educational practice and policy. Rather they all strive to provide readers with the knowledge, skills and *contexts* they will need in order to address and respond to these and other educational discourses in critical, well-informed ways that will enhance both their teaching and their job satisfaction.

UNDERSTANDING SCHOOLS AND SCHOOLING

With this aim in mind, *Understanding Schools and Schooling* sets out to provide readers with a 'contemporary history' of current arrangements for schools and schooling, particularly in the secondary sector, and of the central and local policies that underpin them. In doing this, it provides a historical, political and cultural context within which readers may develop more informed and critical understandings of key issues to do with:

- the ways in which schools are organised and the impact of this on their own practice;
- the ways in which their own working lives are controlled and organised;
- the priorities and values implicit and often contested within schools and schooling, particularly through value-laden educational *policies*.

Understanding Schools and Schooling is broad in its scope, tackling a range of organisational and political issues that will be of central importance to teachers' developing educational philosophies and understandings of their work. These include political and professional attitudes to various forms of prejudice, discrimination and exclusion; issues related to the historical and political underpinnings of the National Curriculum for England and Wales; the philosophy and practical implications of Local Management of Schools and Grant Maintained status; teachers' Conditions of Service; and, at the end of the book, current political agendas and their implications, including the currently popular discourse of 'the Third Way'.

As the title of the book implies, *Understanding Schools and Schooling* does not seek to present contemporary educational history didactically but rather offers a series of critiqued accounts of key issues, events, interviews, political documents, newspaper stories and details of legislative frameworks, by way of inviting readers to construct their own programme for developing better understandings of the broader contexts of their work and of the possibilities for developing more effective individual and collective practice within those contexts. This approach is supported through suggestions for further reading, and through guided activities and discussion topics situated at the end of each chapter. While these readings and activities can be undertaken independently, they are designed so that they can also be completed collaboratively, providing the basis for small-group discussions on BAEd, PGCE, MA and Professional Development courses for teachers. As with other volumes in the *Key Issues in Teaching and Learning* series, boxes have been used in the body of the text to highlight particularly important points or useful summaries.

STRUCTURE AND CONTENT OF THE BOOK

The book begins with an account of the different values behind and rationales for universal formal education, inviting the reader, through reference to the specific values of *individual fulfilment, preparation for the world of work* and *the promotion of social progress and social change*, to consider such questions as 'What is education for?' 'What values might underpin the "contents" of formal education?' 'Whose values might these be?' and 'What and whose interests might they serve?'

These ideas are built on in Chapters 2 and 3, via an insightful account of the ways in which values have underpinned central government policy on education, with particular reference to matters concerning the *organisation* and *administration* of education and schools. These chapters chart the political development of the underlying principle of 'a national system locally administered' that existed at the time of the 1944 Education Act, tracing its history to present-day practices that incorporate such important and contentious matters as greater financial autonomy for schools within an externally driven marketplace, the changing status and role of school governors, increased competition for places, and increased government interference in pedagogy and curriculum content. Effectively describing the history of comprehensive education in England and Wales, these chapters invite readers to assess the extent to which the comprehensive ideal has resisted or succumbed to the pressures of conservative ideologies and the marketplace, and to reassess the extent to which comprehensive schools are addressing – or might address – continuing social problems and the needs of the most underprivileged sections of society.

Chapters 4 and 5 take up and develop the theme of *curriculum* change through an account of the origins and development of the National Curriculum for England and Wales and the various political and ideological arguments that took place during its construction. These chapters offer not only an account of the National

Curriculum for England and Wales as it is currently configured but also of the nature and significance of the changes and developments undergone by the Curriculum since its initial introduction. These chapters prompt readers to debate important questions about the structure and content of the current school curriculum, who should be in 'control' of the curriculum, the value and limitations of standardised testing, and possible alternative curricula based on models rejected or overlooked by central governments.

In Chapter 6, our attention is directed to more immediate educational reforms, concentrating on the educational policies and initiatives of 'New Labour' in the years following the general election of 1997, and the claim to put 'Education, Education, Education' at the top of the political agenda. Exploring such initiatives as Education Action Zones and the attempted reintroduction of setting and streaming, the reader is invited again to consider what comprehensive education means at the start of the new millennium in England and Wales, what it *might* mean in the future, how far it is effective in promoting equality and social justice, and the extent to which the educational policies of New Labour perpetuate or inhibit the efforts of earlier Conservative administrations to modify or undermine the comprehensive system.

Chapters 7 and 8 take our attention away from the broad sweep of educational reform in curriculum and organisation to issues that impact on teachers' and students' lives in very particular, often differentiated, ways. In Chapter 7, we are given a brief but important account of the *status quo* involving teachers' conditions of service, of the ways in which these may be affected by the kind of school or location we are working in, of new requirements in the meeting of professional and pedagogical 'standards', of the expanding role of the teacher, and of the issue of 'performance-related pay'. Chapter 8 focuses on issues of social justice, which, it is argued, are often ignored or underdeveloped within official policy and its legislative frameworks. This chapter encourages readers to ask searching questions about their own and their schools' policies in action with regard to issues of class, 'race', gender and sexuality in educational policy and practice, as well as offering an important elaboration and critique of the questionable notion of 'special needs'.

As with Chapter 8, Chapter 9 prompts us again to question and consider what is meant by – and what we mean by – comprehensive education, and what we might want to include in a 'comprehensive curriculum'. This final chapter leads us in addressing questions not so much about the past as about possible educational *futures* in *relation* to that past. What are the central educational issues *now*? Are governments and teachers *agreed* as to what those issues are and how they might be addressed and resolved? Where do we want to see – or expect to see – education in England and Wales going in the future?

ENVISIONING EDUCATIONAL POSSIBILITIES

Understanding Schools and Schooling provides an invaluable introduction to thinking about current issues in educational organisations and structures as they are experienced by teachers and students at the local, the general and the national level. In doing this, the book supports other titles in the series that seek to formulate – and to help teachers and student-teachers to formulate – informed and principled critiques of dominant discourses in their work and to develop considerations of how and where to make their voices heard within a properly understood context of what is possible and desirable.

In pulling off this task, Clyde Chitty shares with us a scholarship unique in its breadth and detail, which often takes us into the innermost thoughts of politicians, corrects a number of commonly misunderstood or misrepresented beliefs still taken as historical 'facts', and offers critical insights into what has been referred to elsewhere as the 'unofficial official agenda' of educational policy (Moore 2000). Chitty's account of the post-1944 history and development of comprehensive education in England and Wales, which underpins everything else that is discussed in the book, is both meticulous and readable, making this an invaluable book for teachers, parents and educationalists wanting to know more about the history, culture and details of the system in which they work or in which their children spend so much of their waking lives.

REFERENCES

Elliott, J. (1993) 'The relationship between "understanding" and "developing" teachers' thinking.' In Elliott, J. (ed.) *Reconstructing Teacher Education*. London: Falmer Press.

Loughran, J. (1996) *Developing Reflective Practice: Learning about Teaching and Learning through Modelling*. London: Falmer Press.

Moore, A. (2000) *Teaching and Learning: Pedagogy, Curriculum and Culture*. London: RoutledgeFalmer.

Moore, A. and Edwards, G. (2000) 'Compliance, resistance and pragmatism in pedagogic identities.' Paper presented at the Annual Conference of the American Educational Research Association, New Orleans, 24–28 April 2000.

OFSTED/TTA (Office for Standards in Education/Teacher Training Agency) (1996) *Framework for the Assessment of Quality and Standards in Initial Teacher Training 1996/97*. London: OFSTED.

Schon, D.A. (1983) *The Reflective Practitioner: How the Professionals Think in Action*. New York: Basic Books.

Schon, D.A. (1987) *Educating the Reflective Practitioner*. San Francisco: Jossey-Bass.

Valli, L. (ed.) (1992) *Reflective Teacher Education*. New York: State University of New York Press.

1 Introduction: perspectives on schooling

This chapter serves as an introduction to all the chapters in the book by propounding the thesis that educational policy making is influenced both by the events of the past and by current debates about the relationship between education and society. It highlights three broad perspectives on modern schooling: as individual fulfilment and the development of human personality; as preparation for the world of work; and as a crucial element in the process of social change. Within this third view of schooling as a social function, the chapter highlights the right-wing view of schooling and society that was dominant in the 1980s and some of the characteristics of a more dynamic and progressive view of education's social purpose that is often categorised as 'social reconstructionism'.

INTRODUCTION

When we read about, or, in some cases, infer the existence of, fierce and far-reaching debates about educational policy, whether taking place in Parliament, in the DfEE (Department for Education and Employment), recently renamed the DFES (Department for Education and Skills) in state agencies such as OFSTED (Office for Standards in Education) or the TTA (Teaching Training Agency), in the Education Committee of a local authority, or in the governing body of a school, we become acutely aware of widely differing conceptions of schooling – and of its precise role in preparing young people to operate effectively within adult society. One of the main arguments underpinning all the chapters in this book is that educational policy making, *at all levels*, is profoundly influenced *both* by what has happened in past decades *and* by contemporary debates about the exact relationship between schooling and society. At the classroom level, teachers are in the difficult position of having to constantly rethink and reconfigure their role in the light of fresh demands being made upon them by parents, governors, local community leaders and national politicians.

It seems clear that schooling is called upon to perform many essential functions in a sophisticated democratic society. While the forms it takes is a matter that will affect, either directly or indirectly, every member of that society, individual and group analyses of its true nature and purpose will be infinitely varied – in accordance with the social, political and philosophical outlook of the individuals and groups concerned. It does not, of course, follow that all such analyses will be forever competing on *equal* terms; for a study of the history of education in this country reveals that particular views about the function of schooling have tended to be dominant at certain key stages in our historical and social development. The ascendancy of any particular set of ideas, whether long-term or short-lived, will always depend on a variety of factors, the nature of which ensures that the future is always open and problematic.

In this introductory chapter, we will examine concepts of schooling under three broad headings:

1.   as individual fulfilment;
2.   as preparation for the world of work;
3.   as an essential element of social progress and social change.

It is not suggested that these cover *all* the available scenarios, but they do constitute a useful context in which to discuss current debates and controversies in subsequent chapters.

Schooling as human fulfilment

With regard to the first of our categories, education is often said to be about individual fulfilment and the development of human personality. A 'child-centred' approach to schooling seeks to develop the personal qualities and happiness of each individual child and owes much to the writings of Jean-Jacques Rousseau and his romantic stress on self-development and growth. It was Rousseau's book *Emile*, published in 1762, with its belief in the natural goodness of individual human beings, that became the 'bible' of the child–centred movement both in this country and in America. To educate according to this aim would be to reject, or at least severely modify, traditional approaches to education in favour of a philosophy that emphasises individual differences and 'discovery' methods of learning.

> Ideas associated with 'child-centredness' in education, and with what David Hargreaves (1982) has called 'a culture of individualism', had a marked influence on many primary and secondary schools in this country in the years following the Second World War and appeared to receive the official stamp of approval with the publication in 1967 of the Plowden Report, *Children and their Primary Schools* (DES 1967).

Yet acceptance of these ideas without reservations has not been without its pitfalls, and it has sometimes led to what Hargreaves refers to as 'the fallacy of individualism':

> This is the belief that if only our schools can successfully educate every individual child in self-confidence, independence and autonomy, then

society can with confidence be left to take care of itself. The good society will be automatically produced by the creation, through education, of good individuals. Education, it is held, cannot directly change society; it must do so *indirectly*, by creating the kind of individual who will then possess those qualities which are a prerequisite for the realisation of the good society. This belief can then be used to justify a range of divergent teacher perspectives.

(Hargreaves 1982, p.93)

It is Hargreaves' view that an excessive and exclusive attention to individual needs jeopardises those of society. The growth of individualism can be said to have led to the decline of 'community' both in school and in society – with disastrous results.

Schooling as preparation for employment

A second view of the primary role of schooling argues that it is intimately associated with the needs of the national economy. At a time of considerable optimism and hope, the policy makers of the 1960s saw a direct and indisputable correlation between educational reform and economic prosperity. It was generally assumed that an educated workforce would facilitate economic growth, which would, in turn, constitute a firm basis for continuing educational expansion. Education was seen as an important form of investment in 'human capital' – a superficially attractive notion that secured keen converts across the whole political spectrum in both Europe and America. As Karabel and Halsey (1977) have pointed out, it was able to make a direct appeal to right-wing pro-capitalist ideological sentiment through the claim residing in its insistence that:

> The worker is a *holder of capital* (as embodied in his [*sic*] skills and knowledge) and . . . has the *capacity to invest* (in himself). Thus in a single bold conceptual stroke, the *wage-earner*, who holds no property and controls neither the process nor the product of his own labour, is transformed into a *capitalist*. . . . We cannot be surprised, then, that a doctrine re-affirming the American way of life and offering quantitative justification for vast public expenditure on education should receive generous sponsorship in the United States.
>
> (Karabel and Halsey 1977, p.13)

In this country, 'human capital theory' provided the intellectual justification in the 1960s for both widespread comprehensive reorganisation and the rapid expansion of higher education.

In the mid-1970s, as Britain faced economic dislocation, and optimism and hope were replaced by cynicism and despair, the emphasis changed to preparing youngsters *while still at school* for the challenges to be faced in the 'world of work'. It was now widely claimed that too many schools were generally reluctant to train students to meet the needs of wealth-producing industry and could therefore be held at least partly responsible for the rising rate of youth unemployment. Indeed, this was one of the messages that Prime Minister James Callaghan was most anxious to put across in a famous speech he delivered at Ruskin College, Oxford, in October 1976, where he argued that 'there is no virtue in producing socially well-adjusted members of society who are unemployed because they do not have the skills' (quoted in Chitty 1989: p.171). This economic function of education was reiterated in the 1985 DES White Paper *Better Schools*: 'it is vital that schools should always remember that preparation for working life is one of their principal functions' (DES 1985b, para. 46). This could have divisive implications for the organisation of the secondary school curriculum. As Dan Finn commented at the time:

> The guiding philosophy behind educational policy became the creation of appropriate curricula for different groups of pupils, to be derived mainly from their assumed destination in the division of labour.
> (Finn 1987, p.168)

For many young people, this new view of schooling meant little more than the acquisition of a number of low-level transferable skills. And for all those being prepared for 'working life', there was a new emphasis on the need to become part of a highly 'adaptive' workforce. Indeed, this was the message still being highlighted by Gillian Shephard, Conservative Secretary of State for Education and Employment between 1994 and 1997, in her Foreword to the 1996 DfEE consultative document, *Equipping Young People for Working Life*:

> The Government has carried through major reform over the last few years to bring our educational system in line with the needs of a modern competitive economy. Our vision is of a prosperous Britain in the 21st century with a strong economy in which the skills of each individual are developed through education and deployed to the full. Thus, we must do all we can to help . . . young people to acquire the skills, knowledge and understanding they will need to be part of a highly adaptive workforce.
> (DfEE 1996a, p.1)

The social functions of schooling

In the 1960s, the recognition that spending on education was *investment* as well as *consumption* could exist side by side with the realisation that *all* education systems have social functions and consequences. This is our third view of the role of schooling and is obviously capable of an infinite variety of meanings. The early comprehensive schools were welcomed not just because the old selective system had resulted in a great wastage of ability but also because it was felt that society itself would be more stable and cohesive if children from differing backgrounds were able to mix together in the same school. Comprehensive schools could produce a greater degree of social harmony without in any way disturbing the basic class structure of the capitalist system. (This is discussed more fully in Chapter 8.)

But this is a fairly limited and anodyne version of schooling's social function. It was the view of the great American educationist John Dewey that schooling should equip young people with both the ability *and* the determination to improve society according to changing needs. In his words:

> To say that education is a social function, securing direction and develop-ment in the immature through their participation in the life of the group to which they belong, is to say, in effect, that education will vary with the quality of life which prevails in a group. . . . Particularly is it true that a society which not only changes, but which has the ideal of such change as will improve it, will have different standards and methods of education from one which aims simply at the perpetuation of its own customs. . . . The conception of education as a social process and function has no definite meaning until we define the kind of society we have in mind.
>
> (Dewey 1916, pp.94,112)

Here we have the idea that schools have the task of preparing their students *both* to function effectively within society *and* to use their various abilities to change that society in the light of changing circumstances and developing aspirations.

The problem is that even in a comparatively small country like Britain, there is no one clear overriding view about the kind of society we want to live in. The pessimism of the 1970s gave way to the crude certainties of the 1980s, and as we are now in the third millennium, the legacy of that harsh decade is with us still. In the field of education, we seem singularly uncertain as to how to deal with some of the more enduring elements of the Thatcherite vision of schooling, enshrined particularly in the 1988 Education Reform Act and in the original blueprint for the National Curriculum.

THE THATCHERITE VISION OF SCHOOLING AND SOCIETY

In its heyday, Thatcherism was an uneasy attempt to link the principles of a free-market economy with an atavistic emphasis on the family, traditional moral values and the virtues of a strong state. It involved rolling back the frontiers of the state in some areas while pursuing hard-line policies of repression and coercion in others.

There was a marked hostility to all institutions that mediated between the individual and the state, so that the state could emerge as the only collectivity in a society composed – almost exclusively – of autonomous individuals. These individuals would be encouraged to pursue their own self-interest, particularly in financial matters, with minimum concern for their fellow citizens. It followed that the period of the 1980s was something of a golden age for the speculator and the entrepreneur; in the opinion of a sharply worded editorial in *The Independent* dating from 23 May 1988: 'we now live in a society whose representative figure is the moneyed yob'.

> As far as education was concerned, there was a clear emphasis on enhanced parental choice and greater competition between schools, particularly at the secondary level. This was hardly 'privatisation' in the 'pure' form advocated by free-market zealots; but measures promoting independent management of schools and greater diversity of provision within the state system were seen as working towards a situation where, *eventually*, all schools could be in private ownership and parents would be supplied with education 'vouchers' or 'credits' to spend at the school of their choice (see Chapter 3 and Chitty 1997b).

At the same time, that section of the New Right which supported the idea of a national curriculum clearly intended that it should instil in youngsters respect for the traditional family, private property and all those bodies that could be said to uphold the authority of the bourgeois state. As Ken Jones (1989, pp.73–4) has pointed out, the Thatcherite project sought to overturn the 'progressive' trends of previous decades and substitute 'a tradition, bulky with inherited authority', that would 're-establish itself as the universal culture of the school, pushing to or over the margin all alternatives resting on "modish" interests like anti-sexism or anti-racism'. Anti-heterosexualism, for example, could easily be presented by right-wing politicians and sections of the media as the encouragement of homosexuality in students in schools; and anti-racist policies could be portrayed as a cynical attempt to undermine the nation's 'self-respect' and sense of 'identity'. We certainly gain a clear idea of Mrs Thatcher's own determination to exploit popular prejudices from the following extract from her triumphant address to the 1987 Conservative Party Conference.

> Too often, our children don't get the education they need – the education they *deserve*. And in the inner cities – where youngsters must have a decent education if they are to have a better future – that opportunity is all too often snatched from them by hard-left education authorities and extremist teachers. Children who need to be able to count and multiply are learning anti-racist mathematics – whatever that may be. Children who need to be able to express themselves in clear English are being taught political slogans. Children who need to be taught to respect traditional moral values are being taught that they have an inalienable right to be gay.
>
> (Thatcher 1987)

In the light of the above – and whatever one's view of the practices it seeks to ridicule – it is obvious that particular assessments of the role of schooling will generate their own distinctive curricula. Those who share the philosophy of the neo-conservative tendency within the radical Right will see schooling as essentially a tool of social control – with a particular role to play in the moral and economic regeneration of the nation. In the words of the right-wing Hillgate Group, which began publishing manifestos and pamphlets at the end of 1986:

> Children need a firm moral and spiritual basis, which will engender the values on which their future happiness depends: honesty, industry, charity, respect for others and for the law.
>
> (Hillgate Group 1986, p.2)

SOCIAL RECONSTRUCTIONISM

A more 'dynamic' view of the relationship between education and society would tend to stress the role of schooling in promoting or facilitating social change and social progress (an educational ideology that is sometimes referred to as 'social reconstructionism'). It is Denis Lawton's contention that the appropriate curriculum for such a model of schooling will be a common curriculum in which prevailing social norms and practices are analysed, criticised and 'reconstructed' according to rational democratic and communitarian values. In Lawton's words:

> The 'reconstructionist' curriculum will lay stress upon social values – in a democratic society, for example, citizenship and social co-operation; knowledge is not ignored, but a 'why' question is never far away, and knowledge for its own sake is highly questionable; knowledge is justified in terms of individuals' social needs, not in terms of custom, or cultural heritage *per se* (although cultural heritage may have considerable social importance under some circumstances).
>
> (Lawton 1983, pp.10–11)

It was just such a 'reconstructionist' approach that Her Majesty's Inspectorate, along with many classroom teachers, appeared to be groping towards in the late 1970s. The first of the three HMI Red Books, published in December 1977, accepted that the contribution that schooling alone could make to the creation of a fairer society was 'at best limited', but it emphasised that all schools had a responsibility for educating the 'autonomous citizen' – a person 'able to think and act for herself or himself, to resist exploitation, to innovate and to be vigilant in the defence of liberty' (DES 1977b, pp.9,11; see also Edwards and Kelly 1998). Something of the same concern to produce active and caring citizens can be found in the Final Report of the government-appointed Advisory Group on Citizenship, published in September 1998:

> We aim at no less than a change in the political culture of this country, both nationally and locally: for people to think of themselves as active

> citizens, willing, able and equipped to have an influence in public life and with the critical capacities to weigh evidence before speaking and acting; to build on and to extend radically to young people the best in existing traditions of community involvement and public service, and to make them individually confident in finding new forms of involvement and action among themselves.
>
> (DfEE/QCA 1998, pp.7–8)

The relationship between 'education' and 'society' is clearly a problematic one. The terms themselves are used easily enough in casual conversation, but their precise definition is a difficult and continuing exercise, not least because the concepts change over time. A modern society that claims to be 'civilised' is held together by a number of common beliefs and patterns of behaviour, even if and when these are under attack or changing quite rapidly; but we no longer live in the post-war world of taken-for-granted assumptions about class and morality. As HMI used to argue, we have to be clear about the nature and purposes of the 'socialisation' element of education before the more precise obligations of schools can be examined. In particular, we cannot ignore the fact that society is now composed of groups with widely differing backgrounds, traditions, lifestyles and religious beliefs. The plurality of such groups and interests within our society should be seen as a positive source of strength. It must be one of education's many functions to help to create a society in which all forms of diversity – racial, cultural, religious and sexual – are welcomed and 'celebrated'.

SUGGESTED ACTIVITIES

1. With reference to what this chapter argues about the different rationales, functions and values that might be claimed for formal, universal education, discuss and describe what you see education as being principally 'about', both from your own perspective and in the light of your understanding of government policy.

    In particular, try to identify the ways in which each of the following rationales can be found (a) in your own specialist or subject area (if you have one); (b) in the curriculum as a whole:

    ● the individual fulfilment of the student;
    ● preparation for the world of work;
    ● the promotion of social progress and social change.

To what extent do you think these different functions, rationales or values are *mutually compatible*?

    Can you identify any ways or areas in which they may appear to conflict or be in tension with one another? How are such conflicts dealt with (if at all) in your own practice, in the National Curriculum, and in school generally?

2.   Referring back to the references to Dewey in this chapter, discuss the ways
      in which schools – in general or in the particular case of your own school:

      ●   reflect a desire to *reproduce* existing society;
      ●   reflect a desire to help *redefine* or produce a new and 'better' kind of
           society.

      Consider the extent to which schools and teachers can pursue these two
      apparently contradictory agendas simultaneously, and the extent to which
      they can be successful in doing so.

3.   What are the implications of 'individual fulfilment', 'preparation for the
      world of work' and 'promoting social progress and social change' in
      multicultural contexts?
           To what extent can centralised national curricula meet the needs of
      students from a wide range of cultural backgrounds, in each of these three
      categories of purpose?

SUGGESTED READING

Lawton, D. (1994) *The Tory Mind on Education, 1979–94*. This book provides a
powerful insight into the beliefs, values and attitudes of leading Conservative
politicians and their advisers. Although many Conservatives pride themselves on
their 'practical' and 'commonsense' approach to education, it is the author's
contention that, at least since the 1970s, a strong set of ideological standpoints
have underpinned Conservative policies.

Simon, B. (1985) *Does Education Matter?* This important collection of essays by
one of Britain's leading historians of education examines, among other issues, the
role of education in either *hindering* or *promoting* progressive social change. Brian
Simon argues that schools have the function of deliberately promoting not merely
the skills of literacy and numeracy but, through a deepening grasp of knowledge
and culture, the autonomy of the student able *both* to function successfully within
society *and* to use his or her abilities and talents to change that society according
to developing aspirations.

2 A National System, Locally Administered, 1944–79

This chapter argues that for around thirty years after the end of the Second World War, both major political parties in this country shared a three-fold commitment: to full adult employment; to the idea of a Welfare State; and to the co-existence of large public and private sectors in the economy. Education was seen as making a major contribution to social welfare and economic prosperity, and the emphasis was on expansion. The idea of 'a national system, locally administered' was an integral part of the post-war settlement; and the structure of educational decision making that emerged after 1945 involved a rather cosy partnership between central government, local education authorities and individual schools. The 'welfare capitalist consensus' survived almost intact until the mid-1970s, when economic recession fundamentally altered the map of British politics and led to the questioning of many of the tacit assumptions of the post-war era. Within the Conservative Party, a number of right-wing groups with radical ideas began to exercise a powerful influence on policy formation.

INTRODUCTION

Before looking in some detail at the implications for secondary schools of the many and varied Education Acts passed by the Thatcher, Major and Blair administrations since 1979, it is important to devote some space to the principles underpinning the education system in this country in the decades immediately following the end of the Second World War. Some of those principles remain intact, but in many significant ways, we have effectively abandoned the concept of a 'national system, locally administered', which was such an integral part of the post–war settlement. These important modifications will be dealt with in Chapter 3.

THE 1944 EDUCATION ACT

It is a remarkable fact that for a period of nearly fifty years, the education system of England and Wales was dominated by the philosophy and provisions of the so-called Butler Education Act of 1944. This Act owed much to a growing recognition among leading politicians, administrators and teachers of the importance of education to economic advance and social welfare, and it soon established itself as a cornerstone of the post-war Welfare State. It was the product of at least three years of consultation with a variety of interested bodies and was piloted through Parliament by a wartime coalition government that had come to understand, in Brian Simon's words (1991, p.35), that 'it was impossible, if Britain was victorious, to go back to the stagnant, class-ridden depressing society of the 1930s'. In his own book of memoirs, *The Art of the Possible*, published in 1971, R.A. Butler, who became President of the Board of Education in the summer of 1941, talked in terms of his excitement at being given the opportunity to 'harness to the educational system the wartime urge for social reform and greater equality' (Butler 1971, p.86).

The 1944 Act has certainly had lavish praise heaped upon it, acquiring immense social and political significance in the process. It was characterised by Conservative MP Timothy Raison in 1976 as 'a Rolls-Royce among statutes' (Raison 1976, p.76); and according to the late Professor H.C. Dent, it was 'a very great Act' that made possible 'as important and substantial an advance in public education as this country has ever known' (Dent 1968, p.1). Betty Vernon, biographer of Ellen Wilkinson, Labour's first post-war education minister, endorsed a 1944 Workers' Educational Association pamphlet's view of the Act as 'a landmark in English educational history' (Vernon 1982, p.203); while for historian A.J.P. Taylor, it was 'one real advance' of the period among a number of potentially exciting projects that came to nothing (Taylor 1965, p.568). In his 1985 account of the development of the statutory system of schooling in England and Wales, Keith Evans described the Act as 'probably the greatest single advance in English educational history, its provisions showing real breadth of outlook and considerable educational vision' (Evans 1985, p.109); while in his 1986 biography of Conservative Prime Minister Anthony Eden, Robert Rhodes-James labelled it 'the single most important piece of legislation during the War' (Rhodes-James 1986, p.281).

What, then, accounts for such fulsome praise (not to mention the Act's extraordinary longevity)? Can the actual provisions of the legislation be said to justify such widespread approbation?

In a recent reappraisal of the Act, C.H. Batteson argues that '1944 assumed significance because it commanded cross-party support; enjoyed the patronage and benefaction of the wartime coalition; and seemed to overcome the historical leverage of powerful religious interests'. Furthermore, he suggests, 'it became entrenched in folklore as benevolent and accommodating – a grand occasion of consensual celebration – as a golden moment of history' (Batteson 1999, pp.5,7).

At the same time, the main provisions of the 1944 Act were of genuine importance. These include:

- The establishment of secondary education for all students as an integral part of a new educational system that was to be seen as a continuous process – ranging from the primary sector to further education.

- The establishment of a clear distinction between primary and secondary education with the proposed elimination of the former all-age (5–14) elementary sector.
- The stipulation that secondary education was henceforth to be free, with the phasing out of fees charged for students attending publicly provided or grant-aided secondary schools.
- The delegation of a duty to local education authorities to contribute to 'the moral, mental and physical development of their community' by making 'sufficient and satisfactory provision' for the three main stages of education.
- The raising of the school leaving age to 15 in 1947, with the stipulation that this was to be extended to 16 once the Ministry was satisfied that it had become 'a practical proposition' (although this was, in fact, to be postponed until 1972–3).

All that being said, the Act had a number of serious shortcomings and ambiguities, and, for our purposes in this chapter, these largely related to the actual *structure* of the proposed new secondary sector. (The lack of any clear definition of the *content* of secondary education is dealt with in Chapter 4.)

The wording of the Act, and of the 1943 White Paper *Educational Reconstruction* that preceded it, appeared to favour a tripartite system of secondary schools (comprising grammar, technical and secondary modern schools), but the legislation did not officially *proscribe* experiments with multilateral or comprehensive schools. One interpretation of Section 8 of the Act, referring to the provision of opportunities for all pupils 'in view of their different ages, abilities and aptitudes, and of the different periods for which they may be expected to remain at school' (Ministry of Education 1944, p.5), effectively ensured that secondary reform of a radical nature was deferred for many years. Yet it is also true that the ambiguity in the drafting of this section meant that when the pressure for reorganisation became almost irresistible in the 1960s, it could be addressed by *reinterpreting* the formula without the need for further legislation.

It has been convenient to claim that the process of 'reinterpreting' the formula was a clever device later 'invented' by the Labour Party for its own political purposes. But, in fact, attention was drawn to the possibility of having just one secondary school in a given area, even while the Bill was under discussion in the Commons, by an experienced educational administrator, James Chuter Ede, the Labour Parliamentary Secretary to the Board of Education:

> I do not know where people get the idea about three types of school, because I have gone through the Bill with a small toothcomb, and I can find only one school for senior pupils – and that is a secondary school.

What you like to make of it will depend on the way you serve the precise needs of the individual area in the country.

(Speech reported in *The Times*, 14 April 1944, quoted in Rubinstein and Simon 1973, p.31)

> It remains true that the vast majority of local authorities were happy to establish a divided system of secondary schools, although in a *bipartite* rather than a *tripartite* form. Priority was given in the post-war period to creating a new network of secondary modern schools, often dismissed by critics as merely 'the old elementary schools writ large', while most local authorities showed little enthusiasm for spending the money necessary to develop secondary technical education.

The system that emerged in most parts of the country was indeed a bipartite structure comprising grammar schools on the one hand and modern schools on the other – the former taking, in 1950, one in five of all state students at 11. As late as 1958, secondary technical schools still accounted for less than 4 per cent of the secondary age group.

THE WELFARE CAPITALIST CONSENSUS

For around thirty years after the end of the Second World War, both major political parties shared a basic commitment to the underlying principles of the post-war settlement: a set of tacit assumptions that Tony Benn (1987) has described as 'the welfare capitalist consensus'. This involved a three-fold commitment: to full employment, to the Welfare State, and to the co-existence of large public and private sectors in the economy. As far as education was concerned, the general emphasis was to be on expansion, with a marked increase in the number of schools and schoolteachers and of students opting for higher education. Although the Conservative governments of the 1950s were generally hostile to local experiments in comprehensive reorganisation, there is much to be said for Roger Dale's assertion (1983, p.234) that from 1954, when Sir David Eccles was appointed the Minister of Education, until the general election of October 1964, when the Conservatives were narrowly defeated by Harold Wilson's Labour Party, education policy at a national level was essentially 'non-partisan', and even, when Sir Edward Boyle was Conservative Minister of Education from 1962 to 1964, almost 'bi-partisan'.

> It is also important to understand that, until the late 1970s, the role of local education authorities in the national system seemed unassailable, and that the structure of educational decision making that developed in the post-war period involved a tripartite 'partnership' between central government, local government and individual schools and colleges.

According to Vernon Bogdanor (1979), the 'efficient secret' of the post-war settlement was that no *one* individual participant should enjoy 'a monopoly of power' in the decision-making process, so that:

> Power over the distribution of resources, over the organisation and over the content of education was to be diffused amongst the different elements and no *one* of them was to be given a controlling voice. . . . Such a structure . . . offered clear and obvious advantages not only for the administrator concerned with the efficient working of the system, but also for the liberal, anxious to avoid the concentration of power, and the pluralist, insistent that all the different interests should be properly represented. For parallel to the formal relationships between central and local government, embodied in statute and convention, there grew up a network of professional communities whose role it was to soften the political antagonisms which might otherwise have rendered the system unworkable. . . . The diffused structure of decision-making led, it could be argued, to better decisions because it at least ensured a wide basis of agreement before changes were made.
>
> (pp.157–8)

At the same time, this was a period when the number of powerful interest groups was fairly small and it was comparatively easy to secure consensus and co-operation among a cosily restricted network. As Bogdanor goes on to observe:

> The system of consultation worked best when only a small number of interests were involved whose rank and file were content to defer to elites, and could, therefore, be relied upon to act 'sensibly'. This process of elite accommodation reached its apogee during the post-war period when, or so it was believed, many policy decisions in education were taken over lunch at the National Liberal Club by a troika consisting of Sir William Alexander, Secretary of the Association of Education Committees, Sir Ronald Gould, the General Secretary of the National Union of Teachers, and the Permanent Secretary of the Department of Education. If these three agreed on some item of educational policy, it would, more often than not, be implemented. Such at least was the general belief; and even if it was a caricature, it is at least significant that it was widely held.
>
> (*ibid.*, p.161)

This spirit of compromise and consensus was broken only when an issue of *real* political or ideological significance intervened. In 1954, for example, there was a major row when Minister of Education Florence Horsbrugh took action at the last minute to prevent the then London County Council (LCC) closing the Eltham Hill Girls' Grammar School and transferring the students to the new Kidbrooke School. This meant that London's first purpose-built comprehensive school was not as 'comprehensive' as it might have been. But a dispute of this nature, between central and local government or between bodies with differing political allegiances, was the *exception* rather than the *rule*; and, as we have seen, educational policy making had become almost 'bi-partisan' by the time comprehensive schooling became official government policy with the arrival of a Labour government in 1964 and the issuing of Circular 10/65 a year later.

CIRCULAR 10/65

By the time the Conservatives were defeated in the 1964 general election, there was widespread popular disenchantment with the divided system of secondary schools still in existence in most parts of the country. The feature of the system that came in for special criticism was the 'unfair' method of allocating students to the three (or, more commonly, two) types of secondary school.

After the war, all children coming to the end of their period in primary school were subjected to a crucially important examination – the so-called 11-plus – which owed much to the theory that mental abilities were largely, if not wholly, inherited and could be measured easily at this stage in a child's life. With little incentive to indulge in more sophisticated reasoning, educational administrators were hereby provided with a splendid tool that could be used not only in selecting the most 'intelligent' students for a full 'academic' education but also in planning other forms of post-primary education for those whose horizons were thought to be more strictly limited.

> Yet, as the 1950s progressed, the flaws in the new system were becoming woefully apparent. In the first place, it was obvious to a large number of parents and politicians that far too many children were being written off as 'failures' at the age of 11 at a time when new demands were being made on the country's education system as a result of technological change and economic advance.

A series of influential sociological studies (notably Glass 1954; Floud *et al.* 1956) pointed to a direct relationship between social class and educational opportunities, bringing out clearly the extent to which the divided secondary system discriminated against the children of working-class parents and, conversely, favoured the middle-class child. *It was also an iniquitous feature of the system that the number of grammar school places available to 11-year-old students varied between local authorities, with the awarding of 'pass' marks having to take account of specific local circumstances.*

Above all, the successes secured by secondary modern school candidates in the GCE (General Certificate of Education) Ordinary Level Examination, introduced in 1951, had the obvious and immediate effect of exposing the fallibility of the 11-plus selection procedure. It was now clear to all but the most ardent believers in the theory of innate intelligence that it was quite impossible to say, from the results of mental or IQ tests administered at the age of 10 or 11, what a child's future accomplishments might be. It was also impossible to argue that every child was born with a given quota of 'intelligence', which remained constant throughout his or her life and that this key quality was a direct product of genetic endowment and not therefore susceptible to any educational influence. This much was acknowledged by Conservative Education Minister Edward Boyle in his Foreword to the Newsom Report, *Half Our Future*, published in 1963. 'The essential point', he wrote, 'is that all children should have an equal opportunity of acquiring intelligence, and of developing their talents and abilities to the full' (Ministry of Education 1963, p.iv). A famous early section in the report itself was equally forthright in dismissing the more fatalistic notions of the *psychometrists*:

> Intellectual talent is not a fixed quantity with which we have to work but a variable that can be modified by social policy and educational approaches. . . . The results of recent investigations increasingly indicate that the kind of intelligence which is measured by the tests so far applied is largely an acquired characteristic. This is not to deny the existence of a basic genetic endowment; but whereas that endowment, so far, has proved impossible to isolate, other factors can be identified. Particularly significant among them are the influences of the social and physical environment; and, since these are susceptible to modification, they may well prove educationally more important.
>
> (*ibid.*, p.6)

Yet, despite mounting criticism of the defects of the divided system, local experiments with comprehensive education were strictly limited in the 1950s; and by 1960, the number of students in comprehensive schools in England and Wales still amounted to less than 5 per cent of the secondary school population.

Then, however, came the period when what author C.P. Snow described (in his famous 1959 lecture on *The Two Cultures*) as 'the rigid and crystallised pattern' of English education began to break up under the weight of its inherent contradictions. It was in the four years between 1960 and 1964 that roughly a quarter of all local education authorities made major changes in their selection procedures.

Clearly this was a period when a social movement of considerable significance was taking place. Looking back on this defining moment in post-war educational history, in an article published in 1972, Edward Boyle revealed with characteristic candour that, on becoming Education Minister in July 1962, it was obvious to him that 'support for the development of secondary education along comprehensive lines was gaining considerable momentum' (Boyle 1972, p.32). It was therefore possible for reformers to argue that national education policy after 1964, far from being 'radical' or 'revolutionary' in character, was simply responding to, or taking account of, local initiatives of a widespread nature. As Dr I.G.K. Fenwick has pointed out:

> With the advent of a Labour government in 1964, national and local policies came largely into line, and Circular 10/65 seemed an acceptable progression of policy to many in education who were not ardent supporters of comprehensive reorganisation.
>
> (Fenwick 1976, p.158)

It was only when the general commitment to change became specific to individual and often prestigious schools that a focus for local opposition was provided, which, in turn, helped to fuel the national Conservative backlash of the second half of the decade.

The Circular referred to above, published in July 1965 and issued to all 163 local education authorities, was the means chosen by the Wilson government to implement its declared policy of 'reorganising secondary education on comprehensive lines'. In its final form, it appeared to owe much to a touching faith in the durability of the cosy partnership model of educational policy making; but there is also evidence to suggest (see Kogan 1971, pp.189–91) that in the early months of 1965, there was considerable discussion *within* the Department of Education and Science (DES) as to whether the new Circular should *require* or *request* local authorities to prepare plans for comprehensive reorganisation. Anthony Crosland, who had become Education Secretary in January 1965, finally sided with his civil servants and officials and opted for 'request'. He seems to have been convinced that this would be sufficient to take advantage of 'the general mood in the local authority world' and that, in any case, the DES would find it very difficult to cope with the vast number of local proposals resulting from a tougher type of circular. Speaking in the House of Commons towards the end of March, Crosland made it very clear that he was anxious to avoid compulsion:

> I regard compulsion as an academic question at the moment. . . . I am perfectly confident that local authorities will respond voluntarily and co-operatively to our request to submit plans.
>
> (reported in *The Times Educational Supplement*, 26 March 1965)

Two months later, he was determined to play down any suggestions in the national press of bitter conflict between his department and certain recalcitrant LEAs by reminding his audience of parents and local politicians that almost two-thirds of the secondary school population now lived in areas where the LEA was *implementing* or *planning* a comprehensive school policy. It was simply not true, he argued, that the Labour government was *imposing* comprehensive education on a reluctant nation:

> The fact is that there has been a growing movement against the 11-plus examination and all that it implies. This movement has not been politically inspired or imposed from the Centre. It has been a sponta-neous growth at the grassroots of education, leading to a widespread conviction that separation is an offence against the child as well as a brake on social and economic progress. . . . The whole notion of a

selection test at this age belongs to the era when secondary education was a privilege of the few.

(quoted in Kerckhoff *et al.* 1996, p.28)

Circular 10/65 began by announcing that it was the government's declared objective 'to end selection at 11-plus and to eliminate separatism in secondary education'. Local education authorities were *requested* to submit *within a year*, 'plans for reorganising secondary education in their areas on comprehensive lines'. No single pattern of comprehensive organisation was specified; instead, the Circular outlined the 'six main forms' of organisation that had so far emerged from 'experience and discussion'. Two of these would be acceptable only as 'interim solutions', while the 'simplest and best solution' (provided that the authority could devise a viable scheme 'without having to take account of existing buildings') was the 'all-through' 11 to 18 comprehensive school as already established in London, Coventry and elsewhere.

The two patterns regarded as 'acceptable' for only a transitional period involved the use of separate schools for students over the age of 13 or 14 and the continuance of some form of selection.

The four patterns recognised as 'fully comprehensive' were:

1. The orthodox comprehensive school for students aged 11 to 18.
2. A two-tier system whereby all students transferred automatically at 13 or 14, without any form of selection, to a senior comprehensive or upper school.
3. A two-tier system comprising schools for the 11 to 16 age range, combined with new sixth form colleges for students over 16.
4. A two-tier system comprising 'middle schools' for students aged 8 to 12 or 9 to 13, followed by upper schools with an age range of 12 or 13 to 18.

It was accepted that 'the most appropriate system' would depend on 'local circumstances' and that an authority might well decide to adopt 'more than one form of organisation' in a single area. It was made clear that the government did not seek to impose 'destructive or precipitate change on existing schools'; and it was recognised that 'the evolution of separate schools into a comprehensive system must be a constructive process requiring careful planning by local education authorities in consultation with all those concerned' (DES 1965, pp.1,2,10,11).

PROBLEMS FACING COMPREHENSIVE SCHOOLING

Many of the problems facing comprehensive schooling in this country in the second half of the 1960s can be attributed to the cautious and tentative nature of the Circular itself. Characterised in *The Guardian* (14 July 1965) as 'an amiably toothless tiger', and as 'a vague and permissive document' in *The Times Educational Supplement* (31 December 1965), it tried hard to be moderate and conciliatory in tone without *settling* many of the major problems associated with comprehensive reorganisation. It stated that no extra money would be made available to assist the process of change before 1967/68 (*ibid.*, p.11), which effectively meant that many of the new comprehensive schools had to begin life in buildings designed for use as *separate* schools. Then again, the range of patterns that would be considered 'acceptable' as comprehensive schemes – even if only on a temporary basis – was so great as to create the widespread suspicion that the resulting system would resemble 'a patchwork quilt of uneven quality' (see Chitty 1998b). The decision to avoid going down the road of compulsion *might* have worked if the spirit of 'consensus' had been genuinely 'national'; but between 1965 and 1970, a number of local authorities, mainly Conservative-controlled, were able to make eye-catching headlines in the national press by boasting of decisions that appeared to flout the spirit and intentions of the Circular. Many campaigners for comprehensive education would have welcomed the drafting of a solid and cogently worded piece of legislation, particularly after the March 1966 general election, which gave Harold Wilson's Labour Party a House of Commons majority over the Conservatives of more than 100, with the heady prospect of a full five-year term in government.

There was also considerable confusion, both within the government and within the Labour Party at large, as to what comprehensive schooling actually amounted to in practice – beyond the elimination of the 11-plus and the amalgamation, where appropriate, of existing grammar and secondary modern schools.

In the late 1950s, leading members of the Labour Party had been quite happy to exploit public misgivings concerning the unfairness of the 11-plus and the general shortage of grammar school places. Yet being aware of the continued popularity of the grammar schools among a sizeable section of their traditional supporters, they had also been anxious to play down the suggestion that comprehensive reorganisation entailed one type of school being *abolished* in order to create another. Hugh Gaitskell, the Labour leader from 1955 to 1963, had rejected the accusation that the grammar schools would be 'thrown overboard' in a letter he wrote to *The Times* in July 1958:

> It would be much nearer the truth to describe our proposals as amounting to 'a grammar-school education for all'. . . . Our aim is greatly to widen the opportunities to receive what is now called a grammar-school education; and we also want to see grammar-school standards, in the sense of higher quality education, extended far more generally.
>
> (Letter to *The Times*, 5 July 1958)

This interpretation of Labour Party education policy had been taken over by Harold Wilson (Gaitskell's successor as Party leader from 1963 onwards) in speeches made in the period leading up to the 1964 general election. Despite the embarrassment caused to committed educationists – particularly those Party activists who for a decade or more had campaigned for the comprehensive principle for educational and egalitarian reasons and were aware of the limited value of the grammar school model – the slogan of 'grammar schools for all' in fact served a number of useful functions:

- it silenced the opponents of reorganisation within the Party itself;
- it appealed to the growing demands for a more 'meritocratic' system of secondary education;
- it dispelled the fears of all those parents who placed their trust in the traditional grammar school curriculum.

David Hargreaves has summed up its appeal in the following terms:

> The slogan was a sophisticated one for it capitalised on the contradictions in the public's mind: parents were generally in favour of the retention of the grammar schools and their public examinations but opposed to the 11-plus selective test as the basis of a 'once-for-all' allocation. If the new comprehensive schools could be seen by the public as 'grammar schools for all', then the contradictions could be solved.
>
> (1982, p.66)

Significantly, the idea of promoting the new comprehensive schools as 'grammar schools for all', with the clear implication that the grammar school curriculum could now be made more widely available, was also enshrined in the Introduction to Circular 10/65, which reproduced a motion passed by the House of Commons on 21 January 1965 endorsing the government's policy:

> That this House, conscious of the need to raise educational standards at all levels, and regretting that the realisation of this objective is impeded by the separation of children into different types of secondary school, notes with approval the efforts of local authorities to reorganise secondary education on comprehensive lines which will preserve all that is valuable in a grammar-school education for those children who now receive it and make it available to more children.
>
> (*Hansard*, H. of C., Vol. 705, Col. 541, 21 January 1965)

This clear preoccupation with the taken-for-granted 'superiority' of the traditional grammar school curriculum meant that there was a failure to plan a common 11-to-16 programme that would be appropriate for the new type of secondary school, a point we shall return to when we discuss the origins of the National Curriculum in Chapter 4.

THE CONSERVATIVE BACKLASH

By the time Edward Boyle finally relinquished his post as Shadow Education Minister in 1969, he had lost the support of a large number of local Conservative

Party activists for his policy of 'welcoming' experiments in comprehensive school-ing. For some time, he had been aware of the exposed nature of his position on the 'liberal' wing of the Party – a position that became increasingly untenable as large groups of right-wing backbenchers and constituency workers mobilised against him (see Knight 1990, pp.22–60). It was now widely held within the Party that the Conservatives had been defeated in 1964 and 1966 not simply because of perceived internal dissensions or because the public had become bored with them (although there was seen to be some truth in both assertions), but because ministers and later shadow ministers had been content to embrace economic and social policies that were a diluted version of their opponents' ideas. Nowhere did this appear to be more true than in the area of education policy – and Boyle was seen to be the main culprit. At any rate, he was a convenient scapegoat. Matters came to a head at the 1968 Conservative Party Conference, where Boyle was challenged to acknowledge that the Party was hopelessly divided on such important issues as secondary education, the grammar schools and comprehensive reorganisation, and where he made a passionate plea for moderation and consensus:

> I will join with you willingly and wholeheartedly in the fight against Socialist dogmatism wherever it rears its head. But do not ask me to oppose it with an equal and opposite Conservative dogmatism, because in education, it is dogmatism itself which is wrong.
>
> (quoted in Corbett 1969, p.785)

The plea was unsuccessful, and the official motion on education was defeated.

Yet, although the Party seemed determined to reject Boyle's largely 'non-partisan' or even 'bi-partisan' approach, the views of his many and vociferous critics did not yet add up to a coherent rival philosophy. Above all, there was developing a very real split on the right of the Party between the 'preservationists', who simply wanted to 'preserve' the grammar schools, and the so-called 'voucher men', who wanted to experiment with new and untried methods of organising state education – principally with the idea that all parents should be issued with a free basic coupon, fixed at the average cost of schools in their area, to be 'cashed in' at the school of their choice.

It was the 'preservationists' who had the upper hand until at least the mid-1970s. Three Black Papers were published by the opponents of educational reform in 1969 and 1970 (Cox and Dyson 1969a, and 1969b, 1970), and all the contributors were seen as wanting to put back the clock: to the days of formal teaching methods and streaming in primary schools, of high academic standards associated with a grammar school education, and of well-motivated, hard-working and essentially conservative university students. The polemical articles in these three pamphlets were largely devoid of radical, forward-looking ideas; here was the voice of the past bemoaning the loss of a rigid hierarchy of educational establishments. It was only in two further Black Papers published in 1975, 1977 (Cox and Boyson 1975 and 1977) that support was given to the introduction, at least on a trial basis, of education vouchers and to the idea of providing much greater scope for parental choice of schools.

> By the mid-1970s, the Right was no longer on the defensive; the politics of *reaction* were giving way to the politics of *reconstruction*. The ground was certainly being prepared for a more bitter ideological struggle between the two main political parties. Even the very concept of a 'national system, *locally administered*' was now being called into question.

It was the economic recession of the early 1970s that fundamentally altered the map of British politics and provided the necessary conditions for the widespread dissemination of new ideas. The collapse of fixed exchange rates in 1971–2, followed by the quadrupling of the oil price in 1973, resulted in a general world recession and thereby undermined the rather glib assumptions that had been made in a period of relative prosperity. In the UK, the economic downturn exposed all the underlying weaknesses of the post-war welfare capitalist consensus. That consensus relied on an increasing prosperity for any success it might have had in promoting a sense of social unity, and when that prosperity disintegrated, so too did the consensus. As David Marquand has argued (1988), the Keynesian approach to the management of capitalism, with its tacit rejection of the concept of class enmity, simply could not cope with the economic shocks and adjustment problems of the mid-1970s:

> The post-war consensus finally collapsed under the Wilson–Callaghan Government of 1974–79, amid mounting inflation, swelling balance of payments deficits, unprecedented currency depreciation, rising unemployment, bitter industrial conflicts and what seemed to many to be ebbing governability. The Conservative leadership turned towards a new version of the classical market liberalism of the nineteenth century. Though the Labour leadership stuck to the tacit 'revisionism' of the 1950s and 1960s, large sections of the 'rank and file' turned towards a more inchoate mixture of neo-Marxism and the 'fundamentalist' socialism of the 1920s and 1930s.

(p.3)

It is also true that while both major parties contained groups with radical proposals for the future direction of society, it was only in the Conservative Party – at least after the defeat of Edward Heath as leader and his replacement by Margaret Thatcher in February 1975 – that such groups enjoyed easy access to the leadership. It was in the mid-1970s that the Party set about the process of reversing the so-called 'left-wing ratchet' and abandoning the 'middle ground' in politics.

The Labour Party was thrown on the defensive by the ferocity and scale of the right-wing attack on its education and social policies. The leadership appeared to be acutely embarrassed by the association of the Party in the eyes of the public with so-called 'progressive' education – characterised as it often was by a child-centred approach to teaching, informal pedagogic and assessment methods, and a general antipathy to all manifestations of hierarchy and inequality.

There was, therefore, some justification for the triumphant claim made by Rhodes Boyson, a former headteacher and by the mid-1970s a prominent right-wing Conservative MP, at a meeting organised by the National Council for Educational Standards (NCES) in May 1976, that 'The forces of the Right in education are on the offensive. The blood is flowing from the other side now' (reported in *The Times Educational Supplement*, 21 May 1976).

All the education ministers in the 1974–9 Wilson–Callaghan administration were distinctly half-hearted in defence of comprehensive education and of the new advances in primary school teaching made possible by the abolition of the 11-plus selection. Furthermore, they all seemed to work on the assumption that what they were engaged in was largely a 'damage-limitation exercise' fought on Conservative terms.

In particular, the important speech that Prime Minister James Callaghan delivered at Ruskin College, Oxford, in October 1976 signally failed to celebrate the many achievements of the state education system (see Chitty 1993b). Opening, in Callaghan's words, a 'Great Debate' on education, it can be viewed, in part at least, as an attempt to wrest the populist mantle from Margaret Thatcher's Conservative Party and to pander to perceived popular disquiet at the alleged decline in educational standards. It was also designed to highlight the need to make more effective use of the money – roughly £6 billion a year – that the government was spending on the nation's schools. The means of achieving this involved the construction of a new educational consensus around more central control of the school curriculum, greater teacher accountability and the more direct subordination of the secondary school curriculum to the 'needs' of the economy.

In the event, the new 'consensus' that Labour tried to construct in 1976 lasted for little more than ten years and was never truly 'national' in character. Indeed, if Mrs Thatcher's own right-wing supporters had had their way, it would have disintegrated as early as 1979 when Callaghan's Labour government was defeated by a Tory Party that was far more 'ideological' than the body once presided over by Harold Macmillan and Edward Heath.

SUGGESTED ACTIVITIES

1. What do you understand by the term 'comprehensive education'? Discuss this question with reference to:

    ●   school structure and organisation;
    ●   curriculum content;
    ●   pedagogies and classroom organisation.

    In what ways are we moving closer towards or further away from the 'comprehensive ideal' as you see it?

2. With reference to your own practice and to the National Curriculum and any SATs and public examination syllabuses that you are familiar with, what is

your response to the suggestion that schools and education systems continue to discriminate *against* working-class students and *in favour of* middle-class students?

Try to find specific examples where such a charge might be valid, in addition to some where the argument might be challenged.

3.   In terms of the assessment of students, discuss with a colleague or colleagues how far you think we have moved from evaluating ability normatively by such means as 'intelligence testing'.

In your own area of experience, do you feel that assessment is becoming more subtle, formative and tailored to individual achievements and needs, or less so? It might be helpful to support your answer with reference to specific examples.

Discuss with colleagues the pros and cons of SATs assessments and the publication of SATs results. If you support SATs in general terms, outline, with reasons, any improvements that you would like to see in those that you know about. At what age(s) should SATs be set, and at what age(s) should they definitely *not* be set?

SUGGESTED READING

Marquand, D. (1988) *The Unprincipled Society: New Demands and Old Politics*. The first part of this book tackles a number of issues that are essential for understanding educational developments between the mid-1940s and the mid-1970s: the principles underpinning the post-war consensus; the shared values and assumptions of the governing elite in the 1950s and 1960s; and the eventual collapse of Keynesian social democracy amid soaring inflation and ebbing legitimacy. Professor Marquand shows how the economic crisis of the early 1970s paved the way for a return to the old nineteenth-century politics of competitive individualism allied with a new emphasis on the free rein of market forces.

Smith, W.O.L. (1957) *Education: An Introductory Survey*. First published nearly half a century ago, this little book remains a classic text for understanding the organisation of education in the post-war period. As Chief Education Officer for Manchester between 1931 and 1949, Lester Smith was a firm believer in what he called 'the English compromise', whereby the government of education was shared between the state, local authorities and the voluntary bodies.

3 Years of Reconstruction and Conflict, 1979–97

This chapter follows on chronologically from Chapter 2 and argues that the period of partnership and consensus that lasted, despite a number of set-backs, until the mid-1970s was followed by two decades of conflict and radical change. It was in the 1980s that powerful sections of the Conservative Party began to question the very concept of a national education system, locally administered. Legislation passed during the third Thatcher administration (1987–90) represented a very real threat to the power and influence of local education authorities while creating a hierarchical system of secondary schooling subject both to market forces and to much greater control by central government. It was also a powerful objective of Thatcherite policies to create more choice and diversity within the secondary system; and the attack on comprehensive education was continued by the two Major administrations (1990–7) through the promotion of a policy of 'selection by specialisation'.

INTRODUCTION

Margaret Thatcher, who became leader of the Conservative Party in February 1975 and Prime Minister in May 1979, made little secret of her fundamental desire to undermine and eventually destroy both the comprehensive system of secondary schooling and the concept of a 'national system of education, *locally* administered'.

> The first could be achieved by establishing new types of school within the secondary structure and reintroducing (or reinforcing) the principle of selection. The second would involve ensuring that new secondary schools would be completely independent of local authority control, that existing schools could choose to 'opt out of' local authority control and that parents would be given far greater control over the choice of schools and colleges for their children.

As far as Mrs Thatcher and her supporters were concerned, the decline in educational standards, purported to have begun in the 1960s, had been caused by a corrupt alliance between local education authority inspectors and advisers, left-wing educationists and radical or incompetent classroom teachers. The new administration simply could not continue with the cosy traditional 'hands-off' approach, whereby government laid down the broad structure, provided the resources, and then left it to LEAs to run the schools and to teachers to determine what went on in the classroom. What was needed was a profound change in the whole culture of education; the post-war consensus must be overturned.

The new Prime Minister felt a profound sense of shame that during her four-year period as Education Secretary in Edward Heath's administration (1970–4), she had done so little to halt or at least slow down the process of comprehensive reorganisation. Indeed, it was during that period that more secondary schools became comprehensive than either before or since. Plans made under the previous Labour government, by both Labour and Conservative councils, were in the process of being implemented, and many others were waiting to be approved. *In her first thirty-two months in office, Mrs Thatcher received 2,765 schemes for consideration and actually rejected fewer than 5 per cent of them.* The number of comprehensive schools more than doubled in the period of the Heath government and by 1974 accounted for more than 50 per cent of all maintained secondary schools in England and Wales (see Simon 1991, p.586, table 6a). *It is the case, therefore, that, for all her strong opposition to comprehensive schooling, Mrs Thatcher was quite unable to overturn the prevailing 'orthodoxy' that reorganisation was almost inevitable.* There seems, in fact, to be much truth in the suggestion that a lingering resentment over this helped to account for her longstanding and ill-disguised contempt for the independent local education authorities, DES officials, members of Her Majesty's Inspectorate (HMI) and the educational 'establishment' as a whole. This was, after all, a view to which she herself gave some credence with a number of recollections to the effect that she had been up against entrenched conventional wisdom, which effectively prevented her 'saving' the grammar schools. In 1983, she told one interviewer:

> There was a great battle on. It was part of this equalisation rage at the time, that you mustn't select by ability. After all, I had come up by selection by ability. I had to fight it. I had a terrible time.
>
> (quoted in Young 1989, p.68)

In May 1987, she confided to the editor of *The Daily Mail*:

> The universal comprehensive thing started with Tony Crosland's Circular in 1965 and all local education authorities were asked to submit plans in which schools were to go totally comprehensive. When I was Secretary of State for Education in the Heath Government . . . this great roller-coaster of an idea was moving, and I found it difficult, if not impossible, to stop it.
>
> (*The Daily Mail*, 13 May 1987)

Even the education correspondents of the period could not escape some of the blame. In an interview with the Press Association News Agency at the beginning of May 1989, Mrs Thatcher said that she had never forgotten a lunch she had had with a group of prominent education correspondents back in early 1970. Many of them had 'ridiculed' everything she believed in, but now they were the ones having to eat 'humble pie':

> They had swallowed, hook, line and sinker, compulsory comprehensive education. But they and I have lived to know that they were all wrong.
>
> (quoted in *The Independent*, 4 May 1989)

By the time she became Prime Minister, Mrs Thatcher could rely for encouragement and advice on a growing number of right-wing think tanks and study groups, whose power and influence increased remarkably during the eleven-year period of her administration (1979–90). She had herself been instrumental, with Sir Keith Joseph and Alfred Sherman, in the establishment in August 1974 of the Centre for Policy Studies (CPS), a think tank designed to be more radical than the essentially moderate Conservative Research Department. It soon spawned a variety of study groups – among them the Education Research Group – whose brief was to devise new right-wing solutions to existing problems. In the same year, Marjorie Seldon presented a motion in favour of experimental education vouchers at the Annual Conference of the National Council for Women, which led to the setting up in December 1974 of FEVER (Friends of the Education Voucher Experiment in Representative Regions). While all this was going on, the Institute of Economic Affairs (established in 1955) worked tirelessly to persuade the Conservative Party to abandon the corporalist consensus and embrace policies based on nineteenth-century free-market anti-statism. Professor E.G. West's influential book *Education and the State*, arguing that the state should never have concerned itself with education provision back in 1870, was first published by the Institute in 1965 and went through several reprints. It is surely significant that just a few months after becoming Prime Minister, Mrs Thatcher felt moved to write to the IEA's founder to express her appreciation of the Institute's 'magnificent work' in helping to create a 'new intellectual climate':

> I am delighted to underline my admiration for all that the IEA has done over the years for a better understanding of the requirements for a free society. The Institute's publications have not only enabled us to make a start in developing sound economic policies; they have also helped create the intellectual climate within which these policies have commanded increasingly wide acceptance in the universities and the media. I wish you every success in your efforts to advance the principles in which we all believe. I am one of your strongest supporters.
>
> (quoted in Knight, 1990, p.144)

THE FIRST TWO THATCHER ADMINISTRATIONS, 1979–87

Bearing in mind the radical instincts of the new Prime Minister and the scope of the reforms devised by her more right-wing and adventurous supporters, it is a remarkable fact that the first two Thatcher governments achieved comparatively little as far as *radical* educational change was concerned.

The clear priorities of the period 1979–87 were two-fold: to bring down the rate of inflation (even at the risk of sustaining very high levels of unemployment); and to curb the power and influence of such extra-parliamentary institutions as the big trade unions. Much of the post-war Welfare State was left untouched, and there was little evidence of truly innovative planning in the areas of housing, health and education.

Education was accorded comparatively little space in the 1979 Conservative election manifesto; and plans to maintain and improve standards were included as part of a broader section with the title 'Helping the Family'. Here the Conservatives' main proposals involved:

- the repeal of those sections of Labour's 1976 Education Act that had *required* local education authorities to carry out comprehensive reorganisation;
- the more effective use of HMI and of the Assessment of Performance Unit (which had been set up by the DES in 1974 to 'promote the development of methods of assessing and monitoring the achievement of children at school');
- the introduction of a new Parents' Charter;
- the setting up of an Assisted Places Scheme.

(Conservative Party 1979, pp.24–6)

The Assisted Places Scheme was the one radical measure introduced by Margaret Thatcher's first Education Secretary, Mark Carlisle (1979–81), although it was probably the brainchild of Stuart Sexton, then special adviser to Carlisle and throughout the 1980s a leading advocate of right-wing ideas (see Knight 1990, p.148). It was designed, in the words of the 1979 manifesto, to enable 'less well-off parents to claim part or all of the fees at certain independent schools from a special government fund'. It was broadly conceived as a form of 'scholarship ladder' that would benefit 'bright' children from poor homes who would otherwise be inadequately 'stretched' at their local 'under-achieving' comprehensive school. According to Carlisle himself, the purpose behind the scheme was 'to give certain children a greater opportunity to pursue a particular form of academic education that was regrettably not otherwise, particularly in the cities, available to them' (quoted in Griggs 1985, p.89). As far as Labour critics were concerned, the scheme clearly reflected the Conservative government's lack of confidence in the quality of state education and its determination to undermine the comprehensive sector. It was described by Labour peer Lord Alexander during a debate in the House of Lords as 'an offensive public declaration by a government that the national system of education is incapable of providing for our most able children' (reported in *The Times Educational Supplement*, 19 September 1982).

When Sir Keith Joseph replaced Mark Carlisle as Education Secretary in September 1981, it was confidently expected on the right of the Conservative Party that this would mark the beginning of a radical overhaul of the education system. Interviewed after leaving office, Sir Keith went so far as to question the whole *raison d'être* of the system for which he had been responsible:

> We have a bloody state system I wish we hadn't got. I wish we'd taken a different route in 1870. We got the ruddy state involved. I don't want it. I don't think we know how to do it. I certainly don't think Secretaries of State know anything about it. But we are landed with it. If we could move back to 1870, I would take a different route. We've got compulsory education, which is a responsibility of hideous importance, and we tyrannise children to do that which they don't want, and we don't produce results.
>
> (quoted in Chitty 1997, p.80)

In 1981, the main priority for the Right was to encourage Sir Keith to promote 'parent power' by means of the education voucher. The newly appointed Education Secretary received spontaneous applause at the 1981 Conservative Party Conference when he declared:

> I personally have been intellectually attracted to the idea of seeing whether eventually, *eventually*, a voucher might be a way of increasing parental choice even further. . . . I know that there are very great difficulties in making a voucher deliver – in a way that would commend itself to us – more choice than policies already announced will, in fact, deliver. It is now up to the advocates of such a possibility to study the difficulties – and there are *real* difficulties – and then see whether they can develop proposals which will really cope with them.
>
> (Joseph 1981)

Questioned after a speech to the Institute of Directors in March 1982, Sir Keith spoke of the campaign for the education voucher in these terms:

> The voucher, in effect, is a cash facility for all parents, only usable in schools instead of money. It would come from the taxpayer, and, were the campaign to be successful, it would give all parents, however poor, a choice of schools regardless of how much these schools cost, be they in the private sector or the maintained, that is, the public sector. The idea of the voucher is a noble idea. It is the idea of freeing parents from all money considerations in choosing a school for their children. . . . A voucher would provide an equal moral treatment for all parents. It would not, of course, provide an equal background for all children, because the home is very important in the education of a child, and homes differ from one another in the combination of love, discipline and encouragement that is given to the child.
>
> (Joseph 1982)

> In the event, and despite the fervent campaigning of the National Council for Educational Standards (NCES) and the Friends of the Education Voucher Experiment in Representative Regions (FEVER), Sir Keith found it impossible to deliver the longed-for education voucher. In the interesting story of the role of political advisers (see Lawton 1984; Chitty 1989), this appears to have been one of the few occasions in the period from 1979 to 1997 when the civil servants of the DES were able to defeat the schemes of doctrinaire campaigners and right-wing pressure groups.

In fact, DES officials were able to emphasise the very real practical difficulties that would arise from the many and complex changes required to the legal and institutional framework of the education system. They had the support of Labour opponents of such changes and of those Conservative politicians who were worried about the cost of implementing them. Indeed, such was the strength of the opposition that by the end of 1983 the voucher idea had been dropped. Speaking at the 1983 Conservative Party Conference, Sir Keith announced: 'The voucher, at least in the foreseeable future, is dead'; and he repeated this in a written statement to the House of Commons in June 1984:

> I was intellectually attracted to the idea of education vouchers because it seemed to offer the possibility of some kind of market mechanism which would increase the choice and diversity of schools in response to the wishes of parents acting as customers. In the course of my examination of this possibility, it became clear that there would be great practical difficulties in making any voucher system compatible with the requirements that schooling should be available to all without charge, compulsory and of an acceptable standard. These requirements – difficult though the latter two are to achieve effectively under any dispensation – were seen to limit substantially the operation, and indeed the benefits, of free market choices; and to entail an involvement on the part of the state – both centrally and locally – which would be both financial and regulatory and on a scale likely to necessitate an administrative effort as great as under the present system. A change of this magnitude would desirably be preceded by pilot schemes undertaken by a number of volunteer LEAs. These would require legislation, and there was serious doubt whether they could adequately establish the feasibility of a voucher scheme within a manageable time scale.
>
> (*Hansard*, H. of C., Vol. 62, Col. 290,
> written answers to questions, 22 June 1984)

It is sometimes argued (see, for example, Knight 1990, p.161) that the Secretary of State's decision had much to do with the anticipated *financial* cost of a phased changeover to education vouchers, but, after leaving office, Sir Keith himself was anxious to repudiate this suggestion and to emphasise instead the insuperable *political* problems that would have been involved in pressing ahead regardless with the voucher project:

> I wanted vouchers simply because you transfer in one go from the producers to the consumers. . . . But I was a frustrated enthusiast – because I was forced to accept that, largely for political reasons, it wouldn't be practicable. . . . Not, as some think, for financial reasons. . . . Certainly not. . . . Finances didn't enter into it. Finances certainly didn't enter into it. No, it was political. In the sense . . . that you would have very controversial legislation, which would probably take two or three years to carry through, with my party split and the other parties all unanimously hostile on the wrong grounds. . . . And all the producer forces hostile. And then one would have had to decide either to go by way of imposition – from an appointed date there shall be vouchers everywhere – or one could have gone forward with a pilot scheme. And a pilot scheme would probably have been wrecked by producer hostility and could have produced only a mouse. And I didn't think that I had the moral courage to impose the voucher. Of course, it wouldn't have been like imposing comprehensivisation: it would have been imposing *freedom* – that's the main difference between the two.
>
> (quoted in Chitty 1997a, pp.82–3)

Despite winning a substantial victory in the June 1983 general election, with a 42 per cent share of the total vote, the re-elected Thatcher government was clearly not ready in 1983–4 to risk alienating a large number of its traditional supporters. The self-made individuals who had 'captured' the Conservative Party, both at a local and at a national level, were apparently not yet strong enough to proceed with the next stage of their formidable programme: the removal of all obstacles to the exertion of parental preferences and entrepreneurship in schooling. The unexpected abandonment of the voucher project (temporary or otherwise) could therefore be seen as something of a victory for the conservative forces at the very heart of the political establishment in this country. Reviewing the Thatcher government's second term at the beginning of 1986, *The Daily Telegraph* argued that:

> measures dear to the Prime Minister which fell by the wayside include education vouchers, student loans, repeal of rent control. . . . Though it is clear that her own aspirations reflect popular feeling, they run counter to those of the political classes . . . the establishment, by now accustomed to rule whomever *demos* elects.
>
> (*The Daily Telegraph*, 13 January 1986)

There is, however, a further factor, which is often overlooked in critical assessments of Sir Keith Joseph's period at the DES (1981–6), and which helps to explain the abrupt abandonment of the education voucher in 1983–4. This concerns the extent to which Sir Keith himself came under the influence of a powerful group of politicians and industrialists often referred to as Conservative Modernisers (see, for example, Jones 1989, pp.79–116). This group was particularly influential while David (now Lord) Young was chairperson of the Manpower Services Commission (MSC) between 1982 and 1984, and it was in this period that it succeeded in giving the Education Secretary a new set of priorities.

> The main aim of the Modernisers was to see the school curriculum – particularly at secondary level – restructured in order to prepare students for 'the world of work'. Their main achievement in the area of curriculum reform was probably the Technical and Vocational Education Initiative (TVEI), which was introduced as a series of fourteen pilot projects in a number of carefully selected schools in the autumn of 1983.

By 1986, the TVEI scheme involved 65,000 students in 600 institutions, working on two- or four-year programmes designed to stimulate work-related education, make the curriculum more 'relevant' to post-school life and enable students to aim for nationally recognised qualifications in a wide range of technical and vocational subject areas. Significantly, the new TVEI was not a DES policy initiative but emanated from David Young's MSC.

Unlike the supporters of the education voucher, Conservative Modernisers saw no particular virtue in measures designed to *privatise* the education system. Unlike the members of some right-wing campaigning groups, they had little time for the grammar school tradition, which, in their view, could be held at least partly responsible for Britain's long industrial decline. Instead, they particularly admired the tripartite system of secondary schools operating in West Germany – where the *Realschule* or technical school had always been a powerful rival to the *Gymnasium* or grammar school – and saw Britain's educational future in terms of a strictly differentiated secondary curriculum preparing students according to their supposed ability for the varying tasks to be performed in a thriving capitalist economy.

The Modernisers' vision of the ideal system of education and training was neatly summarised by Lord Young in an article in *The Times* in September 1985:

> My idea is that . . . there will be a world in which 15 per cent of our young go into higher education . . . roughly the same proportion as now. Another 30 to 35 per cent will stay on after the age of 16 doing the TVEI, along with other courses, and then ending up with a mixture of vocational and academic qualifications and skills. The remainder, about half, will simply go on to a two-year YTS (Youth Training Scheme).
>
> (*The Times*, 4 September 1985)

Yet, despite opposition from a large body of Conservative opinion, campaigners for the education voucher refused to accept defeat. In February 1986, the Institute of Economic Affairs (IEA) published *The Riddle of the Voucher* by Arthur Seldon

(Seldon 1986), which put forward suggestions for 'halfway houses' and 'stepping stones' – changes in the way education was managed that fell short of the introduction of a fully fledged voucher system but would pave the way for such a move later on.

A year later, Stuart Sexton produced an IEA pamphlet, *Our Schools: A Radical Policy*, in which he conceded that advocates of privatisation had probably attempted to achieve too much too quickly and that what was needed was 'a step-by-step approach' to the introduction of a market system of schooling:

> In pursuit of the 'privatisation' of management, if not of ownership also, the mistake has been to assume that we can get from where we are now to where we want to be in one giant stride, and all in a couple of years. . . . After a hundred years of state-managed education, it will take more time to accommodate the schools, the teachers and, above all, the parents themselves to a system of 'free choice': from a producer-led system to a consumer-led system, which is what it ought to be. . . . Vouchers, or 'education credits' to use a better term, available for every child and usable at any registered school, should be the ultimate objective. That would probably take five years to achieve if a series of measures began to be introduced now, each being a positive constructive step towards that ultimate objective. . . . We need to adopt a step-by-step approach to the eventual introduction of a 'market system', of a system truly based upon the supremacy of parental choice, the supremacy of purchasing power.
>
> (Sexton 1987, pp.10–11)

It can be argued that the Right had now recognised the need for the adoption of more subtle tactics; and, as we shall see, campaigners like Arthur Seldon and Stuart Sexton were indeed to achieve a sort of belated 'victory' with the passing of the mammoth Education Reform Act in 1988. It is an appraisal of this important piece of legislation that forms the substance of the next section.

THE 1988 EDUCATION REFORM ACT

For the various right-wing pressure groups that dominated the educational scene in the late 1980s, the privatisation of schooling *in its purest form* involved creating the ideal situation where all primary and secondary schools would be privately run and all parents would be issued with education vouchers or 'credits' to spend at the schools of their choice. It was becoming increasingly obvious, however, that these objectives could not be achieved overnight, so the legislation of the next ten years, beginning with the 1988 Education Reform Act, can be seen as an attempt at *gradual* privatisation – at blurring the boundaries between the private and state sectors.

Through that legislation, a tougher climate would be created in which the cosy relationships of the post-war years would no longer hold sway. The power and influence of local education authorities would be severely undermined and schools would be pitted against one another in a cut-throat drive to attract students. New types of headteacher would be appointed; new kinds of teacher would be welcomed into the profession; and different kinds of people would be trained for the Inspectorate. *The culture of co-operation and public service would be replaced by one of competition and enterprise.*

It was acknowledged by many leading Conservatives in 1987–8 that education was one of the key areas where Thatcherite principles had not yet been actively applied. In an interview published in *The Independent* on 4 April 1988, former chairperson of the Conservative Party Norman Tebbit argued that, on the whole, the first two Thatcher governments had been 'fairly successful'. The major task ahead was clearly to transform 'the dependency culture'. The climate of opinion *was* improving, but where health and education were concerned, 'ministers still had a way to go in changing public attitudes'. This view that much remained to be done was reiterated by Sir Geoffrey Howe, then Foreign Secretary, in a speech to a meeting of Conservatives in the City of London at the beginning of June 1988:

> The new frontier of Conservatism – or, rather, the later stage in that rolling frontier – is about reforming those parts of the state sector which privatisation has so far left largely untouched: those activities in society such as health and education which together consume a third of our national income, but where market opportunities are still hardly known.
>
> (Quoted in *The Independent*, 7 June 1988)

This view had also been expressed in statements made by the Prime Minister herself in the run-up to the June 1987 general election. In an interview with the editor of the *Daily Mail*, published in May 1987, Margaret Thatcher had said:

> We are going much further with education than we ever thought of doing before. When we've spent all that money per pupil, and when, even with more teachers, there is still so much wrong, it is obvious that we are going to have to do something determined about it. . . . There is going to be a revolution in the running of the schools.
>
> (*Daily Mail*, 13 May 1987)

This 'revolution' would apparently embrace a reduction in the powers of local education authorities, a reversal of this 'universal comprehensive thing' and the 'breaking-up of the giant comprehensives'.

A month later, the same determination was clearly in evidence. Asked by a caller to a pre-election radio and television programme in the BBC series *Election Call*, broadcast on 10 June 1987, what she regretted she had not actually achieved during eight years of Conservative government, the Prime Minister replied:

In some ways, I wish we had begun to tackle education earlier. We have
been content to continue with the policies of our predecessors. But
now we have much worse left-wing Labour authorities than we have
ever had before – so something simply has to be done.

(Reported in *The Guardian*, 11 June 1987)

*That 'something' turned out to be the most far-reaching piece of educational legislation since
the Butler Education Act of 1944.*

The 1988 Education Reform Act, based on the Education Reform Bill of the
previous year, is often seen as the main lasting achievement of Kenneth Baker, who
had replaced Keith Joseph as Education Secretary in May 1986. Reversing many
of the principles of the 1944 Act, it was designed to set a framework for the future
of state education that would last for half a century. Whether or not this intention
was capable of being realised will be discussed later in the chapter.

With its 238 clauses and thirteen schedules, covering everything from the
'spiritual welfare' of the next generation to the definition of a 'half day', the 1988
Act was described by Peter Wilby and Ngaio Crequer in *The Independent* (28 July
1988) as 'a Gothic monstrosity of legislation'. It actually covered England and
Wales only (although parallel bills with many similarities had also been prepared
for Scotland and Northern Ireland). By the time it received the Royal Assent on
29 July 1988, it had occupied over 370 hours of parliamentary time – more than
any other measure since the Second World War. Few other Acts had attempted so
ambitiously to redesign a major public service from top to bottom. No legislation
since Aneurin Bevan's introduction of the National Health Service forty years
earlier had faced such bitter and widespread professional opposition.

For the purposes of this chapter, it will be convenient to discuss the provisions
of the 1988 Act under *three* main headings:

1. the introduction of a national curriculum for all state schools;
2. the introduction of a new system of school management known as LMS
    (Local Management of Schools);
3. the creation of a new tier of schooling, particularly at the secondary level.

A national curriculum

The policy of imposing a national curriculum on all state schools in England and
Wales was the one major provision of the 1988 Act that divided Mrs Thatcher's
right-wing advisers and indeed incurred the wrath of the Prime Minister herself
(a point that will be discussed further in Chapter 4). The one right-wing pressure
group that supported the idea of a state-imposed curriculum on the grounds that
it would emphasise the importance of traditional subject disciplines and a testable
body of knowledge was the Hillgate Group, whose first major pamphlet, *Whose
Schools? A Radical Manifesto*, was published in December 1986; and the concept had
powerful advocates among the civil servants at the DES led by Education Secretary
Kenneth Baker. Those who opposed the policy did so on the basis that it was

inimical to the underlying philosophy of the Act, which laid great stress on choice and diversity and on the right of all schools, especially at secondary level, to develop a distinctive ethos in order to attract as many students as possible.

The National Curriculum defined by the Act required:

- mathematics, English, science, history, geography, technology, music, art and physical education to be taught to students of all ages;
- a modern foreign language to students aged 11 to 16;
- Welsh to students in Welsh-speaking schools;

It also included religious education as an additional compulsory subject (the only subject that had, in fact, been compulsory since 1944) as a result of pressure exerted on the government during the passage of the Education Bill through Parliament in 1987–8. For most subjects, the Secretary of State would lay down programmes of study, with attainment targets and assessment for students at 7, 11, 14 and 16.

A new system of school management

The introduction of LMS, or local management of schools, was the reform that had some of the main features of an educational voucher scheme and thereby pleased those right-wing pressure groups that had felt betrayed by Sir Keith Joseph's rejection of the project in 1983–4. As soon as the new system was fully operational, school budgets for staffing, premises and services would be delegated to individual schools. This new delegated budget would be determined by a formula largely reflecting the number of students on the school roll. At the same time, there would be significant changes to admissions regulations obliging all schools in future to admit students to their full capacity.

A new tier of schooling

The third major change introduced in the late 1980s involved the creation of city technology colleges (CTCs) and grant-maintained (GM) or opted-out schools. The CTC plan had actually been announced by Kenneth Baker, shortly after his appointment as Education Secretary, in a speech he delivered to the 1986 Conservative Party Conference. It had been foreshadowed in a remarkably accurate article that appeared in *The Sunday Times* at the end of 1985. Under the heading 'Technology School Plan for the Young Elite', the article revealed that:

> Plans have been devised for the establishment of 16 to 20 technology schools or colleges in the main urban areas. . . . Each would take around 1,000 pupils, who would be specially selected and would not pay fees. . . . The LEAs would not be responsible for the new schools. . . . They would be funded directly by the taxpayer via a National Education Trust.
>
> (*The Sunday Times*, 22 December 1985)

According to Kenneth Baker, the new colleges – some twenty in number and situated largely in inner-city areas – would indeed be completely independent of local education authority control – the part of his announcement that drew sustained and rapturous applause from his partisan audience at the 1986 Conference. While the Treasury had agreed to make extra public money available to help to finance the new colleges, an important part of the project was that private sector sponsors would be encouraged to contribute to the heavy capital and running costs. The colleges would be designed to develop enterprise, self-reliance and responsibility – and would broaden parental choice. There would be no 11-plus style of entry examination for the new colleges, but there would be selection procedures, and these would lay particular emphasis on the 'attitudes' of students and their parents and on their commitment to making the most of a technology-oriented education. As far as the curriculum was concerned, there would be a large technical and practical element within a broad and balanced diet.

Grant-maintained schools – the second component of the new tier of schooling – would be those schools, both secondary and large primary, where a requisite proportion of parents had voted to take the school out of local authority control. It is true that a certain degree of confusion about the precise advantages of acquiring grant-maintained status had been evident in the run-up to the 1987 general election. At one pre-election press conference, Mrs Thatcher had argued that the heads and governing bodies of those secondary schools that 'opted out' of local authority control should be free to establish their own admissions policies and would not necessarily be prevented from raising extra funds through parents – thereby giving rise to much media speculation that the new plans might include a fee-paying element (reported in *The Guardian*, 23 May 1987). Then Kenneth Baker conceded during a BBC Radio 4 *World at One* discussion, broadcast on 10 June 1987, that there would be nothing to stop 'better-off parents' raising additional resources for a particular 'opted-out' school so that the headteacher would be in a position to purchase particularly expensive books and items of equipment and perhaps even pay some of the teachers higher salaries. It was left to later statements from the DES to play down the fee-paying aspect and even to deny that the whole 'opt-out' policy was really a covert means of reintroducing secondary selection.

DIFFERING INTERPRETATIONS OF THE 1988 ACT

It is possible to view the 1988 Education Reform Act from a number of different perspectives.

A fairly benign view of the legislation – and one encouraged by the government itself – tended to stress that it was all about raising educational standards, producing a better-educated society and improving the management of schools.

These were the sort of objectives cited by Kenneth Baker when he spoke in favour of the Education Bill in the House of Commons in December 1987:

> Our education system has operated over the past 40 years on the basis of the framework laid down by Rab Butler's 1944 Act, which, in turn, built on the Balfour Act of 1902. We need to inject a new vitality into that system. It has become producer-dominated. It has not proved sensitive to the demands for change that have become ever more urgent over the past 10 years. This Bill will create a new framework, which will raise standards, extend choice, and produce a better-educated Britain.
>
> (*Hansard*, H. of C., Vol. 123, Col. 771, 1 December 1987)

Linked to all this were notions of competition and accountability, with one of the main purposes of the 1988 Act being to challenge the 'producer interest' in education (an issue touched upon by the Education Secretary in the House of Commons statement quoted above). It seemed to be the government's view that schools forced into a state of healthy competition with their neighbours would have to be more accountable to their 'customers' − or run the risk of losing large numbers of their students. One of the objectives of the publication of National Curriculum test results was, after all, to provide evidence to parents of the desirability or otherwise of individual schools. According to Nick Stuart, Deputy Secretary at the DES and the man with special responsibility for drafting the final version of the Act: 'accountability was regarded by the Thatcher Government as the linchpin of its education reforms in the late 1980s'. In his view, the legislation was essentially about *three* things:

1. the provision of an improved basic curriculum for schools with the associated publication of relevant test results;
2. increasing parental choice and influence;
3. the better management of institutions.

All of those things were linked together by notions of accountability. In Stuart's words: 'the best curriculum in the world is not going to work where there is inefficient and ineffective management of schools which then fail to be responsive to the needs of parents' (Stuart 1988).

These may have been important and genuine concerns for a number of ministers and civil servants, but it needs to be emphasised that for many teachers and educationists, the legislation had other quite different and more sinister purposes. To opponents of the government's overall philosophy, it seemed to be designed primarily to erect (or, perhaps more accurately, *reinforce*) a hierarchical system of schooling (particularly at the secondary level) subject both to market forces and to greater control by central government.

Genuine comprehensive education, with a strong built-in 'neighbourhood' or 'community' element, was effectively being *circumvented* and *undermined* by the creation of new types of secondary school and by the increasing emphasis on parental choice regardless of local circumstances.

This was perceived, in other words, as the destruction of comprehensive schools by stealth – a point conceded by Kenneth (now Lord) Baker himself in a recent interview with Nick Davies of *The Guardian*:

> The introduction of parental choice was, in fact, part of a much bigger silent coup. My real target . . . was the comprehensive system of schooling itself. I would have liked to bring back selection, but I would have got into such controversy at an early stage that the other reforms would have been lost. . . . I realised that the introduction of parental choice would polarise the system and effectively kill off the comprehensives. Yes – that was deliberate. In order to make important changes, you have to come at them from several points. . . . I had already tried to break things up by introducing the City Technology Colleges and promoting grant-maintained schools. Choice was my other weapon. . . . The political appeal was simple: choice means freedom, and freedom is good. But the real objective was a lot more destructive: I hoped it would open it all up and that it would lead to the poorer comprehensive schools literally having to close. . . . Stealth was essential. I was not going to take on the comprehensive system head-on. I'd had the teachers' strike and the National Curriculum; you can't take on yet another great fight. So I believed that if I set in train certain changes, they would have a cumulative beneficial effect.
>
> (*The Guardian*, 16 September 1999).

Yet the various provisions of the Act meant far more than a simple return to the divided secondary system of the post-war years. What was also under attack was the role (well-executed or otherwise) of local education authorities in devising fair admissions policies and balanced intakes for their schools.

In this respect, the most important proposal in the 1988 Act was that for financial delegation, the chief object of which was to make all local authorities distribute funds to their primary and secondary schools by means of a weighted *per capita* formula. Governing bodies would then be responsible for controlling the budgets delegated to them.

This development, viewed in conjunction with the provision for open enrolment, can fairly be seen as a subtle means of adapting the education system in such a way as to make a later transition to vouchers possible without undue disruption. Under the terms of the Act, the *per capita* payments were still to be paid to the schools, but the circumstances had been engineered in which it would be a relatively simple matter to give the money directly to the parents in the form of vouchers or warrants. Indeed, this very point was made by Kenneth Baker in the course of the highly revealing *Guardian* interview cited above:

> The emphasis on parental choice combined with the new funding formula meant that the vast bulk of each school's budget depended entirely on the recruitment of children, whose parents were now empowered to choose their schools. . . . Well, yes, it was not a formal voucher system, but it was very tantamount! In effect, it *was* a voucher system. I just didn't call it that. Mine was a subtler approach. . . . If I had had the time I *would* have done more. . . . I would have introduced a proper voucher system under which parents could spend their education voucher on the school of their choice, starving unpopular schools of funding. . . . I would have reduced the LEAs to dealing with special educational needs, and not much else. . . . But time was limited, and I believed I had done enough.
>
> (*ibid.*)

Addressing a meeting of right-wing Conservatives in May 1987, junior Education Minister Bob Dunn proudly told his audience that government proposals to allow schools to take as many students as they could physically cope with, in tandem with plans to give heads and governors control of school budgets and the right to 'opt out' of council control, were all parts of a carefully worked out strategy that would eventually lead to 'the denationalisation of education' (reported in *The Times Educational Supplement*, 15 May 1987).

THE 1990–7 MAJOR ADMINISTRATIONS

The 1990–2 and 1992–7 Major governments found themselves in the difficult position of having to cope with the many inadequacies and shortcomings of the 1988 Education Act.

John Major himself, who replaced Margaret Thatcher as Prime Minister (and leader of the Conservative Party) in November 1990, certainly appeared to share his predecessor's ill-founded and uncompromising hostility towards the comprehensive system of secondary schooling. According to his recent biographer Anthony Seldon:

> He saw himself as the champion of the child from the ordinary home; and his determination that the state school system should meet the needs of all its students spurred on his pursuit of more national curriculum testing and the publication of league tables based on the results of those tests.
>
> (Seldon 1997, p.398)

His educational outlook embraced a traditional belief in the values of meritocratic society and a fervent desire to reverse the changes of the 1960s and 1970s. He made his position abundantly clear in a well-publicised speech to the right-wing Centre for Policy Studies delivered at the Café Royal in London (the CPS lacking its own lecture hall) on 3 July 1991. He spoke of the nation's deep-seated low regard for education, the low expectations of far too many students by their teachers and a need to return to more traditional approaches to the teaching of literature and history. According to the Prime Minister, many of the shortcomings of the secondary sector could be attributed to the Left's obsession with comprehensive reorganisation in the 1960s, which had been based on 'a mania for equality'.

> This was equality, not of *opportunity*, but of *outcome*. This was a mania that condemned children to fall short of their potential; that treated them as if they were *identical* – or must be made so. This was a mania that undermined common-sense values in schools, rejected proven teaching methods, debased standards – or disposed of them altogether. A canker in our education system which spread from the 1960s on, and deprived great cohorts of our children of the opportunities they deserved. I, for one, cannot find it easy to forgive the Left for that.
>
> (Major 1991, my italics)

The main proposals in the speech included:

- a hardened-up form of testing of the National Curriculum, which the Prime Minister felt had been 'sabotaged' by the 'educational establishment';
- fresh legislation to 'smooth the path to grant-maintained status';
- a 'tightening up' of written examinations at GCSE level, with 'a diminution of coursework' (see Seldon 1997, p.187).

John Major's obsessive hostility towards comprehensive schooling was further emphasised in a four-page letter to Fred Jarvis, former General Secretary of the National Union of Teachers, released to the press at the end of February 1992. In this remarkably frank letter, the Prime Minister seemed anxious to blame comprehensive schools for *all* the failings of the education system, in a crude blanket condemnation that accused the Labour Party of having ushered in a secondary structure that fostered low standards and low expectations:

> I am . . . drawn to the view that the problem of low standards stems . . . from the nature of the comprehensive system which the Labour Party ushered in in the 1960s, and from the intellectual climate underpinning it that has tended to stress equality of *outcome* at the expense of equality of *opportunity*. . . . The 'orthodoxy' which has grown up around the comprehensive system has, frankly, been an orthodoxy of the Left: hostility to any form of competition *between* schools and *between* pupils, and even in sport; hostility to testing; hostility to genuine parental choice; and a steady infiltration of traditional curriculum subjects such

as history and English literature by some questionable dogmas that fly in the face of common sense. . . . I ask you not to doubt my sincerity and determination to reverse the failings of the comprehensive system and the cycle of low expectations and low standards which it has fostered. I want to ensure that we *actively* recognise pupils' differing abilities and aptitudes and create the means for this diversity to flourish. That is the way to ensure genuine equality of opportunity.

(Jarvis 1993, pp.25–6, my italics)

John Major said that he wanted to see a grammar school restored to every town; and yet his unequivocal respect for the grammar school tradition was curiously at odds with the resentment he clearly felt that his own secondary school, in the 1950s a boys' grammar school in south-west London, had done so little to develop his own abilities and talents. In a 1995 interview with Anthony Seldon, he talked movingly of the sense of alienation he had felt at the school between 1954 and 1959:

I didn't like the school ambience; I didn't like the shepherding together of lesser beings who were told that they had to be subservient to and respect these greater beings who happened to be the schoolmasters. I am not suggesting that the School was harsh or unfair in any way. I am just suggesting that to me the innate view that a certain class of people was 'better' than a certain class of other people was absolute anathema. The reason I didn't work at school was my sense of alienation from this particular school. If you had the sort of difficulties we faced at home at the time, you were alienated. I wasn't interested in school. I wasn't stupid at school. I just didn't work. I couldn't work.

(Seldon 1997, p.12)

> Despite John Major's concern to make continuing education reform one of the key features of his premiership, effective implementation of the 1988 Education Act was running into all manner of difficulties almost from the start of his six-and-a-half year occupancy of Number 10. As we have already seen, there was considerable confusion at the outset about the benefits that would accrue to schools opting for grant-maintained status; and many feared that 'opted-out' secondary schools would soon constitute a privileged tier of schooling.

Partly in order to allay such fears, the original DES Circular on grant-maintained schools, published in October 1988 (DES 1988), stated unequivocally that the new grant-maintained schools would compete '*on equal terms* with LEA-maintained schools' and would be funded '*on the same basis* as other schools in their neighbourhood' (my italics). Yet this was certainly *not* how things turned out. Indeed, it was estimated by Local Schools Information (LSI 1992) that within the first four years of their existence, the new grant-maintained schools had cost the DES more than £30 million in additional expenditure. Such was the strength of the evidence that after a series of denials, John Major himself was forced to concede, in August 1991, that 'opted-out' schools were being given preferential financial treatment in an attempt to encourage more schools to take up the option. In a letter to the General Secretary of the National Union of Teachers, he wrote:

> We have actually made no secret of the fact that grant-maintained schools do indeed get preferential treatment in the allocation of grants for capital expenditure. We look favourably at grant-maintained schools to encourage the growth of the sector, and I am delighted to see that numbers are continuing to grow rapidly.
>
> (Reported in *The Guardian*, 7 August 1991)

There were also issues to be raised with regard to the admissions policies of some of the new grant-maintained schools. Kenneth Baker had given a pre-election assurance that no proposal for 'a change of character' would be entertained within five years of a secondary school acquiring grant-maintained status. Yet this crucial stipulation did not appear in the 1987 Education Bill and was to be widely circumvented in all manner of covert ways. Research carried out by a team at the University of Leicester and published in 1993 revealed that around one-third of the first comprehensive schools to opt out of local authority control used some form of academic or social selection when over-subscribed. Methods for choosing between applicants included parent and/or student interviews, reports from the previous school and, in one case, written examinations (Bush *et al.* 1993, p.95) – all of which seemed to support the contention that the grant-maintained project was leading to the emergence of a new two-tier system of schooling.

Yet, despite fears that the new grant-maintained schools would soon be in a strong position to undermine the comprehensive system, it became apparent in the early 1990s that opting out was *not* taking off all over the country but was, in fact, popular only in local authorities that were either Conservative-run or low-spending – or both. By the beginning of 1992, schools intending to opt out of local control were concentrated in just twelve of the 117 education authorities in England and Wales (LSI 1992; see also Chitty 1999, p.56).

Nor was it necessary to be too alarmed by the threat to the comprehensive ideal posed by the new city technology colleges. The general reaction to the CTC project was certainly not as the government would have desired. Apart from the expected negative response of the main teacher unions, the local education authorities and the Labour Opposition, there were very few industrialists who showed any wish to help to 'extend the range of choice for families in urban areas' – and many who were openly hostile to the concept. Several directors of major companies already involved with state schooling rejected the idea of sponsoring a single school or college and argued the benefits of wider sponsorship. The programme eventually stalled at just fifteen CTCs, with only 20 per cent of capital funding having been provided by private sponsors and the bulk of the capital expenditure and practically all of the current expenditure being provided directly by central government.

All of which caused the Major government of 1992–7 to explore new ways of creating choice and diversity *within* the existing comprehensive framework. By the time John Patten became Education Secretary in April 1992, it was clear that *specialisation* was replacing *selection* as the guiding principle of Conservative education policy.

The details of a new 'schools revolution', introducing 'the British version of the American "magnet school"', were spelled out as a front-page story in *The Mail on Sunday* at the beginning of May 1992:

> Education Secretary John Patten is looking at plans to turn some of our secondary schools into 'centres of excellence' in key subject areas. . . . This means that some schools will specialise in the academic subjects like languages, maths and science; some will be technically-based; and others might offer performing arts or sports as their specialism. . . . This move puts a form of selection back on the education agenda – but it drives a final nail in the coffin of the campaign to bring back grammar schools and the 11-plus.
>
> (*The Mail on Sunday*, 3 May 1992)

The Education Secretary himself argued in an article in the *New Statesman and Society*, published in July 1992, that socialists must now 'come to terms with the concept of specialisation':

> Selection is not, and should not be, a great issue of the 1990s as it was in the 1960s. The S-word for all Socialists to come to terms with is, rather, 'specialisation'. The fact is that children excel at different things; it is foolish to ignore it, and some schools may wish specifically to cater for these differences. Specialisation, underpinned by the National Curriculum, will be the answer for *some* – though not *all* – children, driven by aptitude and interest, as much as by ability. . . .
>
> It is clear that on the foundation stone of the National Curriculum can be built the liberation of all the talents through greater specialisation in our schools. This could be specialisation *within* a large comprehensive, setting for this or that subject – by the pupils self-selecting, or being guided towards their choice by aptitude and commitment. Or it could be something that builds on to the schools – a leading edge in bilingually-taught technology, for example, or in music, or in the area where languages crucially meet business studies.
>
> Such schools are already emerging. They will, as much more than mere exotic educational boutiques, increasingly populate the educational landscape of Britain at the end of the century – a century that introduced universal education at its outset; then tried to grade children like vegetables; then tried to treat them . . . like identical vegetables; and which never ever

gave them the equality of intellectual nourishment that is now being offered by the National Curriculum, encouraged by testing, audited by regular inspection.

(Patten 1992, pp.20–1)

The White Paper *Choice and Diversity*, published in July 1992, attacked the comprehensive system for 'presupposing that children are all basically the same and that all local communities have essentially the same educational needs' (DfE 1992, p.3). It asserted that 'the provision of education should be geared more to local circumstances and individual needs: hence a commitment to diversity in education' (*ibid.*, pp. 3–4). But it went on to argue that *specialisation* should never be confused with *selection*:

> The fact that a school is strong in a particular field may well increase the demand to attend, but it does not necessarily follow that selective entry criteria have to be imposed by the school. The selection that takes place is parent-driven. The principle of open access remains. As demand to attend increases, so the school may simply require extra resources to cope with the range of talent available.
>
> (*ibid.*, p.10)

The 1992 White Paper announced plans to build on the work of the fifteen city technology colleges by establishing a network of maintained secondary schools with enhanced technology facilities, to be known as 'technology schools', and a network of schools established in partnership with business sponsors, to be known as 'technology colleges'. It was anticipated that schools seeking to become new 'technology colleges' would do so as grant-maintained schools. It was also suggested that new grant-maintained schools could be created in response to parental demand and on the basis of local proposals, thereby paving the way for England and Wales to have state-funded schools that aimed to foster, for example, Muslim, Buddhist or evangelical Christian beliefs, or that wished to promote particular educational philosophies.

The principle of providing a greater variety of schools, particularly at the secondary level, was extended still further in a 1996 White Paper, *Self-Government for Schools*, published during Gillian Shephard's period as Education Secretary (1994–7). The general tone of the White Paper was set in an early section with the heading 'Choice, Diversity and Specialisation', where it was argued that:

> Children have different abilities, aptitudes, interests and needs. These cannot all be fully met by a single type of school, at least at secondary level. The Government wants parents to be able to choose from a range of good schools of different types, matching what they want for their child with what a school offers. The choice should include schools which select by academic ability, so that the most able children have the chance to achieve the best of which they are capable. . . . Independent schools, church schools and grammar schools have long offered choice

for some parents. The Government has greatly expanded diversity through the Assisted Places Scheme, by setting up the 15 City Technology Colleges, and by giving all secondary schools the opportunity to become grant-maintained. It has also encouraged schools to specialise in particular subjects such as technology and languages.

(DfEE 1996, pp.2–3)

By the time this White Paper was published, there were 163 grammar schools in England and Wales, concentrated in English counties such as Buckinghamshire, Kent and Lincolnshire and in many of the larger conurbations; there were about 1,100 grant-maintained schools, including 660 secondary schools accounting for almost one in five of all students at the secondary level; and there were 196 specialist schools and colleges: fifteen city technology colleges, thirty language colleges and 151 new technology colleges. If the 1996 White Paper had become law, grant-maintained schools would have been free to select up to 50 per cent of their intake by ability; language and technology colleges up to 30 per cent; and all remaining LEA schools up to 20 per cent. In the event, Conservative plans for an even more divided secondary system had to be jettisoned as a result of the Labour victory in the 1997 general election.

SUGGESTED ACTIVITIES

1. From your reading of this chapter, and with an emphasis on arrangements for the *organisation* and *management* of schools, itemise what you see as the most radical and influential reforms embedded in the 1988 Education Reform Act. (More experienced teachers might wish to justify their choices with reference to their own experience.)

2. What do you see as the main arguments for and against increased financial autonomy for schools? In what ways might such autonomy work to the good and/or harm of student and teachers?

3. To what extent can the development of

    ●   specialist schools and City Technology Colleges; and
    ●   parental choice

    be incorporated within your own vision of comprehensive education? Articulate any aspects of these particular developments that you feel run counter to the comprehensive idea as you envision it.

4. What do you understand by the difference – drawn by John Major and others – between *equality of opportunity* and *equality of outcome*? Is this a defensible distinction?

5   What is your own understanding of *equality of opportunity* in the school and classroom context, and in which ways might this be manifested in your own practice?

SUGGESTED READING

Chitty, C. and Simon, B. (eds) (1993) *Education Answers Back: Critical Responses to Government Policy*. This book performs a useful task by bringing together a number of lectures and essays from a distinguished cross-section of the educational establishment hostile to the policies pursued by the Thatcher and Major governments between 1988 and 1992.

Jones, K. (1989) *Right Turn: The Conservative Revolution in Education*. This book is to be highly recommended as a brilliant analysis of Conservative education policy in the 1980s. Ken Jones points out that while that policy is often viewed as a regression, it did in fact have a number of radical and modernising features. Above all, its main aim was to eliminate the major tendencies that had dominated post-war educational thinking and replace them with a quite different order of priorities.

4 The National Curriculum 1: Origins and Implementation

This chapter points out that for nearly forty-five years after the end of the Second World War, the UK was almost unique in Europe in not possessing any sort of national curriculum. It is argued that this was not an oversight on the government's part but an important feature of a policy of 'non-intervention' where the day-to-day running of schools was concerned. At the same time, it would have to be admitted that it also represented, at least in the 1940s and 1950s, a strong belief in the virtues of a divided system where students would be taught in different types of school according to a set of commonly held views about fixed intelligence. With the growth of comprehensive schools came a movement among educationists and teachers promoting the desirability of a common curriculum; while similar views were circulating in the DES as part of a new-found interest in accountability and 'value for money'. There were at least two models of what a national curriculum should look like; and it was an issue that divided Mrs Thatcher's education advisers.

INTRODUCTION

In the immediate post-war period, the notion of a prescriptive state-imposed curriculum was looked upon as an undesirable alien concept, associated as it was in the official mind with the sort of regimes, be they fascist or communist, to which Britain was implacably opposed. Speaking during the second reading of the Bill that became the 1944 Education Act, R.A. Butler's parliamentary secretary James Chuter Ede declared that 'state control of the school curriculum prevented the development of a wise and sound system of education' (*Hansard*, H. of C., Vol. 396, Col. 497, 20 January 1944). This was indeed the prevailing attitude at the post-war Ministry of Education, which was generally proud of its policy of non-intervention with regard to school curriculum matters, believing that *consensus* was always preferable to *control*. Looking back over the previous ten or so years, in his influential book *Education: An Introductory Survey*, first published in 1957, W.O. Lester Smith, who had served as Chief Education Officer for Manchester for eighteen years, articulated this consensus viewpoint when he argued that 'no freedom that teachers in this country possess is so important as that of determining the curriculum and methods of teaching' (Smith 1957, p.161).

> Despite the far-reaching nature of its main proposals (see Chapter 2), the 1944 Act epitomised the contemporary attitude towards curriculum control by making no attempt to define – or even offer advice about – the actual *content* of primary and secondary schooling. The word 'curriculum' *does* appear in the Act (on page 20), but only in passing – and at the end of a section (Section 23) giving responsibility for secular instruction in state schools (although not in voluntary-aided secondary schools) to local education authorities. Since the Elementary Regulations had been abolished in 1926 and the Secondary Regulations were simply allowed to lapse in 1944, the Act established a unique situation where there was to be *no* statutory requirement for the inclusion of any subject in the school timetable, except that of religious education or instruction.

The absence of curriculum guidelines meant that, in practice, and despite the clear reference in the Act to the role of LEAs, day-to-day decisions about the content and timetabling of the school curriculum were invariably taken by headteachers and teachers under the nominal oversight of the school governing body. (Indeed, when the Labour government of James Callaghan asked LEAs for information about their curriculum policies at the end of the 1970s, many of the replies they received were politely worded 'nil returns'.) Post-war governments, whether Labour or Conservative, were well aware of the considerable autonomy granted to schools and teachers in curriculum matters and saw nothing strange in adopting this *laissez-faire* approach to such a crucial aspect of education. Labour Minister of Education George Tomlinson (1947–51) once disposed of an importunate questioner with the curt remark 'Minister's now't to do with curriculum' (quoted in Smith 1957, p.163).

In 1950, the Ministry of Education celebrated its jubilee: there had been a unified central department for half a century as a consequence of the Board of Education Act of 1899. George Tomlinson and the Permanent Secretary, Sir John Maud, crystallised the story of those fifty years in their joint introduction to the Ministry's Report for 1950, published in 1951:

> This is the story of a progressive partnership between the central department, the local education authorities and all the teachers. To build a single, but not uniform, system out of so many diverse elements; to widen educational opportunity and, at the same time, to raise standards; to knit the educational system more closely into the life of an increasingly democratic and industrialised community: these are among the main ideas which, despite two major wars, have moved legislators and administrators alike.
>
> (Ministry of Education 1951, p.1)

They went on to emphasise the absence from the report of any specific reference to the school curriculum:

> If this Report comes into the hands of readers from overseas, as we hope it will, they may be expected to look first for a substantial chapter on educational method and the curriculum of the schools. They will not find it. This does not, of course, mean that the schools have made no response to the new knowledge about the nature and needs of children or to the changing conceptions of the function of education in a democratic community. The reason is that the Department has traditionally valued the life of institutions more highly than systems and has been jealous for the freedom of schools and teachers.
>
> (*ibid.*)

In 1951, a party of schoolteachers from Britain visited Stalin's Russia to study its education system at first hand. Sir Ronald Gould, the General Secretary of the National Union of Teachers (NUT), was a member of the party, and on his return he gave a talk on the radio to explain the contrast, as he saw it, between the Russian and the British systems of education. After remarking on the generous staffing there, the cleanliness of all the schools, the well-stocked school libraries and the ample equipment, he spoke of the uniform and rigid pattern of the school curriculum. What could be the advantages of this rigidity? 'I was given only one answer', he reported to his listeners, 'namely, that when a child moves from place to place, it is easy to pick up the work in his [*sic*] new school'. Gould went on to comment: 'No doubt that is so, but is it sufficient – or even the main – reason for the enforcement of uniformity?' He then gave its flexibility and its diversity as his main reasons for preferring the curriculum set-up in this country. 'I make no bones about it', he concluded, 'give me the English approach' (quoted in Smith 1957, pp. 164–5).

This then was the period (1944 to the mid-1970s) when, in theory at least, both primary and secondary teachers were able to enjoy a remarkable degree of autonomy in curriculum planning, even though, or so it has been argued, they failed to take advantage of the situation in any meaningful sense. In Denis Lawton's famous phrase, this was, in fact, 'the Golden Age of teacher control (or non-control) of the curriculum' (Lawton 1980, p.22).

TEACHER 'CONTROL' OF THE CURRICULUM

It has to be borne in mind that, despite the absence of firm curriculum directives or guidelines from central and local government in the post-war period, there were a number of important practical considerations that severely restricted the range of options available to schools, and particularly at the secondary level. These included:

- examination syllabuses;
- university and other entrance requirements;

- the subject choices of parents and students;
- the availability of teachers and teaching materials;
- the advice and criticisms of local and government inspectors.

At the same time, most secondary schools in the 1940s and 1950s were expected to teach their students according to a set of (dubious) assumptions that were common at the time. As we saw in Chapter 2, these included fatalistic theories about fixed innate intelligence, which were used to justify the whole process of 11-plus selection for different types of secondary school.

On the one hand, post-war grammar schools were expected to provide courses of a predominantly 'academic' nature. Secure in their position as constituting the most respected type of state secondary school, these schools were able to concentrate on developing the 'cognitive–intellectual' skills associated with an 'academic' curriculum; and it was clearly assumed that most students would stay on into the sixth form and then move on to an elite form of higher education. Older students were invariably permitted a fair degree of freedom in their choice of subjects; and the replacement (in 1951) of the School Certificate, which had been a group examination requiring at least five passes, including English, by the new single-subject GCE Ordinary Level Examination meant the virtual abandonment of any idea of implementing a uniform curriculum for 'able' 11- to 16-year-olds.

The late Edward Blishen's two very successful novels, *Roaring Boys* (1955) and *This Right Soft Lot* (1969), were based, at least partly, on his experience of teaching in a demanding secondary modern school in a neglected, deprived part of London from 1949 until the late 1950s, and from this vantage point, he was able to write (in 1957) of the remarkable esteem in which local grammar schools were held:

> What does 'secondary education' mean? In the districts with which I am familiar, the people, justly enough, take it to mean a *grammar-school* education. ('I mean, this isn't a real secondary school', said a parent to me once, stubbornly incognisant of the signboard at the school entrance.) And they don't precisely mean grammar-school education in its every detail. They have in mind the fact that grammar schools take their pupils somewhere, strengthen them, and add to them, palpably and measurably. The grammar school has managed to become something much more than a place to which you have, by law, to send your child for a specified period. It's a road that forks out in so many directions, not one that comes to a single dead end.
>
> (Blishen 1957, p.75)

These illuminating comments were later confirmed by sociologist William Taylor in his 1963 study of the problems facing the secondary modern school:

> It is clear that, for the working-class child, the grammar school not only provides education that makes upward social and occupational mobility practicable, but also furnishes an educational and social environment which encourages the formulation of upwardly mobile vocational aspirations.
>
> (Taylor 1963, p.80)

The new secondary modern schools, on the other hand, which catered for the education of the vast majority of the nation's secondary-age students, were expected to provide less well-defined courses of a practical and vocational nature, although it was not always clear what this meant in terms of subjects, and, in any case, it soon became apparent that there were large numbers of so-called 11-plus failures who could cope with something far more demanding. Lacking a clear sense of their aims and objectives, what were the new schools to do: should they opt for a diluted version of the traditional grammar school curriculum, particularly for their more 'able' students; or should they plan something completely different with scant regard to the demands created by preparing youngsters for public examinations?

The problems facing the new secondary moderns (seen by many as merely the old elementary schools 'writ large') were highlighted in a special inset devoted to these schools in *The Times Educational Supplement* in June 1956. The teachers, it was argued, had had 'to fashion a new sort of school, knowing all the while that it was being measured against the old . . . to build a new Jerusalem with the one hand and fend off the critics with the other'. Clearly, there was no shortage of opinions as to what the secondary modern school should be aiming to achieve:

> Never were labourers in the vineyard subject to so much advice. The secondary modern school has been the target of every new-fangled theory, every half-digested, ill-assorted idea . . . if ever it has seen a settled objective, half the busybodies in the world of education have rushed in to save it from itself. Turn out citizens. Turn out literates. Turn out technicians. Be more vocational. Prepare for leisure. Stick to the wider view. . . . The wonder is that with all this, and with all the difficulties of the post-war world, the secondary modern schools have got anywhere at all. . . . But they have.
>
> (*The Times Educational Supplement*, 8 June 1956)

It needs to be emphasised that many politicians, particularly on the Right, were slow to realise that the 11-plus selection procedure was a deeply flawed exercise, legitimating an academic/vocational divide that was ultimately harmful to *all* students. In a debate in the House of Commons in January 1965, Conservative politician Quintin Hogg (later to become Lord Hailsham) articulated a commonly held view about the low aspirations and capabilities of secondary modern students when he launched an attack on Labour MPs for supporting secondary reorganisation:

I can assure Hon. Members opposite that if they would go to study what is now being done in good secondary modern schools, they would not find a lot of pupils biting their nails in frustration because they had failed the 11-plus. The pleasant noise of banging metal and sawing wood would greet their ears, and a smell of cooking with rather expensive equipment would come out of the front door to greet them. They would find that these boys and girls were getting an education tailor-made to their desires, their bents and their requirements. . . . I am not prepared to admit that the Party opposite has done a good service to education, or to the children of this country, by attacking that form of school, or seeking to denigrate it.

(*Hansard*, H. of C., Vol. 705, Cols 423–4, 21 January 1965)

So the absence of any form of centrally imposed national curriculum in the post-war period did *not* mean the complete lack of national assumptions and expectations about appropriate curricula for different groups of students. Then in 1960, there was some indication that the era of teacher 'control' of the curriculum might be coming to a premature end and that the government was contemplating a more positive role in the process of curriculum planning. Debating the 1959 Crowther Report (on the education of 15- to 18-year-olds) in the House of Commons in March 1960, Sir David Eccles (Conservative Minister of Education from 1959 to 1962) made it clear that there was a desire at the Ministry to make its own voice heard on matters of content – in Sir David Eccles' famous phrase, to enter 'the secret garden of the curriculum':

I regret that so many of our education debates have had to be devoted almost entirely to bricks and mortar and to the organisation of the system. We hardly ever discuss what is taught to the seven million boys and girls in the maintained schools. We treat the curriculum as though it were a subject, like 'the other place' [that is, the House of Lords], about which it is 'not done' for us to make remarks. I should like the House to say that this reticence has been overdone. Of course, Parliament would never attempt to dictate the curriculum, but, from time to time, we could, with advantage, express our views on what is taught in schools and in training colleges. As for the Ministry of Education itself, my Department has the unique advantage of the countrywide experience of Her Majesty's Inspectorate. Nowhere in the kingdom is there such a rich source of information or such a constant exchange of ideas on all that goes on in the schools. I shall, therefore, try in the future to make the Ministry's own voice heard rather more often, more positively, and, no doubt, sometimes more controversially. For this purpose, we shall need to undertake inside the Department more educational research and to strengthen our statistical services. Crowther . . . prodded us to do this, and action is now in hand. In the meantime, the section in the Report on the Sixth Form is an irresistible invitation for a sally into the secret garden of the curriculum.

(*Hansard*, H. of C., Vol. 620, Cols 51–2, 21 March 1960)

Two years later, in 1962, after much discussion within the Inspectorate, the government announced the setting up of the Curriculum Study Group, although without prior consultation with organised educational interests. The new group was to involve HMIs, administrators and experts co-opted from the outside. It would provide a nucleus of full-time staff to organise and co-ordinate research studies. Its work would be linked with that of the universities, practising teachers, local authorities, research organisations, professional institutes and others concerned with the content of education and examinations. According to Ronald A. Manzer, the group was conceived by Sir David Eccles as 'a relatively small, "commando-like unit", making raids into the curriculum' (Manzer 1970, p.91). It certainly marked a definite departure in the Ministry's conception of its role in the formulation of an important area of educational policy. To quote Manzer again: 'it involved the insertion of an agent of the community into what had previously been regarded almost entirely as a technical or administrative problem' (*ibid.*, p.92).

Such was the hostility of professional educators to the government's new body that in 1963, the new Minister of Education, Sir Edward Boyle, concluded that it would have to be replaced by a more representative organisation. The Lockwood Committee was set up and quickly recommended that there should be a Schools Council for the Curriculum and Examinations.

Meeting for the first time in October 1964, with Sir John Maud as its chairperson, this new council was not at all the sort of body that Sir David Eccles had had in mind in 1962. It was an independent body with a majority of teacher members. Its declared purpose was to undertake research and development work in curricula, teaching methods and examinations in schools. Most important of all, it aimed to adhere to the general principle, expressed in its constitution, that each school should have the fullest possible measure of responsibility for its own curriculum and teaching methods based on the needs of its own students and evolved by its own staff. In, for example, Working Paper 53 *The Whole Curriculum 13–16*, published in 1975, it was argued that the aims of each school should be stated in a 'covenant' to which parents, students, teachers and society at large could easily subscribe. At the same time, the paper was anxious to uphold the principle of teacher autonomy in all matters relating to the curriculum:

> British schools have for long been jealous of their independence in curricular matters. However much they may turn to outside bodies for resources, information and advice, they insist that the curriculum must be of their own making. We strongly affirm our support for this position for . . . we believe the surest hope for the improvement of the secondary-school curriculum lies in the continuing professional growth of the teacher, which, in turn, implies that teachers take even greater responsibility for the development of schools' curriculum policies. Moreover, we have stressed the distinctive nature of the curriculum policies appropriate to particular schools, and it would be a denial of this to attempt to prescribe the sort of policies they should adopt.
>
> (Schools Council 1975, p.30)

Yet, despite the clear stand taken by the Schools Council in this 1975 document, it was in the mid-1970s that more central control of the school curriculum became a real possibility, with intimations of a new interventionist stance by central government that were far more positive and challenging than were the rather vague 'threats' uttered by Sir David Eccles back in 1960.

The country's straitened economic circumstances following the OPEC (Organization of Petroleum Exporting Countries) oil crisis of 1973 (already discussed in Chapter 2) meant that ministers felt under considerable pressure to account for the efficient use of the £6 billion of resources devoted to education. Similarly, the new centralising ambitions of DES civil servants could be viewed as part of a new-found interest in policy, efficiency and 'value for money'. At the same time, education ministers were being advised by a number of influential industrialists and employers that secondary schools had a vital role to play in preparing their students for entry into the world of work, and this constituted an additional reason for ways having to be found of directly influencing the aims and content of the school curriculum. It was no longer considered good practice to leave important curriculum decisions in the hands of classroom teachers.

It was the 1976–9 Labour government of James Callaghan that first made a concerted effort to challenge the concept of 'teacher control of the curriculum'. The confidential Yellow Book on the current state of the education service, compiled for the Prime Minister by DES civil servants and completed in July 1976, addressed a number of the thorny problems that were preoccupying central government. In particular, it was quite frank about the need for more positive initiatives from the centre – and especially in the areas of curriculum content and teaching methods:

> It would . . . be good to get on record from ministers, and in particular, the Prime Minister, an authoritative pronouncement on the division of responsibility for what goes on in schools, suggesting that the Department should give a firmer lead. Such a pronouncement would have to respect legitimate claims made by the teachers as to the exercise of their professional judgement, but should firmly refute any argument – and this is what they have sought to establish – that no one except teachers has any right to any say in what goes on in schools. The climate for a declaration on these lines may, in fact, now be relatively favourable. Nor need there be any inhibition for fear that the Department could not make use of this enhanced opportunity to exercise influence over curriculum content and teaching methods: the Inspectorate would have a leading role to play in bringing forward ideas in these areas and is ready to fulfil that new responsibility.
>
> (DES 1976, p.25)

Then in the speech delivered at Ruskin College, Oxford, in October 1976 (already referred to in Chapter 2), the Prime Minister himself was anxious to repudiate the suggestion that education policy in general, and curriculum policy in particular, could be said to be the exclusive concern of any one group:

> If everything is reduced to such phrases as 'educational freedom versus
> state control', we shall get nowhere. . . . Parents, teachers, learned and
> professional bodies, representatives of higher education and both sides of
> industry, together with the Government, all have an important part to
> play in formulating and expressing the purpose of education and the
> standards that we need.
>
> (quoted in Chitty 1989, p.139)

It was also in the mid-1970s that the issue of central control became inextricably linked with the debate over the desirability or otherwise of establishing the principles for the composition of a common or common-core curriculum for all state secondary schools; and for many teachers and administrators, this marked a new stage in the evolution of the comprehensive school, by 1975 accounting for the education of around 70 per cent of the secondary school population (DES 1976, p.5).

DIFFERENT CONCEPTS OF A COMPREHENSIVE CURRICULUM

In the early days of comprehensive reorganisation, comparatively little attention had been paid to the nature of the curriculum for the new 'all-ability' schools. Few had argued that a new comprehensive school might require a new *comprehensive* or *whole-school* curriculum; and, significantly, Circular 10/65 (already discussed in Chapter 2) had had *nothing* to say about curriculum and assessment. Comprehensive reorganisation had been promoted as a largely *institutional* reform – as if comprehensive schools were simply a good thing *in themselves*. Writing at the end of the 1960s, politics lecturer Anthony Arblaster had bemoaned the fact that:

> The long fight over comprehensive secondary education and virtually
> all the discussion and activity provoked by the series of official reports –
> Plowden on primary, Newsom on secondary and Robbins on higher
> education – has revolved around questions of organisation and structure,
> principles of selection, equality of opportunity, numerical expansion,
> standards of teaching and accommodation, and so on.
>
> (Arblaster 1970, p.49)

The absence of a nationwide debate about the content of secondary education meant that for many years, the majority of the new comprehensive schools simply tried to assimilate the two existing curriculum traditions derived from the grammar and modern schools.

There was, after all, no blueprint for a successful comprehensive school; and in the 1960s and early 1970s, the DES was too busy scrutinising the reorganisation plans submitted by co-operating local authorities to give any thought to the curriculum implications of the move away from selection. Even the Schools

Council, potentially an important agent for curriculum planning and development, failed to produce any kind of basis for a whole-school curriculum for the early comprehensives. In 1973, Denis Lawton could lament both the 'elitist mentality' inspired by 'the post–war tripartite system' and 'the consistent failure to re-think the curriculum and plan a programme which would be appropriate for universal secondary education' (Lawton 1973, p.101).

As late as 1979, an HMI survey of the nation's secondary schools (DES 1979) reported that although some form of common curriculum could invariably be found in the first year or two of secondary schooling (now usually referred to as Years 7 and 8), curricular differentiation began to operate from the third year (Year 9) onwards. Students in the 'higher' streams or 'bands' were often given the opportunity to start one or more additional foreign languages – additional, that is, to French; while their 'less able' contemporaries might well be encouraged to drop French altogether. Similarly, a select group of students could be found studying separate physics, chemistry and biology, while the 'science' on offer to the 'bottom' streams took the form of general science, rural science or science incorporated into something called 'environmental studies'. While the emphasis in the 'top' streams or bands was on developing the cognitive-intellectual skills, only the 'less able' were thought to derive benefit from extended contact with the creative-aesthetic areas of the curriculum. Whatever form the differentiated curriculum then took in the last two years of compulsory schooling (Years 10 and 11) – whether organised around completely segregated courses or a wide variety of option schemes – it was obvious that, in reality, the 'top' streams or classes were following a grammar school curriculum with its emphasis on the traditional academic school subjects, while those below had to be content with either a diluted version of that curriculum or a programme of work much influenced by the recommendations of the 1963 Newsom Report, with its tacit support for non–academic, 'life-adjustment' courses of a relatively undemanding nature.

Somewhat paradoxically, the period of the mid–1970s when, largely for political and economic reasons, central government began to seek ways of directly influencing the composition of the school curriculum was also the time when a number of teachers and educationists were beginning to question the approaches outlined above. John White had produced *Towards a Compulsory Curriculum* in 1973; and for some time, Denis Lawton had been writing in terms of an integrated curriculum (1969) or a common-culture individualised curriculum (1973), acknowledging his debt to the work of Broudy *et al.* in America (1964) and to the more accessible writings of Raymond Williams in this country (1958, 1961). All of this exerted a powerful influence on a small but growing group of teachers who were now beginning to write of their experiences in trying to implement a unified curriculum appropriate to an age of comprehensive secondary schools (see, for example, Holt 1976, 1978; Chitty 1979). Here at last was evidence that teachers wanted to prove themselves worthy, so to speak, of the power that they wielded over the curriculum; but the effects of the new thinking were to be both localised and relatively short-lived, for influential civil servants at the DES were soon to argue that curriculum content was far too important to be left totally in the hands of pioneering schools.

> When the curriculum debate moved out of the control of a limited number of teachers and educationists and became a matter of government concern, reflected in the terms of the so-called 'Great Debate' following the 1976 Ruskin speech, it was often seen as focusing on a single identifiable concept, whereas it is important to stress that there were, in fact, at least two different official versions of what a national or common curriculum should look like. Specifically, we need to be clear about the major distinctions between the *professional* concept of a 'common entitlement' curriculum embodied in material prepared within Her Majesty's Inspectorate and the *bureaucratic* concept of a 'core' curriculum to be discerned in curriculum documents emanating from the DES itself.

THE HMI MODEL

The professional common–curriculum approach, as depicted, for example, in the three HMI Red Books concerned with the secondary school curriculum published between 1977 and 1983 (DES 1977b, 1981b, 1983), reflected a genuine concern with the quality of the teaching process in schools and with the needs of individual students. It sought to transcend traditional subject boundaries and saw the use of subjects on the timetable as simply a convenient means of achieving higher–level aims. It presupposed that teachers were well motivated, well trained and generally skilled in identifying individual problems and needs. It was concerned with students as developing individuals and opposed to any system of assessment that resulted in large sections of the school population being dismissed as 'failures'.

Without arguing that there was only *one* model of 'good practice', the HMI approach suggested the adoption by schools of a number of so-called 'areas of experience', to be used as the basis of curriculum construction or of reshaping and refining existing curricula (see also Edwards and Kelly 1998; Moore 2000). In the 1977 Red Book, eight such areas were recommended:

- the aesthetic and creative
- the ethical
- the linguistic
- the mathematical
- the physical
- the scientific
- the social and political
- the spiritual.

(DES 1977b, p.6)

These 'areas of experience' were deliberately listed as above in alphabetical order so that no particular order of importance could be inferred: in the view of the Inspectorate, they were all to be considered equally important. Then, in a later HMI document, *The Curriculum from 5 to 16*, published in March 1985 (DES 1985b), the 1977 checklist was expanded to nine areas of learning and experience. The ethical became the moral; the linguistic became the linguistic and literary; the social and political became (significantly) the human and social; and the additional area of experience was the technological (*ibid.*, p.16).

The 1977 checklist could be translated into a timetable for the older students in a comprehensive school in a number of ways, but the one shown in Table 4.1 is the one suggested in Red Book 1. Based on a forty-period week, this model would satisfy the basic HMI requirement that the common curriculum should always occupy the major part of the total time available. The eight remaining periods could be used for the provision of two option blocks, allowing students to choose additional subjects (for example, a second foreign language, a classical study or another science) or devote more time to subjects already being studied.

Yet the authors of the 1977 Red Book were anxious to make it clear that, in its crude form, this timetable model fell far short of what they would like to see in practice. Curriculum construction in terms of subjects was acceptable when, but only when, teachers were quite clear what was to be achieved through them:

> It is . . . important to emphasise the fact that subject or 'course' labels often tell us surprisingly little about the objectives to be pursued or the activities to be introduced, still less about the likely or expected levels of achievement. An individual subject may make valid, although varied, contributions in different schools; or to different pupils in the same school; or to the same pupils at different ages or stages of individual development. Any framework to be constructed for the curriculum must be able to accommodate shifts of purpose, content and method in subjects, and of emphasis between subjects. In other words, it is not proposed that schools should plan and construct a common curriculum in terms of subject labels only: that would be to risk becoming trapped in discussions about the relative importance of this subject or that. Rather, it is necessary to look through the subject or discipline to the

Table 4.1 A typical timetable for older students in a comprehensive school

Subject	Periods
English	5
Mathematics	5
A modern language	4
A science	5
Religious education and a social study	4
Art/craft/music	4
Careers education	2
Physical activities	3
Total	32

Source: (DES 1977b, p.7).

areas of experience and knowledge to which it may provide access, and
to the skills and attitudes which it may assist to develop.

(DES 1977b, p.6)

Red Book 3, *Curriculum 11–16: Towards a Statement of Entitlement*, published in
1983 (DES 1983), provided HMI with an opportunity to highlight the principles
that had underpinned its curricular thinking for more than a decade and to lay
particular emphasis on the concept of 'entitlement':

> It seems essential to us that all pupils should be guaranteed a curriculum
> of a distinctive breadth and depth to which they should be entitled,
> irrespective of the type of school they attend or their level of ability or
> their social circumstances – and that failure to provide such a
> curriculum is unacceptable. . . . The conviction has grown that all
> pupils are entitled to a broad compulsory common curriculum to the
> age of 16 which introduces them to a range of experiences, makes them
> aware of the kind of society in which they are going to live and gives
> them the skills necessary to live in it. Any curriculum which fails to
> provide this balance and is over-weighted in any particular direction,
> whether vocational, technical or academic, is to be seriously questioned.
> Any measures which restrict the access of all pupils to a wide-ranging
> curriculum or which focus too narrowly on specific skills are in direct
> conflict with the entitlement curriculum envisaged here.
>
> (DES 1983, pp. 25,26)

The DES model

The bureaucratic core–curriculum approach, as depicted in a number of key DES
documents (for example, DES 1977a, 1980, 1981a), was primarily concerned with
the 'efficiency' of the education system and with the need to obtain precise
information to *demonstrate* that efficiency. It was concerned with controlling what
was taught in schools, particularly secondary schools, and making teachers generally
more accountable for their work in the classroom.

Whereas the professional approach was concerned with individual differences
and the learning process, the bureaucratic approach was associated with norms
or benchmarks, norm-related criteria and judgements based on the expectations of how a 'statistically normal' child should perform.

Whereas the professional viewpoint saw the school curriculum as a broad
synthesis of the academic, the technical, the vocational and the practical, the
bureaucratic approach was concerned to vocationalise the secondary curriculum
for students of 'average' and 'below-average' ability.

> Whereas the professional approach was concerned to define 'areas of learning and experience', the ideal bureaucratic curriculum was based largely on traditional subjects.

Both the 1976 Yellow Book and the 1976 Ruskin College speech talked in terms of investigating the nature of a so-called 'core curriculum' of basic knowledge; and a 1977 Green Paper made references to five subjects that had a right to be included in the 'protected' or 'core' element of the secondary curriculum:

> English and religious education are in most secondary schools a standard part of the curriculum for all pupils up to the age of sixteen, and it is simply not true that many pupils drop mathematics at an early stage. . . . Few, inside or outside the schools, would contest that alongside English and mathematics, science should find a secure place for all pupils at least to the age of sixteen, and that a modern language should do so for as high a proportion as practical.
>
> (DES 1977a, p.11)

The 'core curriculum' concept was developed further in two DES documents: *A Framework for the School Curriculum*, published in January 1980 (DES 1980), and *The School Curriculum*, published in March 1981 (DES 1981a). The first of these documents went so far as to specify what proportion of time should be spent on the core subjects, but this idea came in for wide criticism. A year later, the idea was quietly dropped, and *The School Curriculum* conceded that the issue of minimum time allocations should be left to the discretion of local education authorities and teachers:

> English, mathematics, science and modern languages are generally treated as separate items in school timetables. . . . It is important that every school should ensure that each pupil's programme includes a substantial and well-distributed time allocation for English, mathematics and science up to the age of sixteen, and that those pupils who do take a modern language should devote sufficient time to it to make the study worthwhile. The two Secretaries of State do not suggest minimum times which should be devoted to these subjects. Any suggested minima might too easily become norms, or be interpreted too rigidly. It is for the local education authorities to consider, in consultation with the teachers in their areas, whether to suggest minimum time allocations in these subjects, as broad guidance for schools.
>
> (DES 1981a, p.14)

In the years following 1976, a stream of documents on the school curriculum flowed from the DES, invariably falling neatly into one or other of the two categories outlined above. Yet it was not until the second half of the 1980s that DES civil servants were successful in their advocacy of widening the centralising process. As late as March 1985, the government was anxious to disclaim any intention of altering the terms of the curriculum debate to include legislation to control the school curriculum. The DES White Paper *Better Schools* (published in that month) contained a number of unequivocal statements:

> It would not in the view of the Government be right for the Secretaries of State's policy for the range and pattern of the 5–16 curriculum to amount to the determination of national syllabuses for that period. It would, however, be appropriate for the curricular policy of the LEA, on the basis of broadly agreed principles about range and pattern, to be more precise about, for example, the balance between curricular elements and the age and pace at which pupils are introduced to particular subject areas (e.g. a foreign language). . . . The establishment of broadly agreed objectives would not mean that the curricular policies of the Secretaries of State, the LEA and the school should relate to each other in a nationally uniform way. . . . The Government does not propose to introduce legislation affecting the powers of the Secretaries of State in relation to the curriculum.
>
> (DES 1985b, pp.11–12)

At the same time, it was clear that if the Thatcher government *did* decide to abandon the commitment highlighted above, it would opt for the DES rather than the HMI approach to curriculum planning. The long-awaited announcement by Sir Keith Joseph, in June 1984, of a new examination to be known as the GCSE (General Certificate of Secondary Education), to replace the GCE Ordinary Level and CSE examinations, was seen by many as marking the triumph of a *subject-dominated* curriculum. In the words of an editorial in *The Times Educational Supplement* at the end of November 1985:

> It is now clear that all the Inspectorate's efforts to steer curriculum planning towards an exploration of a full range of areas of experience have failed to lift the secondary-school programme out of its entrenched subject-defined tradition. By the time the SEC (Secondary Examinations Council) has done its best (or worst), any notion of a national core curriculum will have to be found in the form of a spread of GCSE entries.
>
> (*The Times Educational Supplement*, 29 November 1985)

It was only after Kenneth Baker replaced Sir Keith Joseph as Education Secretary in May 1986 that the idea of a national curriculum moved into the realm of practical policies. Yet, as we saw in Chapter 3, it was an issue that divided the Prime Minister's right-wing advisers and incurred the deep hostility of all those for whom the whole concept of a state-imposed curriculum was frankly incompatible with the provision of greater variety and choice in education.

TOWARDS A NATIONAL CURRICULUM

It seems clear that it was only in the second half of 1986 that serious consideration was given to the idea of overcoming the opposition of right-wing libertarians and imposing on schools, both primary and secondary, a centrally determined curriculum framework. Education Secretary Kenneth Baker gave his staunch support to the broad concept of a subject-based national curriculum, and so too did the newly formed Hillgate Group of right-wing political theorists (comprising Caroline Cox, Jessica Douglas-Home, John Marks, Lawrence Norcross and Roger Scruton), which (as we saw in Chapters 1 and 3) viewed it chiefly as a useful form of social control and as a means of increasing teacher accountability (see Hillgate Group 1986, 1987). Such a curriculum would, in the group's view, uphold the values of a traditional education and instil respect for all the institutions of the bourgeois state. At the same time, it would preach the moral virtue of free enterprise and the pursuit of profit – a concept designed to appeal to the neo-liberal wing of the far Right.

As discussion continued, the group's arguments failed to convince those who played leading roles in devising measures for inclusion in the 1987 Education Reform Bill. Members of the Centre for Policy Studies (CPS) and of the Education Unit of the Institute of Economic Affairs (IEA) adhered to the view that a school's individual curriculum structure should always be seen as one of its major 'selling points' with prospective parents and *not* as something to be determined by the DES. When he was asked on a BBC Television *Panorama* programme 'A Class Revolution', broadcast on 2 November 1987, about the planning for the Bill, which had taken place in Downing Street since the summer of 1986, Stuart Sexton, director of the IEA's Education Unit, revealed that he and many of his colleagues had remained deeply sceptical about the desirability of a government-imposed curriculum – and particularly one with as many as ten compulsory subjects. There was strong support for the Hillgate Group's emphasis on social order and moral values, but it was argued that a return to basic values could be accomplished quite easily by requiring schools to give sufficient time to certain essential disciplines. On one occasion, according to Sexton, the Prime Minister had made it clear that her idea of a decent 'core' curriculum was the effective teaching of the six Rs: 'reading, writing, arithmetic, religious education and right and wrong'.

As it became increasingly obvious that agreement on the precise format of a national curriculum could not be reached within a suitable time-span, Kenneth Baker took the bold decision to pre-empt any further discussion on the matter by simply announcing his proposals for a 'national core curriculum' on the prestigious London Weekend Television programme *Weekend World*, broadcast on 7 December 1986. He informed his interviewer, Matthew Parris (a former Conservative MP and since the early 1990s a *Times* sketch writer), that his proposed curriculum should be viewed by the public as a crucial aspect of the move towards 'more central control of education' in the interest primarily of the school students themselves, far too many of whom were allowed to be 'aimless and drifting' (reported in *The Times*, 8 December 1986).

This announcement shocked the neo-liberal members of the far Right and even came as a surprise to fellow members of the government. Writing in *The Guardian* six years later, Kenneth Baker admitted that he had decided to keep his Cabinet colleagues in the dark about his curriculum plans, for he had not relished 'holding a series of seminars for them on the differences between a curriculum and a syllabus, the purposes of testing, and the teaching methods needed to deliver a curriculum in the schools'. Baker had realised that his opponents would continue to argue that if there had to be a national curriculum as part of the new Bill, it should concentrate on the three 'core' subjects of English, science and mathematics, leaving all the rest to flexible interpretation. He had 'set his mind against this' and had even 'argued fiercely with Margaret Thatcher' (*The Guardian*, 24 November 1992).

In his 1993 autobiography *The Turbulent Years: My Life in Politics*, Kenneth Baker revealed that as late as October 1987 – only three weeks before the introduction of the Education Reform Bill into the House of Commons – he had been obliged to use the threat of his resignation to prevent his broad-based curriculum being eroded by Mrs Thatcher:

> I saw the Prime Minister privately. I said to her: 'If you want me to continue as your Education Secretary, then we will have to stick to the Curriculum that I have set out in the Consultative Paper. I and my ministerial colleagues have advocated and stoutly defended the broad curriculum. We have listed the ten subjects, and I set them out before the Select Committee in April. You will recall, Prime Minister, that I specifically cleared my statement with you'. . . . This was a tough meeting, but I was simply not prepared to give in to a last-minute rearguard action, even when waged by the Prime Minister herself. The broad-based curriculum was saved – for the time being.
>
> (Baker 1993, p.197)

Even in 1993, when the National Curriculum was already beginning to fall apart, Baker was not to know just how short-lived his 'victory' would prove to be.

As we saw in Chapter 3, the original National Curriculum that found its way into the 1987 Bill consisted of ten foundation subjects to be taken by all students during their compulsory education: English, mathematics and science (constituting the 'core'), a modern foreign language (except in primary schools), technology, history, geography, art, music and physical education – with religious education added later as the one and only *basic* subject. It was originally intended that the majority of curriculum time at primary school level would be spent on the three subjects making up the 'core' of the curriculum.

All the available evidence suggests (see Chitty 1988, 1989) that the 1987 National Curriculum Consultation Document (DES 1987) was prepared in great haste and with little regard for the principles underpinning previous government policy.

For one thing, the 'core' was defined far more rigidly than would have been thought 'desirable' over the previous ten years. At the same time, there were few references in the document to the need for the curriculum to be made more relevant to adult and working life, a key concept that had found its way into all DES statements published since 1976, culminating with the appearance of *Better Schools* in March 1985. And in this respect, it is particularly interesting to examine the treatment of the Technical and Vocational Education Initiative (TVEI) as indicative of a marked change in emphasis. A major curriculum project that had been awarded many column inches in the 1985 White Paper warranted only two brief mentions in 1987. Nowhere in the consultation document was there any reference to the many new subjects, such as hotel and food services, robotics, microelectronics or manufacturing technology, that teachers had been able to introduce – for at least some of their students – as part of the TVEI scheme.

It has been suggested (see Aldrich 1988) that, as part of its refusal to embark on a period of *genuine* consultation with all interested parties, the DES simply looked for a 'suitable' national curriculum among the regulations issued earlier in the century. It is certainly instructive to compare the curriculum outlined in the 1987 document with the syllabus prescribed in the 1904 Regulations for students in the state secondary schools established by the 1902 Education Act (see Table 4.2):

Table 4.2 A comparison of curricula, 1904 and 1987

1904	1987
English	English
Mathematics	Mathematics
Science	Science
History	History
Geography	Geography
Foreign language	*Modern* foreign language
Drawing	Art
Physical exercise	Physical education
Manual work/housewifery	Technology
	Music

There is certainly a striking similarity between these two lists of subjects, notwithstanding a few *minor* differences: the term '*modern* foreign language' in the 1987 list excluded Latin, which featured prominently in the secondary school curriculum of 1904; 'manual work/housewifery' from the 1904 list had become 'technology' in 1987; and music, which appeared in the 1987 list, had not been a compulsory subject in 1904.

Richard Aldrich has observed with some justification that the new National Curriculum, 'in so far as it was expressed in terms of core and foundation subjects', appeared as 'a simple reassertion of the basic grammar-school curriculum devised at the beginning of the twentieth century' (Aldrich 1988, p.23). This grammar school curriculum was now to be extended to all state primary and comprehensive secondary schools.

Many teachers and educationists have shared Professor Aldrich's views about the unsuitability of the 1987/88 National Curriculum framework. Delivering the Raymond Priestley Lecture at the University of Birmingham on 14 November 1991, Peter Watkins, the former Deputy Chief Executive of the National Curriculum Council, commented on the failure of the Thatcher government to treat the process of curriculum construction with the seriousness and sense of purpose it so clearly demanded:

> There is . . . one fundamental problem from which all others stem. The National Curriculum had no architect, only builders. Many people were surprised at the lack of sophistication in the original model: ten subjects, attainment targets and programmes of study defined in a few words in the 1987 Bill, that was all.
>
> (Watkins 1993, p.73)

During his three-year period as Education Secretary (May 1986 to July 1989), Kenneth Baker tried to 'sell' his curriculum package to his vociferous critics on the Far Right on the grounds that it would serve as ideal justification for a massive programme of national testing at 7, 11, 14 and 16. This, in turn, would provide the raw data for the compilation of national league tables, whose publication in the local and national press would furnish valuable evidence to parents as to the desirability or otherwise of individual schools.

However, Baker's opponents were not to be quite so easily assuaged, particularly as it was becoming apparent that the original simplistic curriculum framework was being rapidly transformed into a rigid, content-specific *national syllabus*.

What was not foreseen was that each one of the subject working groups appointed by the government would attempt to pack everything that it considered important into its own curriculum. Neither these subject groups nor the ministers to whom they were responsible paid any regard to whether or not all the various subjects taken together made a workable or coherent whole. It soon became obvious to both politicians and headteachers that the new curriculum was seriously overloaded – particularly in the primary sector and at Key Stage 4.

All this provided valuable ammunition to a number of prominent figures on the Right, who were not reticent about voicing their strong opposition to the unwieldy structure that was clearly emerging. Contributing to a debate in the House of Lords in April 1988, former Education Secretary Keith Joseph argued that the government's policies were in danger of putting the school curriculum into 'too tight a straitjacket'. He told his fellow peers that he was a strong supporter of most of the clauses in the 1987 Bill but felt obliged to warn that the new curriculum was already too detailed and 'far too rigid' (reported in *The Guardian*, 19 April 1988). In the following month, Stuart Sexton, Director of the Education Unit of the Institute of Economic Affairs, made his own views clear in a hard-hitting article that appeared in *The Times* under the heading 'No nationalised curriculum':

> What Kenneth Baker proposes is a *nationalised* curriculum set down in detail by a committee of so-called experts and endorsed by him with the

force of law. . . . The Government's proposals will put the schools' curriculum into a straitjacket, removing all flexibility and retarding the continual process of improvement and updating. Once these proposals are put into tablets of legislative stone, it will be years before the bureaucracy wakes up both to its own mistakes and to necessary changes. . . . A compromise now would be either to scrap the National Curriculum Council altogether, and that would be most welcome, or to make its recommendations advisory upon the schools, but nothing more. . . . The opportunity remains for the Government to respond to its critics by returning to a *national* curriculum dictated by the 'market' instead of a *nationalised* one dictated by government.

(*The Times*, 9 May 1988)

Even the Prime Minister herself was prepared to voice her opposition to the prescriptive nature of the National Curriculum. In a controversial interview with the editor of *The Sunday Telegraph*, published in April 1990, she was keen to emphasise that she had never agreed to the National Curriculum becoming a national syllabus, and she drew a distinction between the 'core' subjects of the curriculum and the seven other 'foundation' subjects:

> The core curriculum, so far as we have the English one out, the mathematics and the science – now that originally was what I meant by a national curriculum. Everyone simply must be trained in mathematics up to a certain standard. You must be trained in language, and I would say some literature up to a certain standard, you really must. It is your own tongue. . . . Now that is to me the core curriculum. And it is so important that you simply must be tested on it. . . . Going on to all the other things in the curriculum, when we first started on this, I do not think I ever thought they would work out the syllabus in such detail, as they are doing now. . . . Now the history report has just come out. . . . My worry is whether we should put out such a detailed one. You see, once you put out an approved curriculum, if you have got it wrong, the situation is worse afterwards than it was before.

(*The Sunday Telegraph*, 15 April 1990)

Within a few years of this interview, and much to the delight of those who continued to think of themselves as Thatcherites, the National Curriculum was being steadily dismantled. And that constitutes the main theme of Chapter 5.

SUGGESTED ACTIVITIES

1.   Starting with the arguments elaborated in this chapter and the various perspectives given, discuss who you think should be 'in control of' the curriculum.

To what extent should the curriculum be imposed, and to what extent should it be a negotiated, collaborative construct arrived at through discussion between interested parties?

Who might these parties be?

2.   Identify the specific advantages and disadvantages of:
    ● a centralised national curriculum such as now exists in England and Wales, in which curriculum content is spelt out in considerable detail and is common across schools;
    ● a decentralised curriculum, in which schools decide pretty much for themselves (with or without the constraints of public examination systems) exactly what to teach;
    ● a national 'minimum' curriculum, in which the broad principles and content of the curriculum are imposed externally and are common across schools but it is left to schools to translate these principles and guidelines into practice in the light of perceived local needs.

3.   What do you understand by the term 'comprehensive curriculum'?
    What would you personally want to see included in a 'comprehensive curriculum'? What, for you, would be its non-negotiable elements?
    From your experience, how close does the current school curriculum appear to be to your own preferred comprehensive curriculum? Are you able to identify any 'gaps' or any areas that you feel are currently over- or under-represented in the curriculum?

4.   With reference to question 2 and to points made in Chapter 4, what do you understand to be the main difference between 'syllabus' and 'curriculum'?

SUGGESTED READING

Chitty, C. (1989) *Towards a New Education System: The Victory of the New Right?* The main part of this book looks at the period before the introduction of the National Curriculum, when the very idea of state control of the curriculum was not considered to be either necessary or desirable. It also examines the reasons why there was a sudden reversal of government policy between 1985 and 1988.

Lawton, D. (1980) *The Politics of the School Curriculum*. This book is a lucid and challenging study of the period that the author describes as 'the Golden Age of teacher control (*or non-control*) of the curriculum'. Professor Lawton is concerned to explain why schools and teachers made such limited use of their 'control' of the curriculum and why there was a consistent failure to rethink the curriculum and plan a programme that would be appropriate for a new age of comprehensive secondary schools. He also examines the dangers of an 'accountability' model of education.

5 The National Curriculum 2: Reversals and Amendments

This chapter follows on from Chapter 4 and traces the development of the National Curriculum since its introduction in the late 1980s. There were initial difficulties over the structure and implementation of the testing programme; and the so-called TGAT Report prepared by Professor Paul Black was viewed by many as an uneasy compromise between the view of professional educators, that testing's main function was to diagnose individual strengths and weaknesses, and the government's wish to evaluate the effectiveness of individual schools. At the same time, it soon became clear that there was a real problem of 'overload' with the structure envisaged for Key Stage 4. In desperation, the Major government turned to Sir Ron Dearing to help it out of its difficulties and was happy to accept most of the key recommendations contained in the Final Report of the Dearing Committee published at the end of 1993. It was now possible for schools to adopt a more flexible approach to the education of 14- to 16-year-olds.

INTRODUCTION

Initial difficulties with the implementation of the National Curriculum centred on two major issues: National Curriculum testing and the nature of the arrangements for Key Stage 4.

NATIONAL CURRICULUM TESTING

As we saw in Chapter 4, Kenneth Baker had tried to 'sell' the National Curriculum to his influential critics on the far Right of the Conservative establishment (including the Prime Minister herself) on the grounds that it would serve as convenient justification for a massive new programme of national testing at 7, 11, 14 and 16. As part of the bargaining process, it followed that the price of the right-wingers' support was the *precise nature* of the tests to be imposed on all schools: these 'free-marketers' were opposed to anything more sophisticated than cheap standardised tests ('paper-and-pencil' tests) capable of yielding results that could be published in the form of simple league tables of schools. Only in this way could a centrally determined curriculum be rendered compatible with the tenets of the free market. Other Conservatives with a less doctrinaire approach were chiefly interested in a school system that was demonstrably more efficient and with enhanced accountability. As Denis Lawton argued in 1993:

> The different sections of the Conservative Party were promised greater national accountability *and* more market competition. A new assessment system was needed which could deliver data demonstrating the efficiency (or lack of it) in every state school, as well as providing test scores which could be used *competitively* and then published in league table form. . . .
>
> (Lawton 1993, p.65)

To make things even more complex and problematic, it was considered necessary by Baker and his civil servants to try to secure the support of sceptical teachers and educationists by claiming that the *real* purpose of the government's proposed testing arrangements was to monitor and improve student progress and achievement. In his 1993 autobiography, Baker argued that 'the absence in Britain of any regular standard assessment of children's school performance was unique for a developed country'. But he went on to concede that trying to introduce such a system was to become 'one of the most emotive aspects' of his reforms. It was not easy to convince the teachers that the government was genuinely interested in ascertaining what children had 'actually been able to absorb and assimilate at a particular time in their education'. In his view, 'far too many teachers were suspicious of testing because, despite its diagnostic function, it might also reflect badly upon their own teaching ability, and would, moreover, highlight one school's performance relative to another with a similar pupil intake' (Baker 1993, p.199).

   The task of devising a workable structure for National Curriculum assessment was entrusted to an expert Task Group on Assessment and Testing (TGAT) chaired by Professor Paul Black of King's College, University of London. In a letter to the group offering detailed guidance on its task (reproduced in full in the published report as Appendix B), Kenneth Baker outlined the often conflicting purposes that the new structure of assessment, including testing, was expected to fulfil:

> These include diagnostic or formative purposes, mainly concerned with ascertaining what stage a pupil has reached, identifying strengths and weaknesses and then planning the appropriate next steps in the pupil's education; summative purposes, concerned with recording in a systematic way the pupil's achievement overall, particularly compared with attainment targets for each subject; and purposes mainly concerned with publicising and evaluating the work of the education service and its various parts in the light of pupils' achievements. I attach importance to all of these, and I expect your recommendations to cover all.
>
> (DES 1988, Appendix B)

In the event, the TGAT Report, published in January 1988, turned out to be an uneasy compromise between the various purposes of assessment: appearing to find a role for *professional* expertise and showing a fitting concern for *formative* assessment while giving civil servants and politicians the sort of information necessary for the purposes of accountability, control and the efficient running of a market system of schools.

As Caroline Gipps argued in an article published in *Forum* in 1988:

> TGAT's forms of assessment can be used *formatively* and perhaps even *diagnostically*, but make no mistake: the competition and comparison will be malign for many children and are likely to be more powerful in their impact than will be any of the positive aspects.
>
> (Gipps 1988, p.6)

Despite Baker's comments in his book of memoirs (quoted above), it was certainly not clear that the government was chiefly concerned to compare the performance of schools with *similar student intakes*; nor was there any attempt at this stage to measure a school's performance according to its success in actively raising its students' attainment levels (the so-called 'value-added' factor). As things turned out, the report was a compromise that satisfied very few people: politicians on the Right swiftly dismissed the TGAT proposals as being far too costly and sophisticated, while many classroom teachers found all the Standard Assessment Tasks (SATs) difficult to carry out with scant resources and within a limited timescale.

In March 1988, the right-wing Centre for Policy Studies published a short pamphlet, *Correct Core: Simple Curricula for English, Maths and Science* (CPS 1988), which rejected complex assessment procedures and contained simple examples of what about 85 per cent of students could be expected to do by the ages of 7, 11, 14 and 16. For pressure groups like the CPS, it already seemed clear that Baker had allowed the government's assessment plans to be 'hijacked' by detested 'professionals'.

We know from a letter from the Prime Minister's Office to Kenneth Baker's private secretary, dated 21 January 1988 and 'leaked' to *The Independent* in March of that year, that Mrs Thatcher herself was profoundly unhappy with the main proposals in the TGAT Report, with four main reservations:

1. The system is enormously elaborate and complex and seems to require the setting up *two* new powerful bodies – the School Examinations and Assessment Council (SEAC) and the National Curriculum Council (NCC) – and a major new role for the LEAs.
2. Tests are only a part of assessment, and the method of assessment places a heavy responsibility on teachers' judgement and general impressions. There was also concern about the major role envisaged for the LEAs in the implementation of the whole system.

3.   The overall costs of the exercise would be very large.
4.   The new assessment system would not be introduced in less than five years.

A compromise was eventually reached: a shorter time for implementation was accepted; and the extent to which teachers' judgements would be externally moderated was to be more precisely determined. In practice, it was usually found that when teachers were in doubt, they tended to refer to external standards to confirm or adjust their own judgements.

Other more fundamental problems were not so easily solved, and by the beginning of 1993, the testing programme was in danger of falling apart under the weight of its own internal contradictions. Speaking at a Centre for Policy Studies seminar in London in March, Lord Skidelsky argued that the tests deserved to fail since they were essentially 'a fudge between the professional educator's doctrine that testing should diagnose individual strengths and weaknesses and the Government's wish to evaluate the effectiveness of teaching and schools' (reported in *The Guardian*, 18 March 1993). Initial teacher concern about the nature of the English and technology tests for 14-year-olds broadened with remarkable speed into a decision by the three largest teaching unions – the National Union of Teachers, the National Association of Schoolmasters/Union of Women Teachers and the Association of Teachers and Lecturers – to ballot their numbers on a boycott of *all* National Curriculum tests. The NASUWT was largely concerned with the issue of *workload*; the NUT argued that it was opposed *both* to Standard Assessment Tasks because they involved 'an excessive workload' *and* to 'paper-and-pencil' tests because they were 'educationally unsound'. Finally, at its annual conference in June, the National Association of Head Teachers launched a campaign against the compilation of *all* test and examination league tables.

THE CHANGING NATURE OF KEY STAGE 4

It can be argued (see Campbell 1992; Chitty 1992) that the 1987–8 National Curriculum, and particularly the arrangements for Key Stage 4, represented a 'defeat' for the thinking of two major groups: Her Majesty's Inspectorate and that faction within the Conservative Party of the 1980s often referred to as the 'Conservative Modernisers'.

As we saw in Chapter 4, the 1977 HMI model of a common 'entitlement' curriculum for all students aged 11 to 16 (later modified in 1985 to embrace all students aged 5 to 16) was very different from the DES concept of a compulsory 'core' curriculum that eventually found its way into the thinking underpinning the 1987 DES Consultation Document *The National Curriculum 5–16* (DES 1987). This was to have important implications for the construction of the curriculum for the last two years of compulsory schooling.

- Whereas the HMI approach was concerned to develop and exploit the quality of input and the skills, knowledge and expertise of classroom teachers, the DES was preoccupied chiefly with securing improved standards and accountability.
- Whereas the HMI approach was based on individual differences and the learning process, the major concern of the DES was to find ways of monitoring the coherence and efficiency of the education system.
- Whereas the professional common-curriculum approach was concerned with promoting the idea of 'areas of learning and experience', the DES thinking was never able to break out of the straitjacket imposed by viewing the school curriculum in terms of traditional subject disciplines.

Civil servants were well aware of the conflict between the DES and the HMI approaches to curriculum planning, but the DES Discussion Document *The School Curriculum*, published in March 1981 (DES 1981a), made no attempt to resolve the issue, talking in terms of both subjects and 'areas of experience'. As Janet Maw (1985) has argued: '*The School Curriculum* could be seen to *incorporate* two views of a national curriculum framework without actually *reconciling* them' (p.97). In one particular paragraph, it was conveniently suggested that each school could easily sidestep the problem by developing more than one kind of curriculum analysis:

> The Secretaries of State recognise that the curriculum can be described and analysed in several ways, each of which has its advantages and limitations. They have thought it most helpful to express much of their guidance in terms of subjects, because secondary school timetables are almost always devised in subject terms, they are readily recognised by parents and employers, and most secondary school teachers are trained in subjects. But a subject title hardly indicates the content or level of study, or the extent to which teaching and learning meet particular objectives. Moreover, many important elements of the curriculum are to be found 'across the curriculum', rather than exclusively within any one subject. A subject title is therefore a kind of shorthand, whose real educational meaning depends on the school's definition of what it expects children will learn and be able to do as a result of their studies in the subject in question. Some subjects contribute to more than one aim of the curriculum; some aims need a contribution from more than one subject. In analysing the curriculum, therefore, other frames of reference are also required. These may be in terms of the skills required at particular stages of a pupil's career; or of 'areas of experience' such as the eight used in HM Inspectors' Working Papers on the 11–16 Curriculum. . . . In translating general principles into practice, schools need to develop more than one kind of analysis as working tools of curriculum planning.
>
> (DES 1981a, p.6)

This could be said to be a wonderful example of the art of pandering to all bodies of opinion without attempting to arbitrate on their worth!

There was, of course, no evidence of HMI influence on the construction or implementation of the 1987–8 National Curriculum. The original DES idea of a limited 'core' of four or five subjects had been modified in the course of a decade to arrive at an unwieldy structure of ten foundation subjects, posing particular difficulties for the planning of the Key Stage 4 timetable; but there were very few other signs of a change in bureaucratic philosophy.

HMI *did*, in fact, try to make its voice heard in the early months of 1987, but the entreaties of Chief Inspector Eric Bolton (who had replaced the formidable Sheila Browne in 1983) had an air of desperation about them. Speaking to the Mathematical Association in April 1987, he argued that politicians must *not* be allowed to take control of the National Curriculum and dictate what was to be taught in schools. Some kind of national framework was probably inevitable, since all political parties had expressed a desire to see it happen. But whatever the 'frights and horrors' it might cause the teaching profession:

> It will be a better curriculum coming from people who know what they are talking about, than if it is left to be decided by politicians and administrators.
>
> (report in *The Times Educational Supplement*, 17 April 1987)

The debate was clearly going ahead; but teachers must not be intimidated into remaining silent:

> Don't wait to be asked to make your views known . . . It is silly politicians indeed who fly totally in the face of the best professional advice they can get.
>
> (*ibid.*)

If Kenneth Baker read this speech, it certainly did nothing to persuade him to seek professional approval for his new curriculum policies.

The marginalisation of HMI thinking at the end of the 1980s was a significant but not altogether surprising feature of the educational scene. Occupying a unique position as an independent member of the 'educational establishment', the Inspectorate was almost bound to incur the hostility and resentment of all those right-wing pressure groups that were anxious to undermine the influence of professional educationists. In a study of HMI published in 1987 (Lawton and Gordon 1987), it was argued that the autonomy and independence of the Inspectorate could not be taken for granted: as a body of experienced educationists and curriculum specialists, HMI still had to guard against 'bureaucratic opposition and insensitivity' on the one hand and political interference on the other (p.153). As if to prove the point, the authors of the 1986 Hillgate Group pamphlet *Whose Schools? A Radical Manifesto* argued the case for a full-scale investigation into the activities of the Inspectorate:

> We believe the time has come for a full and independent survey of the
> Inspectors, whose role has undergone considerable unsupervised change
> since the institution was first established in 1839. . . . The time has
> clearly come to define the procedures, criteria and accountability of the
> Inspectors, who are as likely as any other section of the educational
> establishment to be subverted by bureaucratic self-interest and
> fashionable ideology.
>
> (Hillgate Group 1986, p.14)

In a later Hillgate pamphlet, *The Reform of British Education: From Principles to Practice*,
published in 1987, the ranks of those who were said to have worked hard to
undermine traditional values in education and frustrate the pursuit of excellence
were extended to embrace the civil servants of the DES. HMI advisers and DES
civil servants must not, it was argued, be allowed to take control of the new statutory
bodies, principally the National Curriculum Council (NCC) and the School
Examinations and Assessment Council (SEAC), set up as a result of the introduction
of the National Curriculum.

> We are particularly concerned about the proliferation of new bodies
> with statutory advisory powers. If so many bodies are really necessary,
> then we hope that several members of each of them will be appointed
> from *outside* the educational establishment, whose collective failure over
> the past decades has virtually forced the Government to put forward its
> current reforms. And it is important that the proceedings of these
> bodies should not be dominated by the Secretariat provided by the
> DES, or by their HMI advisers. . . . We emphasise that we have no
> confidence in the educational establishment, which has acted as an
> ideological interest group, and which is most unlikely to further the
> Government's aim of providing *real* education for all. It would be worth
> insisting that the new bodies should be enabled to function wholly
> independently of the DES, and with HMI present, where necessary, in
> an advisory capacity only.
>
> (Hillgate Group 1987, pp.9–10)

The Right's 'vendetta' against HMI culminated in 1992 with the passing of the
Education (Schools) Act, which effectively 'privatised' the inspection process for
all schools. The number of inspectors was to be greatly reduced, from nearly 500
to 175, and the new Office for Standards in Education (OFSTED) was to become
the 'independent' body responsible for contracting independent teams to inspect
all primary and secondary schools. HMI/OFSTED would train the new inspectors
and require them to work to a new *Framework for the Inspection of Schools*.

The other contributors to the curriculum debate whose views were largely
disregarded at the end of the 1980s were the so-called Conservative Modernisers,
who, as we saw in Chapter 3, exerted a powerful influence on the policy-making
process in the first half of the decade.

The debate within the Conservative Party of the 1980s is often and rightly seen as one between the neo-conservative and the neo-liberal elements of the Thatcherite New Right – an essential point of conflict as far as education policy was concerned being the desirability or otherwise of a state-imposed national curriculum. The neo-conservatives of the cultural Right, and particularly the members of the Hillgate Group, were in favour of a national curriculum on the grounds that it would stress the importance of traditional subject disciplines and enhance teacher accountability. The neo-liberals, on the other hand, laid their special emphasis on choice, diversity and the free play of market forces.

> Both groups were anxious to undermine the power and influence of the local education authorities; and both groups hated the so-called educational establishment of DES civil servants, HMI and university academics.

All this is a useful way of analysing the educational scene of the 1980s, but as Ken Jones has pointed out (1989, p.79), it ignores the fact that Conservatism in education – as elsewhere – was essentially 'three-headed' rather than 'double-faced'. A group of 'modernising' Conservatives, led by David (later Lord) Young and not really part of the New Right as such, became particularly influential during Keith Joseph's five-year period at the DES (1981–86) – a factor that, as we saw in Chapter 3, helps to account for Joseph's curious and unexpected failure to implement the sort of privatising measures much favoured by his former allies in the Centre for Policy Studies.

Writing at the end of the 1980s, Ken Jones summarised the main assumptions and preoccupations of the 'modernising tendency' in the following terms:

> While no opponent of selection, the modernising tendency has no time for the grammar-school tradition. Unlike the Cultural Right, it considers it to be *part of the problem*, not the *solution*. It is thoroughly critical of the 'anti-industrial' values of a liberal education: the state schools of the present century have reproduced many of the failings of the public schools that some of them have tried to emulate, and have preserved a rigid distinction between 'high-status' academic knowledge and 'low-status' practical training. Adhering to a book-bound curriculum, they offer to students an education which many find both irrelevant and demotivating. The modernisers, by contrast, present their programme as a means not only of serving industry but – by knocking down the academic/practical barrier – of democratising knowledge, and of enabling students to demonstrate kinds of achievement which the old education neither fostered nor recognised.
>
> (*ibid.*, p.82)

The Modernisers' main achievement in the area of curriculum initiatives was the introduction of the Technical and Vocational Education Initiative (TVEI) in the autumn of 1983, but, despite the enthusiastic support of a number of committed teachers and employers, this MSC project played little part in the government's plans for a national curriculum, warranting, as we noted in Chapter 4, only two brief mentions in the 1987 DES Consultation Document. What then accounts for the rapid decline in the Modernisers' influence in the late 1980s?

For one thing, employment prospects appeared to be improving after 1987, and, paradoxically, there was therefore *less* need to be concerned about vocational training in secondary schools. Then again, the Manpower Services Commission – which was the Modernisers' chief power base – never regained the authority and influence it had wielded while David Young was its chairperson from 1982 to 1984. The MSC lost a powerful ally when Keith Joseph was replaced as Education Secretary by Kenneth Baker in May 1986; from that date, policy making came more and more under the control of the Downing Street Policy Unit, with radical ideas being fed in by the various right-wing think tanks. Those in favour of 'modernising' the curriculum, particularly for older students, increasingly lost ground after 1986 to those members of the New Right who had always resented the MSC's interference in the education service and saw no virtue anyway in an undue emphasis on technical and vocational subjects – except perhaps for 'non-examination' students. The object now was to fashion a new education system, celebrating unconfined individualism on the one hand while specifying a curriculum that would regard cultural cohesion as an essential prop of state authority.

Yet this subject-based National Curriculum was still in the initial stages of implementation when it became obvious, even to the government, that Key Stage 4 at least could not survive in the form envisaged by Kenneth Baker and his allies. The last two years of compulsory schooling rapidly became the most problematic area of the government's hastily conceived curriculum project. To begin with, there were severe practical problems involved in fitting so many separate subjects (along with a number of cross-curricular themes) into a finite amount of curriculum time. On top of this, many teachers complained that it was simply not possible to teach all ten core and foundation subjects (as well as religious education) to students of all abilities without risking a fair amount of student resentment and indiscipline. Furthermore, as general economic prospects worsened and young people were once again experiencing difficulties in finding suitable employment, it seemed that the 'modernised' curriculum favoured by the MSC in the early 1980s was not necessarily an idea whose time had gone. In other words, the battle for the high policy ground was about to be fought all over again in the changed conditions of the early 1990s.

Speaking at the Conference of the Society of Education Officers in London in January 1990, John MacGregor, who had replaced Kenneth Baker as Education Secretary in July 1989, announced that he was looking again at the requirement that schools should teach 14- to 16-year-olds *all* national curriculum subjects 'for a reasonable time'. He revealed that he had asked vocational examination bodies such as the Business and Technician Education Council (BTEC) and the Royal Society of Arts (RSA) to submit new qualifications for approval as part of a policy of 'providing a wider range of options for older students' (reported in *The Times Educational Supplement*, 2 February 1990).

At the end of July 1990, in a speech to the Conference of the Professional Association of Teachers (PAT) in Nottingham, the Education Secretary signalled a further strategic retreat on the arrangements for the National Curriculum by suggesting that some students might be allowed to 'drop' certain subjects from the age of 14. The most likely subjects to be 'dropped' were art, music and physical education, but the position of history and geography was also in doubt. Mr MacGregor made it clear that the National Curriculum would remain intact up to the age of 14, but after that, students might well be obliged to study only *five* of the original foundation subjects: the three core subjects of English, maths and science, together with technology and a modern foreign language. The Education Secretary admitted in his speech that Key Stage 4 posed its own very real problems:

> Essentially, the question is one of fit – how to achieve a broad balanced curriculum for all pupils without sacrificing worthwhile options. . . . There is a genuine dilemma here.
>
> (Reported in *The Guardian*, 1 August 1990)

Then, in an interview with John Clare of *The Daily Telegraph* at the end of October 1990, Education Minister Tim Eggar made it clear that the government was now proposing to encourage secondary schools to develop a vocational alternative to the academic curriculum. In his words:

> Far too many children from the age of 14 upwards are studying things which they and their teachers do not regard as appropriate. . . . We have to offer these youngsters the sort of vocational courses and qualifications that will make sense to them – and encourage them to stay on in full-time education after 16.

Schools would now be encouraged to develop parallel 'academic' and 'vocational' streams, with the main objective being to raise the status of vocational qualifications:

> That is the main issue facing us in education today. That is the area where we are so much weaker than Germany – not in turning out graduates, but in producing skilled workers and supervisors. . . . To achieve that, we must now have two parallel streams – the vocational and the academic – from half-way through secondary school, so that children can concentrate on what really interests them.
>
> (*The Daily Telegraph*, 30 October 1990)

Finally, Kenneth Clarke, who took over from John MacGregor as Education Secretary in November 1990, effectively abandoned Key Stage 4 of the National Curriculum in his speech to the North of England Education Conference meeting in Leeds in January 1991.

Ignoring the advice of the National Curriculum Council for all ten subjects of the National Curriculum to remain compulsory for all students to the age of 16, Clarke announced that:

- Only English, maths and science would remain 'sacrosanct' in the last two years of schooling.
- Students would now be able to 'drop' art, music and history *or* geography, with physical education being treated 'flexibly'.
- All students would still have to study technology and a modern foreign language in addition to the 'core', but not necessarily to GCSE level.

The new structure was put forward as a victory for common sense and as a means of ensuring that, once again, schools would be able to cater for students according to their talents and their differing job prospects. In the words of the Education Secretary:

> I believe we should not impose on young people a rigid curriculum that leaves little scope for choice. By the age of 14, young people are beginning to look at what lies beyond compulsory schooling, whether in work or further study. We must harness that sense of anticipation if every pupil is to have the chance of developing to the full.
>
> (Reported in *The Guardian*, 5 January 1991)

In the light of the above comments by Tim Eggar and Kenneth Clarke, the idea of a subject-based curriculum for all 14- to 16-year-olds of the type specified in the 1988 Education Act appears as something of an *aberration*, with the government now anxious to revive some of the proposals for separate academic, technical and vocational 'pathways' put forward by David Young and his allies in the first half of the 1980s. The MSC would doubtless have approved of many of the substantial changes to the National Curriculum recommended by Sir Ron Dearing in 1993; and it is the Dearing Review of the National Curriculum and its assessment that forms the subject of the next section.

THE 1993 DEARING REVIEW AND ITS AFTERMATH

By the spring of 1993, there was mounting criticism of several aspects of the Major government's education agenda; and, as we have seen, several teaching unions had launched concerted campaigns against the National Curriculum tests and proposed examination league tables. John Patten, meanwhile, had replaced Kenneth Clarke as Education Secretary in April 1992 and was finding it very difficult to command the respect of both teachers and parents.

Realising that the framework for the National Curriculum and the related testing arrangements could not survive in their existing form, the Major government asked Sir Ron Dearing, chairperson-designate of the new School Curriculum and Assessment Authority (SCAA) to be established in October 1993, to carry out a full-scale review of the National Curriculum and its assessment. John Patten's remit letter of 7 April 1993 outlined four *main* issues that the review should cover:

1.   the scope for slimming down the curriculum;
2.   the future of the 10-level scale for graduating children's attainments recommended by TGAT;
3.   the means by which the testing arrangements themselves could be simplified;
4.   the means by which central administration of the National Curriculum and testing could be improved.

The letter made it clear that the review's initial objective should be:

> to map out a strategy for simplifying the current framework so as to remove needless over-elaboration and over-prescription, while retaining clear teaching objectives which lever up national standards and underpin robust testing arrangements.
>
> (NCC/SEAC 1993, p.65)

Sir Ron Dearing's Interim Report, *The National Curriculum and its Assessment*, was published on 2 August 1993 (with the Final Report expected at the end of the year). It accepted as an initial premise that the National Curriculum had become overloaded in the process of its evolution, and it put forward a number of reasonable explanations for this phenomenon:

> This problem of curriculum overload stems, in part, from the fact that the original Working Groups established to define the content of each Order were not able to judge the collective weight in teaching terms of the Curriculum *as a whole*. Neither was it possible to avoid some overlap of content *between* subjects. A further problem stems from the fact that the attempt to spell out the requirements of each National Curriculum subject in a clear, unambiguous manner has led to a level of prescription that many teachers find unacceptably constricting. The balance between what is defined nationally and what is left to the exercise of professional judgement needs to be reviewed.
>
> (*ibid.*, pp.5–6)

The report proceeded to recommend that there should be a slimmer, less tightly prescribed curriculum, with some of the existing content becoming optional. Each National Curriculum Order should be revised to divide the content into a *statutory core*, which *must* be taught, and optional studies, which could be covered *at the discretion of the individual teacher*. The central importance of English, mathematics and science meant that there would have to be a larger statutory element in each of these three subjects than would be necessary in the remaining seven. The percentage of time freed for work of teachers' own choice could amount to as much as 20 to 25 per cent at Key Stage 3.

As far as national tests were concerned, the report conceded that these had been 'a matter of public controversy throughout the Review'. It recommended that the time taken for the tests at 7 and 14 should be cut by half, and that teacher assessment should be upgraded. At the same time, it accepted that there *was* a case for using so-called 'value-added' assessment methods as a more sophisticated and defensible means of measuring a school's performance. It recommended that the School Curriculum and Assessment Authority (SCAA), in collaboration with the Office for Standards in Education (OFSTED), should commission research into 'operational approaches to a measure of "value-added"'.

Three major issues were identified in the Interim Report as suitable for serious consideration in the second stage of the review. These took the form of *three questions* with far-reaching implications:

1. Should the ten-level scale be modified to make it more effective, or should a new approach to the assessment of pupil progress be developed?
2. Would the revision of the ten National Curriculum subjects be best undertaken through a simultaneous review of each subject, through a two-stage review separating the *core* from the *non-core* foundation subjects, or through a rolling review occupying, say, five years?
3. Should there be a modified approach to the curriculum at Key Stage 4 to enable older students to choose from a number of separate 'pathways', thereby providing 'a smoother transition to study post–16' and responding sensitively to 'the developing needs of all our young people'?

The report argued that:

> The strengths and weaknesses of these options must be examined very carefully before any decisions are reached. We must be confident that the changes which eventually emerge can be managed in the classroom and by the newly-created School Curriculum and Assessment Authority. One of the lessons to be learned from the past is that of misjudging the manageability of change.
>
> (*ibid.*, p.8)

The Major government moved quickly to endorse all the firm recommendations in Sir Ron Dearing's Interim Report, with Baroness Blatch deputising for Secretary of State John Patten, who was ill at the time of the report's publication in early August. With the full support of the Prime Minister, she said: 'We accept the Report in its entirety'. Speaking on the BBC Radio 4 *World at One* programme on 2 August 1993, she voiced government annoyance that education ministers were now having to cope with the consequences of mistakes made by the National Curriculum's early enthusiasts:

> The early architects of the whole system built into it too much bureaucracy and too much convolution. . . . That has substantially been addressed by Sir Ron Dearing.

Although John Patten's remit for the review did *not* include consideration of the contentious league tables, the fact that the report called for the influence of 'value-added' factors to be explored in some detail gave the government a useful pretext for the announcement of the abandonment of national league tables for students at age 7 and 14. In the event, this decision captured the newspaper headlines and provoked more discussion than any proposal in the report itself. It was described in *The Guardian* (3 August 1993) as 'a volte-face on what had been one of the central tenets of the Government's legislative programme'. Some writers viewed it as 'an embarrassing retreat', but for other commentators, it was 'a clever and astute move', designed primarily to destroy the united front that had made the teachers' summer boycott of testing undeniably so successful. It was predicted, for example, in *The Observer* (1 August 1993) that 'the government retreat would make it very difficult for the union militants to win support for a continuation of the boycott'.

In the post-Dearing debate, the report's call for more simplified testing arrangements was indeed welcomed by the National Association of Schoolmasters/ Union of Women Teachers, which had built its campaign against testing on the narrow issue of 'workload'. The National Union of Teachers, on the other hand, reiterated its longstanding opposition to all types of formal national test on the philosophical grounds that they were both 'educationally flawed' and 'designed primarily to compare one school's performance with another'. In the words of NUT General Secretary Doug McAvoy:

> These tests will not inform parents about their child's development; nor will they assist the teachers in diagnosing their pupils' educational needs. . . . While the reduction in their scope might be welcome, they can never serve *educational* purposes, designed as they are to be turned into league tables of school performance.
>
> (Reported in *The Independent*, 3 August 1993)

It was the government's determination to retain league tables for 11-year-olds that provoked strong opposition from the powerful National Association of Head Teachers. In the words of Deputy General Secretary David Burbidge:

> All league tables should be abolished entirely. The criticisms which ministers appear to accept about league tables for 7 and 14-year-olds can equally be levelled at those for 11-year-olds.
>
> (Reported in *The Times Educational Supplement*, 6 August 1993)

The Final Report of the Dearing review, although dated December 1993, was published on 5 January 1994 and was greeted by teachers, parents' organisations and large numbers of politicians with a mixture of enthusiasm and relief. After a year of unremitting conflict between government and teachers over the issue of testing, it was accepted gratefully by beleaguered Education Secretary John Patten as a 'political lifeline' – even before it was published. For many teachers' leaders, it appeared to represent a hard-earned 'victory' for *professional* opinion. (Indeed, an ill-informed editorial in *The Independent* (6 January 1994), which was hardly sympathetic to the teachers' campaign, was headed 'Capitulation to the Professionals'.)

In his Introduction to the Final Report, Sir Ron Dearing argued that it was now possible to make the National Curriculum more manageable by:

- reducing the volume of material required by law to be taught;
- simplifing and clarifying the programmes of study;
- reducing prescription so as to give more scope for professional judgement;
- drafting the Orders in a way that offered maximum support to the classroom teacher.

(SCAA 1993, p.17)

He went on to emphasise that it was not part of his brief to produce 'a less rigorous and less demanding curriculum':

> My concern is, rather, to release more of teachers' energies for teaching. . . . I believe that the reductions proposed will lift the burden of anxiety felt by many teachers . . . because of their current inability to teach the whole of an over-provided curriculum. . . . Moreover, I believe that the trust this places in teachers will serve to encourage the profession in its vital task of raising educational standards.
>
> (*ibid.*, p.23)

It was proposed in the report that the existing National Curriculum at Key Stage 3 be cut back to 80 per cent of taught time, leaving the equivalent of a day a week for schools to use at their own discretion.

At Key Stage 4:

- The minimum National Curriculum would be reduced to about 60 per cent of the timetable for *some* students, with even history and geography becoming *optional* subjects – leaving secondary schools with greater flexibility to introduce either vocational courses or alternative academic options.
- Working parties would begin an immediate review of all National Curriculum subjects, and the new arrangements would be introduced in September 1995, with the promise of no further changes for at least five years.

- A core of *compulsory* material would be separated from *optional* subject matter.
- As far as the assessment procedures were concerned, national tests in the core subjects would be simplified as far as possible without sacrificing validity and reliability, with a reduction in the time required to administer them.
- The ten-level scale for assessing students would be retained but would be simplified and would end at the age of 14.

A number of local and national newspapers covering the report (see, for example, the report in *The Guardian*, 6 January 1994) implied that the government had decided to abandon school-by-school league tables of *all* test results. This was, in fact, a mistaken impression. While abandoning them for children aged 7 and 14, the government actually said it intended to continue with school-by-school league tables for 11-year-olds. This was, of course, a source of great anxiety for both primary and secondary delegates to the annual conference of the National Association of Headteachers (NAHT) meeting in Eastbourne at the beginning of June 1994. David Hart, the NAHT General Secretary, said that the publication of Key Stage 2 test results would be 'a flashpoint for further dispute in schools' and argued that the prospects for the tests were 'not good' (reported in *The Times Educational Supplement*, 10 June 1994). Such concern was echoed by leaders of the National Union of Teachers (NUT), the key union that had been consistent in opposing the government's testing programme for all age groups on *educational* grounds. When Gillian Shephard, who replaced John Patten as Education Secretary in July 1994, finally announced in September of that year that tests for all 11-year-olds would go ahead in 1995, she agreed to postpone including the test results in league tables for a further year 'in response to teachers' concerns' (reported in *The Guardian*, 6 September 1994).

The new National Curriculum, based on Sir Ron Dearing's recommendations and amendments, was officially announced by the Major government on 10 November 1994. In revealing details of the new programme, Mrs Shephard emphasised that this was indeed 'the final peace offering to teachers'. She conceded that the original National Curriculum had become overloaded but said the 'reformed version' gave all children 'a minimum entitlement to education'. In her view, the National Curriculum had already raised educational standards by 'setting clear targets and testing performance'. Now the revised package would 'continue the drive to raise standards' by 'removing overload, stripping out unnecessary bureaucracy and giving more freedom for teachers to exercise their professional judgement' (reported in *The Guardian*, 11 November 1994).

As far as the provision for older students was concerned, it is fair to say that Sir Ron Dearing's Final Report effectively marked the end of the National Curriculum for those beyond the age of 14. Yet, as we have seen earlier in the chapter, it is also important to note that Key Stage 4 *never*, in fact, took the precise

In the revised version of the National Curriculum, designed to take both primary and secondary schools into the twenty-first century, the detailed prescription of the content of lessons was to be reduced by about a third. At the same time, the old ten-level scale of knowledge and ability, covering all students from ages 5 to 16, would be replaced by an eight-level scale for 5 to 14-year-olds, with GCSEs (and, where appropriate, other qualifications) used to assess 16-year-olds.

form envisaged by Kenneth Baker and his civil servants. Kenneth Clarke's interventionist strategy was particularly in evidence where Key Stage 4 was concerned; and by the time the Dearing review was set up in April 1993, there had already been a considerable slimming down of the proposals contained in the 1987 Consultation Document, with a number of foundation subjects no longer forming part of the statutory requirements (see Table 5.1).

The Final Report proposed that the process of reduction and simplification be accelerated; and most media reports emphasised that the National Curriculum for Years 10 and 11 would now occupy students for only about 60 per cent of the normal school week (see Table 5.2). This, however, assumed that the majority of older students would choose no more than the *minimum* statutory requirement. As Table 5.2 shows, the National Curriculum could still, in fact, take up between 70 and 80 per cent of the timetable if students opted to follow a double course in science and full courses in technology and a modern foreign language.

Table 5.1 The National Curriculum at Key Stage 4: the situation in 1993

	Proportion of curriculum time (%)	
	Minimum requirement	Extended requirement
English	12.5	12.5
Mathematics	12.5	12.5
Science*	12.5	20.0
Technology (single subject or as part of a combined-subject course)	5.0	10.0
Modern foreign language (single subject or as part of a combined-subject course)	5.0	10.0
History and/or geography (single subject or as part of a combined-subject course)	10.0	10.0
Physical education	5.0	5.0
Religious education	5.0	5.0
TOTALS	67.5	85.0

Source: *Final Report of the Dearing Review, 1993, p.41*.

* Most students follow the recommended double course in science.

Table 5.2 Two versions of the Dearing proposals at Key Stage 4

Subject	Proportion of curriculum time (%)	
	Minimum requirement proposal	Extended requirement proposal
• English	12.5	12.5
• Mathematics	12.5	12.5
• Science	12.5	20.0
• Technology	5.0	10.0
• Modern foreign language	5.0	10.0
• Physical education	5.0	5.0
• Religious education	5.0	5.0
• Sex education and careers	2.5	5.0
TOTALS	60.0	80.0

Column 1 would leave 40.0% of the timetable free for other options, Column 2 only 20.0%.

Source: *Final Report of the Dearing Review, 1993, p.52*.

The Final Report justified the abandonment of Key Stage 4 in its original form on the grounds of allowing 'greater scope for academic and vocational options'. It identified *three* broad pathways in post-16 education and training:

1. the 'craft' or 'occupational', linked to NVQs (National Vocational Qualifications);
2. the 'vocational', linked to GNVQs (General National Vocational Qualifications);
3. the 'academic', leading to 'A' and 'AS' levels.

It was recognised that the development of these three broad pathways raised the issue of whether younger students (those aged 14 to 16) should be allowed to follow a well-devised vocational course as *one* element in a broadly based curriculum. In the words of the Final Report:

> It will be a particular challenge to establish how a vocational pathway which maintains a broad educational component might be developed at Key Stage Four over the next few years as part of a 14–19 continuum. . . . Such a pathway is already a feature in many European countries, and headteachers and others have clearly indicated their interest in the opportunities which these courses can offer to young people.
>
> (SCAA 1993, p.47)

The report went on to recommend that the School Curriculum and Assessment Authority (SCAA) be asked to work 'closely and urgently' with the National Council for Vocational Qualifications (NCVQ) to identify whether various possibilities concerning GNVQs could now be developed (SCAA 1993, p.49).

In an address to the Secondary Heads Association's annual conference in Bournemouth in March 1994, Sir Ron Dearing announced that 14–year-old students would soon be able to study for qualifications in five vocational areas:

1. manufacturing;
2. art and design;
3. health and social care;
4. leisure and tourism;
5. business and finance.

(report in *The Financial Times*, 21 March 1994)

Then, in December 1994, Schools Minister Eric Forth announced the names of the 118 schools that would be 'piloting' *three* of the new two-year GNVQ courses to be offered as alternatives to GCSE courses from September 1995. The GNVQ Part One would be offered at *two* levels:

1. *foundation*, or the equivalent of two GCSEs below Grade C;
2. *intermediate*, equivalent to two GCSEs at Grade C or above.

Schools would receive £10,000 grants to 'pilot' business and finance or health and social care courses and £12,000 for new courses in manufacturing. Schools offering two subject areas would receive £15,000 (or £17,000 if this included manufacturing) and £20,000 for offering all three courses (report in *The Guardian*, 22 December 1994).

To sum up: after September 1996, maintained secondary schools in England and Wales were required to teach the revised programmes of study at Key Stage 4 in the following subjects (with Welsh as an additional 'core' subject for students in those parts of Wales where Welsh was spoken):

- English;
- mathematics;
- science (as a 'single' or 'double' programme, although with the expectation that the majority of students would choose to take double science);
- design and technology (a short course being the minimum requirement);
- information technology (as a separate subject or co-ordinated across other subjects);
- a modern foreign language;
- physical education.

Secondary schools also had a statutory obligation to provide clearly identified religious education, in accordance with a locally agreed syllabus, and a programme of carefully structured sex education (although, in accordance with Section 241 of the 1993 Education Act, parents now had the right to withdraw their children from *all* or *part* of this programme). Careers education would become a statutory part of the curriculum in maintained secondary schools from September 1998.

In addition to the above subjects, a Part One GNVQ course at either *intermediate* or *foundation* level would be expected to take about the same time as *two* GCSEs and occupy a maximum of 20 per cent of curriculum time. It was *not* intended in the Dearing Report that secondary schools would be in a position to offer any *full* GNVQs at Key Stage 4, because each of these would occupy at least 40 per cent of curriculum time and leave no time for other subject options, even if students opted for only the minimum National Curriculum requirement.

These, then, were the various curriculum changes introduced by the 1992–7 Major government as a result of the wide-ranging 1993 Dearing review and, as we have seen, having a particular impact on the package offered to students in the last two years of compulsory schooling. The National Curriculum at Key Stage 4 was to face a number of further significant modifications under New Labour, but it is fair to say that it had already been drastically changed and slimmed down by the time of the 1997 general election.

SUGGESTED ACTIVITIES

1. Sir Ron Dearing's Interim Report on the National Curriculum (1993) identified three questions related to possible changes to the original National Curriculum for England and Wales. These are listed below. Look at each one, and discuss:

    - how *you* might have answered these questions;
    - the extent to which some of the changes implied in the questions have been successfully and effectively introduced in the period following the publication of the report;
    - the extent to which some of the proposals implicit in the questions have subsequently been abandoned.

    Do you think that these were the right questions for the report to be addressing, or would you have identified different questions? If so, what would they have been?
       The three questions:

    - Should the ten-level scale be modified to make it more effective, or should a new approach to the assessment of pupil progress be developed?
    - Would the revision of the ten National Curriculum subjects be best undertaken through a simultaneous review of each subject, through a two-stage review separating the core from the non-core foundation subjects, or through a rolling review?
    - Should there be a modified approach to the curriculum Key Stage 4 to enable older students to choose from a number of separate 'pathways',

thereby providing 'a smoother transition to study at post-16' and responding sensitively to 'the developing needs of all young people'?

2.   As this chapter has indicated, some politicians have suggested that teachers are opposed to standardised 'pencil-and-paper' tests not for educational or ideological reasons but because they think the tests will show up their own inadequacies as teachers.

   Most readers of this book will recognise such claims as simplistic, misleading and false. But what would you identify as the actual criticisms that teachers might level against such testing, and to what extent would you agree with these criticisms?

SUGGESTED READING

Chitty, C. (ed.) (1993) *The National Curriculum: Is it Working?* This collection of essays is chiefly concerned to explain why the National Curriculum was facing such major problems of implementation within just *five* years of its introduction. In particular, it traces the process by which the original model for Key Stage 4 was already disintegrating under pressure from a number of powerful interests.

Graham, D. and Tytler, D. (1993) *A Lesson for Us All: The Making of the National Curriculum.* Co-authored by Duncan Graham, who was chairperson and Chief Executive of the National Curriculum Council from 1988 to 1991, this is very much an insider's account of the creation of the National Curriculum. It describes the intrigues and pressures that surrounded it and the clashes of ideals and ideologies that shaped it.

6 School Reform Under New Labour

The Labour Party was returned to power in May 1997 with a pledge to make education its top priority in government. One of its first publications was an education White Paper, Excellence in Schools, *which became the basis of the School Standards and Framework Act of 1998. This White Paper outlined many of the themes that would dominate New Labour education policy: the need to 'modernise' the comprehensive principle; the importance of 'standards' rather than 'structures'; the need to tackle the high levels of under-achievement in many inner city areas; and a determination to tolerate no excuses for educational failure. Since 1997, the government has devised a number of new schemes for raising educational standards: education action zones, beacon schools, city academies, the 'Fresh Start' initiative, and a growing network of specialist schools and colleges. Grammar schools have been left untouched; and grant-maintained schools have retained some of their privileges as 'foundation schools'.*

INTRODUCTION

At the general election held on 1 May 1997, the Labour Party gained a landslide victory, with the election of 419 Labour MPs – resulting in a House of Commons majority over all the other parties of 179. With the election of only 165 MPs and the receipt of just 31 per cent of the national vote, this was the Conservatives' most depressing performance in a general election since their defeat at the hands of the Liberals in January 1906. Yet it is still not clear exactly what caused this remarkable and largely unexpected election result: did it represent a massive endorsement of the policies of the Labour Party that Tony Blair had taken over and transformed after the untimely death of John Smith in May 1994; or should it be viewed as a massive rejection of the economic and social policies of the 1992–7 Major administration and of the hugely unpopular ministers who attempted to implement them?

Throughout the election campaign, Tony Blair repeatedly declared that 'education, education, education' were to be 'the top three priorities' of a Labour government; and this was also a key theme of the New Labour election manifesto, *Because Britain Deserves Better.*

THE NEW LABOUR MANIFESTO

Tony Blair's Introduction to the New Labour manifesto argued that Britain *could* and *must* be better: with 'better schools, better hospitals, better ways of tackling crime, of building a modern welfare state, of equipping herself for a new world economy'. The chief purpose of New Labour was to give Britain a new political choice: the choice between 'a failed Conservative government, exhausted and divided in everything, other than its desire to cling on to power' and 'a new and revitalised Labour Party' that had been resolute in 'transforming itself into a party of the future'. This new dynamic Party was putting forward a programme for 'a new centre and centre-left politics' – a set of proposals in each area of policy that differed '*both* from the solutions of the old Left *and* from those of the Conservative Right'. This was essentially why New Labour *was* new. It believed in 'the strength of its values', but it also recognised that the policies of 1997 could not be those of 1947 or 1967. The Labour leader went on to promise – as an essential part of the Party's new 'contract with the people' – that education would be 'the number one priority' and that the Party would 'increase the share of national income spent on education' while decreasing it on 'the bills of economic and social failure' (Labour Party 1997, pp. 1,2,3,5)

Six policies were highlighted as indicative of New Labour's determination to make education its 'number one priority':

1. a reduction in class sizes to thirty or under for all 5-, 6- and 7-year-olds;
2. nursery places for all 4-year-olds;
3. an attack on low standards in schools;
4. access for all to computer technology;
5. lifelong learning through the establishment of a new University for Industry;
6. increased spending on education as a direct consequence of a fall in the cost of employment.

(ibid., p.7)

As far as secondary education was concerned, clear distaste was expressed for the 'monolithic comprehensive schools' that had apparently thrived in the 1960s. But this did *not* mean that New Labour was in favour of a return to *overt* selection:

> In education, we reject *both* the idea of a return to the 11–plus *and* monolithic comprehensive schools that take no account of children's differing abilities. Instead, we favour all-in schooling which identifies the distinct abilities of individual pupils. . . .
>
> *(ibid.*, p.3)

There was an obvious need to 'modernise' the comprehensive principle, learning from the experience of the last thirty years. This would entail recognising the importance of differentiation *within* comprehensive schools:

> We must modernise all our comprehensive schools. Children are *not* all of the same ability; nor do they learn at the same speed. That means 'setting' children in classes to maximise progress, for the benefit of 'high-fliers' and slower learners alike. The focus must be on levelling up, *not* levelling down.
>
> (*ibid.*, p.7)

New Labour believed that '*standards*, more than *structures*', were 'the real key to success'. A Labour administration would *never* 'put dogma before children's education', and therefore there would be no attempt to abolish 'good schools', whether in the private or in the state sector. Any changes in the admissions policies of grammar schools would be decided by local parents. Schools that enjoyed 'grant-maintained' status would continue to prosper, although under a new system of funding that did not discriminate unfairly between schools or between students. Church schools would be able to retain their distinctive religious ethos. At the same time, attempts would also be made to 'build bridges' across such education divides as that between the public and private sectors. On the other hand, the Assisted Places Scheme, the cost of which was set to rise to £180 million per year, would be phased out, in order to reduce class sizes for all 5-, 6- and 7-year-olds to thirty or under.

As part of a well-organised attack on 'under-achievement' in urban areas, new 'education action zones' would be established, charged with the crucial task of developing new and imaginative ways of helping 'under-performing schools' in areas of disadvantage. There would be 'zero tolerance' of under-achievement; and a 'failing school' unable or unwilling to improve would be closed – to be replaced by a new establishment on the same site.

A Labour government would set up a General Teaching Council to 'speak for and raise standards in the profession'. A new grade of teachers would be created to 'recognise the best'; but there would also be speedy, but fair, procedures to remove incompetent and lazy teachers.

The manifesto laid particular stress on realising the potential of new technology. All schools would be linked to the Internet; and lottery money would be used to improve the skills of existing teachers in information technology.

THE 1997 WHITE PAPER

One of the first measures of the new Blair administration was to introduce a short Bill phasing out the Conservatives' Assisted Places Scheme, with the intention of using the money thereby released to reduce the class sizes for 5-, 6- and 7-year-olds.

Then in July, 67 days after assuming office, the government produced an 84-page White Paper, *Excellence in Schools*, setting out the education agenda for the early years of the new administration.

In his Foreword to this document, the new Secretary of State, David Blunkett, stressed the importance of rejecting all excuses for under-performance in schools:

> To overcome economic and social disadvantage and to make equality of opportunity a reality, we must strive to eliminate, and never excuse, under-achievement in the most deprived parts of our country. Educational attainment encourages aspiration and self-belief in the next generation; and it is through family learning, as well as scholarship through formal schooling, that success will come. . . . We must overcome the spiral of disadvantage in which alienation from, or failure within, the education system is passed from one generation to the next.
>
> (DfEE 1997, p.3)

In the first chapter, entitled 'A New Approach', the White Paper listed the *six* principles that would be underpinning New Labour's reform agenda:

1. Education will be at the heart of government.
2. Policies will be designed to benefit the many, not just the few.
3. Standards will matter more than structures.
4. Intervention will be in inverse proportion to success.
5. There will be zero tolerance of under-performance.
6. Government will work in partnership with all those committed to raising standards.

(*ibid.*, pp.11–12)

Chapter 1 also contained confident predictions as to what could be achieved over the lifetime of a parliament (1997–2002):

- There will be a greater awareness across society of the importance of education and increased expectations of what can be achieved.
- Standards of performance will be higher.

(*ibid.*, p.14)

The White Paper was to contain a number of references to the importance of '*standards not structures*' – a somewhat ambiguous catchphrase that had appeared in New Labour's election manifesto and had earlier featured prominently in *The Blair Revolution: Can New Labour Deliver?* co-authored by Peter Mandelson and Roger Liddle and published in May 1996. In this influential book, Mandelson and Liddle set much of the tone of the new educational agenda, arguing that a preoccupation with 'structure' in education had absorbed a great deal of energy to little effect and that the first priority of a Labour government must be to raise general educational standards:

> New Labour now believes that, throughout schooling, standards are more important than structures. Each school should be made clearly

responsible for its own performance and be subject to a mixture of external pressure and support in order to raise it. Performance must be regularly assessed in objective terms that parents can understand and compare with elsewhere. . . . New Labour must now spell out with greater clarity what its new educational policies mean in practice and how its new emphasis on standards, not structures, can, in time, transform state education.

(Mandelson and Liddle 1996, pp.92–3)

As things turned out, the White Paper of July 1997 did exactly what Mandelson and Liddle had called for: under the banner of 'zero tolerance of failure', it paved the way for a school system in which tough improvement targets would be set at every level, from the government, through local education authorities and schools, down to individual classroom teachers.

The document contained a number of important proposals affecting secondary schools, and these are highlighted below.

- The comprehensive principle would be 'modernised' to ensure that all children, whatever their talents, would be able to develop their diverse abilities. Comprehensive education would henceforth be expected to provide 'a broad, flexible and motivating education' that recognised 'the different talents of all children' and delivered 'excellence for everyone'.
- Setting of students by ability should be 'the norm' in all secondary schools. The government was not prepared to 'ignore existing shortcomings' and 'defend the failings of across-the-board mixed-ability teaching'.
- There would be a pilot programme of about twenty-five Education Action Zones (EAZs) charged with the key task of 'motivating young people in tough inner-city areas'. These would be phased in over two to three years and set up in areas with a mixture of 'under-performing schools and the highest levels of disadvantage'. Each would operate on the basis of an 'action forum', which would include parents and 'representatives from the local business and social community', as well as 'representatives from the constituent schools and the LEA'. A typical zone would probably have two or three secondary schools with supporting primaries and associated SEN (special educational needs) provision.
- There would be 'an extensive network of specialist schools' developing their own distinctive identity and expertise. These would focus on technology, languages, sports or arts and would be 'a resource for local people and the neighbouring schools to draw on'. They would be able to give priority to students who demonstrated 'the relevant aptitude'.
- Every school would be inspected by OFSTED at least once every six years. Between these inspections, the performance of schools would be monitored regularly by LEAs on the basis of objective performance information. By April 1999, each LEA would be working to an Education

Development Plan (EDP) agreed with the DfEE and the schools, showing how educational standards in all schools could rise.

- LEAs would be expected to give early warnings to governors of schools causing concern and then be prepared to intervene if necessary. Where schools showed insufficient evidence of tangible recovery, it might then be necessary to consider a 'fresh start' policy. This 'fresh start' could take one or other of a variety of different forms. It could mean closing the school and transferring all the students to nearby 'successful' schools. In less extreme cases, it might involve another school taking over the 'under-performing' school to 'set it on a new path'; or closing the school temporarily and then reopening it on either the same or a different site, but with a new name and new management.

- The DfEE would be encouraged to become more pro-active and outward-looking through the work of the Standards Task Force (STF) and the Standards and Effectiveness Unit. The task force would unite the various educational interests in a new drive to raise standards, carry the crusade to every part of the education service and advise the Secretary of State on the development and implementation of policies to improve school standards in both the primary and the secondary sectors.

- There would be *three* types of secondary school: community, aided and foundation. Community schools would be based on the existing county schools; aided schools would be based on the existing voluntary-aided schools; and foundation schools would offer a new bridge between the powers available to secular and church schools. These three categories would embrace all local authority and grant-maintained schools; and it was anticipated that foundation school status would have particular attractions for most GM establishments. Unlike community schools, aided and foundation schools would be able to employ their own staff and own their premises.

- New national guidelines on school admissions policies would be set by the Secretary of State; aided and foundation schools would be able to put forward their own policies in the light of the DfEE guidelines.

- Where grammar schools still existed in England, their future would be decided by ballots of eligible local parents, and *not* by LEAs.

- Ways would be found of creating new partnerships between state and independent schools. There should be a more positive contribution from independent schools to the government's goal of raising educational standards for *all* children.

Many of these important policy proposals, along with those affecting the primary sector, found their way into the School Standards and Framework Act of 1998 and were then developed and elaborated upon in the early years of the new administration. It is worth examining some of them in greater detail.

STANDARDS NOT STRUCTURES

As we have already seen, the White Paper took its oft-repeated and somewhat ambiguous 'standards not structures' mantra from a 1996 book co-authored by Peter Mandelson and Roger Liddle, which attacked 'educational egalitarians' for regarding 'the structure of schools as far more important than the quality of what is learned' and for showing 'a far greater concern for the social balance of a school's admissions than for the destination of a school's graduates' (Mandelson and Liddle 1996, p.91).

Yet, as I have argued elsewhere (Chitty 1997c), attempts to define the word 'structure' in this context succeed only in adding to the banality of the catchphrase:

> If the term refers to the structure of the education system *as a whole*, one is tempted to ask what sort of national framework we would now have in this country if large numbers of parents, teachers, local education authorities and politicians had not cared about 'structure' in the 1950s and 1960s and campaigned for a comprehensive system of secondary schooling. If it refers to the 'structure' of individual schools (which in any case cannot be viewed in isolation from the system as a whole), then we are being asked to consider a false dichotomy. Standards and structures are inter-related and can be understood only in relation to each other. A comprehensive school which is in reality a secondary modern school in a still selective local system with inadequate resources to perform a wide variety of tasks is less likely to achieve excellent results of the kind measured by OFSTED than will another school in the same area which occupies a safe and privileged position in the local hierarchy of schools. It is one of the major shortcomings of the school improvement/school effectiveness movement that it often treats schools as if they operated in some sort of social and political vacuum.
>
> (*ibid.*, p.71)

A survey of comprehensive education in Britain undertaken in the academic year 1993–4 (reported in Benn and Chitty 1996) emphasised the crucial importance of related issues concerning structure, selection and admissions criteria, which the White Paper neatly sidestepped – a point to which we will return in subsequent sections of this chapter.

SELECTION, DIVERSITY AND SPECIALISATION

As we saw at the end of Chapter 3, the Major government of 1992–97 bequeathed to New Labour a sharply divided system of secondary state schools in England and Wales. Any attempt by David Blunkett to create a unified comprehensive structure subject to fair and transparent admissions rules could not ignore the existence of 163 grammar schools concentrated in English counties such as Buckinghamshire, Kent and Lincolnshire and in many of the larger conurbations; fifteen city technology colleges and 1,155 grant-maintained schools accounting for 19.6 per cent of the students in secondary schools and for 2.8 per cent of those in primary schools; and a growing number of specialist schools and colleges that were now able to 'select' students at the age of 11 on the basis of their 'aptitude' for particular subjects such as technology, languages, sports or arts. In addition, the Major government had issued guidance in June 1996 (DfEE 1996) by which comprehensive schools were able to 'select' up to 15 per cent of their 11-year-old students by 'general academic ability', without the need to publish statutory proposals. Of course, if the Conservatives had won the 1997 general election, the comprehensive principle would have been totally undermined, with grant-maintained schools able to select up to 50 per cent of their intake by general ability, language and technology colleges up to 30 per cent, and all remaining LEA schools up to 20 per cent.

In the event, the Blair administration has proved singularly reluctant to tackle the administrative confusion caused largely by Conservative policies. Indeed, the 1997 White Paper itself was distinctly lukewarm in its defence of comprehensive schooling, arguing that progress towards a more unified system in the 1950s and 1960s had served to undermine 'the pursuit of excellence':

> The demands for equality and increased opportunity in the 1950s and 1960s led to the introduction of comprehensive schools. All-in secondary schooling rightly became the normal pattern, but the search for equality of opportunity in some cases became a tendency to uniformity. The idea that all our children had the same rights to develop their abilities led too easily to the doctrine that all had the same ability. The pursuit of excellence was too often equated with elitism.
>
> (DfEE 1997, p.11)

This curious defensiveness about the comprehensive reform was accompanied by *both* a failure to give a clear lead on the question of grammar schools and their future *and* a determination to persist with the Conservative policy of 'selection by specialisation'.

Many supporters of a *genuine* comprehensive system *without* selective enclaves were already unhappy with the strategy for dealing with selection first outlined in the 1995 Labour policy document *Diversity and Excellence: A New Partnership for Schools*. Here it was argued that the Labour Party was 'implacably opposed to a return to selection by the 11-plus'; but it was also made clear that the grammar schools would *not* be dealt with as an issue of national policy:

> While we have never supported grammar schools in their exclusion of children by examination, change can come only through local agreement. Such a change in the character of a school could follow only a clear demonstration of support from the parents affected by such a decision.
>
> (Labour Party 1995, p.11)

Delegates to the October 1995 Labour Party Conference were clearly unhappy with this clumsy formula, which had been announced the previous June. Accordingly, in his reply to the acrimonious education debate on 4 October, Shadow Education Secretary David Blunkett sought to placate his restless audience by saying: 'Read my lips. No selection, either by examination or interview, under a Labour government'. That categorical assurance won the day for the Labour leadership; and a revolt, organised around demands for the remaining 163 grammar schools to be incorporated into the comprehensive system, collapsed – on the understanding that its chief purpose seemed to have been achieved.

It soon became clear, however, that 'no selection' actually meant 'no *further* selection'; and when David Blunkett began using this new slogan in speeches and media interviews, he was not guilty of a simple slip of the tongue: he was, in effect, announcing a *change of education policy*. As Roy Hattersley has pointed out on a number of occasions, 'no selection' signified an end to the existing grammar schools; 'no *further* selection' was *a guarantee of their retention*. In Mr Hattersley's view, David Blunkett made a specific pledge to see him through a very difficult education debate knowing full well that Tony Blair would not allow him to honour it. But, replying to this charge on the BBC Television *Breakfast with Frost* programme on 30 November 1997, the new Education Secretary protested that when he had used the words 'no selection' in the 1995 debate, he had actually intended them to mean 'no *further* selection'. There had, therefore, been *no* change of policy.

More recently, in a well-publicised interview with *The Sunday Telegraph* (12 March 2000), David Blunkett claimed that his 1995 'Read my lips' selection pledge was 'a joke'. This revelation caused some bitterness among the former Education Secretary's many critics within the Labour Party; but it is important to cite the *actual words* used in the interview, rather than the headlines of rival newspapers:

> The 1995 Conference Debate amuses me now because people haven't got the joke. I was obviously parodying George Bush. The Conference laughed at the time, but, since then, nobody has got it. Read my lips was a joke. As for the second part, if I were doing it again I would say 'no *more* selection'.

At the same time, David Blunkett left the readers of *The Sunday Telegraph* in no doubt that it was time to 'bury the dated arguments of previous decades' and reverse 'the outright opposition to grammars' that had been 'a touchstone of Labour politics for at least 35 years'.

> I'm not interested in hunting the grammar schools. . . . I'm desperately trying to avoid the whole debate in education once again, as it was in the 1960s and 1970s, concentrating on the issue of selection, when it *should* be concentrating on the raising of standards. . . . Arguments about selection are part of a past agenda. We have set up a system which says 'if you don't like grammar schools, you can get rid of them'; but it

isn't really the key issue for the year 2000. The real issue is what we are going to do about the whole of secondary education.

(*The Sunday Telegraph*, 12 March 2000)

This interview was given just two days after the announcement of the voting figures in the first ballot on the future of a grammar school held as a result of the government's policy of leaving the future of 11-plus selection in the hands of local parents. The future of Ripon Grammar School in north Yorkshire, founded in 1556 and one of the oldest in England, was assured as parents decided by a majority of two to one to reject the proposition that the school be required in future to 'admit children of all abilities'. On a 75 per cent turnout, 1,493 of the 3,000 parents who were entitled to vote because their children attended one of fourteen 'feeder' state primary or independent preparatory schools voted to reject the proposition, with only 748 voting in favour – a majority so decisive that the pro-comprehensive 'lobby' immediately abandoned plans to challenge the result. Nevertheless, the Ripon branch of the Campaign for State Education (CASE) complained that more than 25 per cent of those parents eligible to vote came from *outside* the area, while the same proportion educated their primary-age children in the independent sector. It was also significant that the secondary modern school in Ripon had recently been 'upgraded' by being given 'specialist school' status. Responding to the Ripon voting figures, Education Minister Estelle Morris saw no need to take account of the anomalies highlighted by CASE:

> The Government respects the decision of parents to retain the current admission arrangements at Ripon Grammar School. . . . At all stages of the debate, the decision has been a matter for the parents, and they have all had the chance to express their views
>
> (reported in *The Daily Telegraph*, 11 March 2000)

Yet, whatever education ministers might feel obliged to say in public, it can be argued that the future of 11-plus selection is simply too important to be surrendered to the vagaries of local campaigns, affected as they will be by a number of esoteric local factors, especially since research shows that it is not true that the continued existence of selective schools makes no difference to the success or otherwise of neighbouring comprehensives.

The 1994 survey of comprehensive education in this country, to which reference has already been made, emphasised the educationally depressing effect that the 163 remaining grammar schools had upon the comprehensive schools in their own vicinities. With statistics taken from that survey, Table 6.1 shows that where grammar schools were present in an area, the percentage of students in the neighbouring comprehensives falling in the top 20 per cent of the attainment range was 12 – compared with 24 for those comprehensives where there was no competition from selective schools. For those going on from 11–16 schools to

Table 6.1 Statistics for comprehensive schools with and without grammar schools in the area

	Grammar schools present in the area	Grammar schools absent from the area
Average size	801	1,052
Percentage		
In top 20 per cent of attainment	12	24
Going on from 11–16 schools	57	69
Staying on in 11–18 schools	49	60
Gaining five GCSEs A–C	29	48
'A'-level point score average	10.6	13.4

some form of post-16 education and training, the figure was 57 as against 69; for those staying on in 11–18 schools, 49 as against 60; and for those gaining five or more GCSE passes at grades A to C, 29 as against 48. The A-level point score averages were 10.6 and 13.4, respectively. The authors of the survey concluded that:

> Selection at secondary-school level did *not* render comprehensive education impossible or deny it to parents and children; what it did do, however, wherever it was taking place, was decrease comprehensive education's effectiveness *for the majority* – and, in some cases, severely depress outcomes in neighbouring schools.
>
> (Benn and Chitty 1996, p.465)

The other aspect of education policy that seems to point up New Labour's reluctance to abandon entirely the concept of selection by ability (or aptitude) concerns the continuing emphasis on 'specialisation'. The 1997 White Paper argued that 'there is value in encouraging diversity by allowing secondary schools to develop a particular identity, character and expertise' (DfEE 1997, p.66). It went on to give an assurance that schools with a specialism would continue to be able to give priority to children who demonstrated 'the relevant aptitude', as long as that was not misused to select on the basis of 'general academic ability' (p.71). From all this, it seems clear that the concept of 'selection by specialisation', first promoted by Conservative Education Secretary John Patten in 1992, did not become redundant with the end of eighteen years of Conservative rule.

The White Paper pledge was given legislative backing in Clause 93 of the School Standards and Framework Bill, published on 4 December 1997, which said that a maintained secondary school could 'make provision for the selection of pupils for admission to the school by reference to their aptitude for one or more prescribed subjects, where:

- the admission authority for the school is satisfied that the school has a specialism in the subject or subjects in question; and

> • the proportion of selective admissions in any relevant age group does not exceed 10 per cent.

The 10 per cent limit on 'selection by aptitude' was justified by the Government as sufficient to support 'diversity' but low enough *not* to change the basic 'character' of the school. Specialist schools and colleges would be at the heart of a new drive for diversity and excellence within a 'modernised' secondary school system that would now be able to cater for individual strengths, rather than offering a bland sameness for all. *What education ministers failed to acknowledge was that in a class-divided and highly competitive society, specialisms could never be equal, with specialist schools rapidly becoming ranked in a hierarchy of status.* They also made the false assumption that children could actually be tested for *particular talents* rather than for *general ability*. As Professor Peter Mortimore argued in an article published in *Education Guardian* in March 1998, the body of research evidence suggested otherwise:

> Except in music and perhaps art, it does not seem possible to diagnose specific aptitudes for most school curriculum subjects. Instead, what emerges from such testing is a general ability to learn, which is often, but not always, associated with the various 'advantages' of coming from a middle-class home. How can headteachers know if the 'aptitude' of a 10-year-old in German shows anything more than the parents' ability to pay for extra language lessons?
>
> (*The Guardian*, 24 March 1998)

In a pamphlet produced by RISE (the Research and Information on State Education Trust) and published in May 1998, Professor Tony Edwards reviewed all the recent research evidence with regard to specialisation and selection. Without seeking to argue *for* or *against* the Labour government's specialist schools policy, Professor Edwards organised his review around *three* of the main claims made in support of what has appeared to successive governments to be 'an evidently good thing':

1. that parents actually *want* greater curriculum choice;
2. that specialisation is quite different from selection;
3. that diversity through specialisation will raise educational standards *in* and *beyond* the specialist schools themselves.

> While conceding that it was too early for a *decisive* assessment of the validity of these three claims, Professor Edwards found that the weight of evidence supported the following *six* conclusions:
>
> 1. There is no evident parental demand for more specialised forms of curriculum.

> 2.   In the British, and particularly the English, context, specialisation as a means of 'diversifying' and 'modernising' the school curriculum confronts a formidable obstacle – the continuing high prestige of the 'traditional academic' curriculum.
>
> 3.   Specialisation is hard to separate from straightforward selection, and certainly in conditions where schools compete for students.
>
> 4.   'Selection by interest' also tends to produce socially segregated intakes.
>
> 5.   The early identification of 'aptitude' for particular subjects, defined as *promise* rather than *achievement*, remains a problem without technically well-grounded and educationally acceptable solutions.
>
> 6.   Without valid evidence that 'specialist schools' are in fact more effective, the extent to which they are preferentially funded is inequitable.
>
> (RISE 1998)

The Labour government, like its Conservative predecessors, has shown little inclination to take account of those research findings that do not support is own educational agenda. When it took office in May 1997, it inherited 196 specialist schools and colleges established, in the main, by John Patten and Gillian Shephard: fifteen city technology colleges (dating back to the period before 1992), thirty language colleges and 151 new technology colleges (see Chapter 3). By January 1998, 290 specialist colleges had been designated in 100 English local education authorities: 210 technology colleges, 50 language colleges, 17 sports colleges and 13 arts colleges. A further fifty-one specialist colleges were named in June 1998, with Education Minister Estelle Morris announcing a broader remit for these new schools:

> Specialist schools and colleges will have a key contribution to make in raising standards and delivering excellence in schools. . . . They will help thousands of young people to learn new skills and progress into employment, further training and higher education, according to their individual abilities, aptitudes and ambitions.
>
> (reported in *The Evening Standard*, 16 June 1998)

It had been decided that these specialist colleges would also have a role to play in providing programmes of 'masterclasses' for 'gifted' children as young as 5 in a bid to 'improve the education of "bright" pupils in state schools'. The extra lessons, in subjects as diverse as mathematics, foreign languages and sport, would be held after school for those youngsters who were not being sufficiently 'stretched' by the normal timetable. These proposals received special attention at the DfEE in the months that followed and were highlighted as part of a drive to 'rescue the reputation of inner city comprehensives' launched by the government in March 1999.

Finally, in an interview with David Frost on the BBC Television *Breakfast with Frost* programme on 16 January 2000, the Prime Minister announced that hundreds of comprehensive schools would be turned into specialist colleges over the next three years as the government switched its focus from primary to secondary education. The government was on target to have 500 in place by September 2000 and 800 by September 2003, which meant that, by then, nearly one in four state secondary schools would have a specialism in technology, languages, sport or the creative arts. At the same time, the DfEE announced that schools could achieve 'specialist status' by raising £50,000 in business sponsorship, setting realisable but ambitious improvement targets and involving the local community. In return, they would receive a £100,000 capital grant and an extra £120 per student per year for at least four years. According to the DfEE, specialist colleges were already developing useful links with their feeder primaries. For example, Langley Park Technology College in Burnley was running information technology courses for sixty local primary teachers, while Prudhoe Community High School in Northumberland had established links with eleven primaries and was setting up a computer learning site for all adults and children in the community. Alongside these specialist schools, the government programme of 'beacon schools' – centres of excellence for spreading best practice – was also intended to raise educational standards, particularly in inner city areas.

Selection within schools

Not only was continued selection *between* different types of secondary school an important part of New Labour's education policy; it was also made clear in the 1997 White Paper that the government was concerned about the grouping of students for all or most academic subjects *within* schools. Indeed, the one aspect of the White Paper that became a headline story in all the early morning Radio 4 news bulletins on the day the document was published was the rejection of mixed-ability teaching, particularly in secondary schools. Writing on the same day in *The Times* (7 July 1997), Prime Minister Tony Blair urged teachers to abandon mixed-ability classes in favour of homogeneous groups allowing children to 'develop as fast as they can'. In an uncompromising article ('Schools told to break with the past'), he called for 'a determined break' from 'the system of monolithic mixed-ability comprehensives that symbolised Labour's past'.

The government's firm stance on mixed-ability groupings had, in fact, been foreshadowed in a much-publicised speech delivered by Tony Blair, when still leader of the Opposition, in Oxfordshire in June 1996. There he argued that academic standards in comprehensive schools could not be improved if teachers persisted with mixed-ability classes:

> Not to take account of the obvious common-sense that different children move at different speeds and have differing abilities is to give idealism a bad name. The modernisation of the comprehensive principle requires that all pupils are encouraged to progress as far and as fast as they are able. Grouping children according to ability is an important way of making that happen.
>
> (Reported in *The Guardian*, 8 June 1996)

The same line was adopted in *The Blair Revolution*, which confidently asserted that 'where teachers have ideological presumptions in favour of mixed-ability teaching, these should be abandoned in favour of what achieves the best results in schools'. As students got older, streams and sets should be transformed into 'separate routes specialising in a range of either vocational, technological or academic options' – with students still having the chance to combine them (Mandelson and Liddle 1996, p.94).

According to the White Paper itself, mixed-ability teaching had simply *not* proved capable of ensuring that 'all schools play to the strengths of every child'. It went on to claim that 'in too many cases, it has failed *both* to stretch the brightest *and* to respond to the needs of those who have fallen behind'. Setting, on the other hand, *was* proving effective in many schools – and particularly in science, maths and languages. It was *not* suggested that 'any single model of grouping students should be *imposed* on secondary schools'; but, nonetheless, setting should be 'the norm', unless a school could demonstrate that 'it was getting *better than expected results* through a different approach'.

> The White Paper also felt that it would be worth considering a move back to setting in primary schools; and all schools, both primary and secondary, should make it clear in reports to parents what grouping policies they were adopting. This was a matter that OFSTED inspections would be expected to focus on (DfEE 1997, p.38).

In an article published in *The Times Educational Supplement* in July 1997, education journalist Peter Wilby argued that all this fuss about mixed-ability teaching in secondary schools was a classic case of 'tilting at windmills', with the government's anxiety appearing to exist 'in a sort of event bubble of its own, without any reference to past, present or future reality'. Here was another example of governments, whether Conservative or Labour, 'refusing to take notice of the findings of reputable research studies' (*The Times Educational Supplement*, 18 July 1997).

Peter Wilby's comments in this article were in fact largely based on the findings of the large-scale survey of comprehensive schools carried out in 1993–4, which showed that there was very little mixed-ability work in comprehensive schools after Year 7, where it was to be found being used in *all* subjects in just over 50 per cent of all schools. Even here, there was evidence that the use of mixed-ability groups was not necessarily the result of a total commitment to non-streaming as such. Interviews with teachers confirmed that with many comprehensive schools taking students from a wide range of primary schools, there was felt to be the need for a period of assessment by subject teachers in the secondary school before final (or even tentative) decisions could be made about the allocation of students to 'appropriate' sets or streams. In many comprehensive schools, the use of setting in at least two subjects then began in the second year (Year 8) where the proportion of schools using mixed-ability groups in *all* subjects was as low as 16.8 per cent. By Year 9, this figure had fallen to 6.5 per cent; and by Years 10 and 11 (Key Stage 4), it was just 3 per cent – with the vast majority of comprehensives using various forms of streaming, banding and setting.

> At the same time, the research study could find no evidence of a correlation between a school or subject department's grouping policy and its GCSE or A-level results (Benn and Chitty 1996, pp.255,276,287,513).

TACKLING UNDER-ACHIEVEMENT IN INNER-CITY SCHOOLS

One of the six principles underpinning New Labour's reform agenda in the White Paper boldly stated that there would be 'zero tolerance of under-performance'; and this has been a major theme of the government's education policy over the past five years. In particular, this has meant finding new ways of 'motivating young people in tough inner-city areas'.

Back in 1997, the most innovative method for achieving this was the controversial idea of 'Education Action Zones'. These zones were highlighted in New Labour's election manifesto as part of an attack on 'low standards' and 'under-achieving schools'; and they then appeared with more details attached in the chapter of the 1997 White Paper called 'Modernising the Comprehensive Principle'.

According to the White Paper, there would be a pilot programme of up to twenty-five action zones 'phased in over two to three years and set up in areas with a mix of under-performing schools and the highest levels of disadvantage'. At this stage, the exact relationship of a zone to the local education authority was left distinctly vague. The new action zones would be expected to operate on the basis of an action forum, which would include 'parents and representatives from the local business and social community, as well as representation from the constituent schools and the LEA'. It was also clear that the government itself intended to play a direct role in the new project. Once an action zone had been established, representatives of the Secretary of State – 'for example, someone from one of our most successful schools' – would be appointed to the action team to provide 'advice and support'. The operation of the action zone would be monitored by the Standards and Effectiveness Unit of the DfEE.

Zones would have financial attractions for potential bidders: they would have 'first call on funds from all relevant central programmes – for example, the literacy and numeracy initiatives aimed at primary schools, the homework centres, the specialist schools initiative – provided that satisfactory proposals are put forward'. It was also suggested that an action zone might be given 'additional flexibility in matters of staffing or the organisation of schools'; but it was not made clear at this stage exactly what this meant (DfEE 1997, pp.39–40).

The School Standards and Framework Bill, published in December 1997, dealt with Education Action Zones in Chapter 3 (pages 9–11). This added little to the information contained in the White Paper, although it did cover in some detail the proposal to allow the disapplication of the Teachers' Pay and Conditions Order in relation to teachers at participating schools.

It was only on 5 January 1998 that the government's plans for the new EAZs became clearer, when the DfEE sent a letter to colleagues in the LEAs, TECs, government offices, health authorities, business, religious, community and other organisations inviting bids, for which the closing date was 20 March, less than three months later.

> What this letter revealed for the first time was that private companies could have a major role to play in the running of at least *some* of the new zones, thereby exerting a direct influence on the curriculum and the ethos of the participating schools. Indeed, this was the feature of the EAZ project picked up and discussed in the national press. *It was now clear that not only would an action forum be given powers to offer 'a new pay and conditions package for teachers'; it would also be able to 'tailor or radically alter parts of the National Curriculum'.* As has been argued elsewhere (Chitty 1998a, p.80), all this gave rise to fears that the government's plans could 'undermine the role of the Local Education Authority and open the door to the further privatisation of the education service'.

Launching the EAZ project at the North of England Education Conference meeting in Bradford in January 1998, Professor Michael Barber, head of the Government's Standards and Effectiveness Unit, was proud to announce that the new zones would be 'test-beds for innovation in a post-modern world'. The first five zones would begin operation in September 1998 – with a further twenty following in September 1999. Schools in a zone would be allowed to dispense with the National Curriculum and, where appropriate, focus on 'the rudiments of literacy and numeracy'. They would also be able to ignore national agreements on teachers' pay and conditions to extend the working week into early mornings, evenings and/or weekends.

Professor Barber revealed in his speech that the initiative was to be modelled on existing schemes in the United States, where detergent group Procter & Gamble and management consultants Arthur Anderson already ran schools. Apparently, interest had been expressed by a number of 'household names' – multinationals involved in manufacturing, commerce, insurance and information technology. Examples of companies showing a willingness to be involved included Capita, which ran the nursery vouchers scheme and administered council payrolls; Nord Anglia plc, the stock-market-listed education provider; and the Centre for British Teachers (CFBT), which ran careers services and carried out school inspections for OFSTED. According to Professor Barber, 'successful companies are uniquely able to manage change and innovation' (reported in *The Guardian*, 7 January 1998).

As *The Times Educational Supplement* shrewdly observed in an editorial on 9 January 1998, it was 'somewhat ironic' that the North of England Education

Conference, 'the premier showcase for local authorities', was the chosen venue to make an announcement that could lead to 'the break-up of those very authorities'. Typical of the jubilant headlines in the right-wing national press was 'Private Firms to Run State Schools' in *The Daily Mail* (7 January 1998), which went on to argue in an editorial that 'emergency measures have long been needed to make good the damage inflicted by bad teaching and bureaucratic domination'. David Blunkett was to be congratulated for being 'radical and brave', for 'rescuing children imprisoned in dud schools' and for 'tearing up the rule book'. No less jubilant was the tone of Boris Johnson's opinion column in *The Daily Telegraph* of 12 January 1998:

> The EAZ Project is nothing less than a triumph of Tory free-market ideology and, on the face of it, a brutal snub to core Labour voters. . . . Ex-comrade Blunkett has paved the way for the new Cadbury's Comprehensive, with the choc machines in the gym, or for Texaco's hostile bid for Grange Hill.

During the early months of 1998, the government changed the rules and arrangements for the new zones laid down in its early announcements. As we have seen, the original idea was that there was to be an initial tranche of five zones in operation by September 1998, with a further twenty to begin work in September 1999. Each was to receive £250,000 of public money to match £250,000 from the private sector. Then in the late spring, it was decided that there would now be twelve zones in operation in September 1998, with another thirteen in January 1999. All would be chosen from the first sixty bids that had been received by the end of March. At the same time, David Blunkett increased the amount of money on offer. Instead of £250,000 of public money, there would be £750,000 to add to the £250,000 from the private sector. That would help to provide the level of resources needed to fund some of the more 'radical' developments, such as recruiting 'advanced skill teachers' on higher salaries, negotiating a longer school day or changes in traditional holiday patterns, and appointing new classes of 'managers' and support staff.

   The EAZ initiative seemed to many to mark a significant new stage in the ability of business to participate in the core educational functions of schools, but in the event, the worst fears of the government's left-wing critics were not realised when details of the first twenty-five action zones were announced on 23 June 1998. Companies backing the successful bids included Blackburn Rovers, Cadbury Schweppes, Nissan, Rolls Royce, Kellogg, British Aerospace, Tate & Lyle, American Express and Brittany Ferries.

> But in the vast majority of cases, the leading role in the zone partnerships was to be taken by the local authorities themselves, one exception being the zone located in the London borough of Lambeth, which would be led by Shell International and managed by private-sector consultants.

Announcing the locations, not all of them areas of great disadvantage, David Blunkett called the action zones 'test-beds for the school system of the 21st century'. Schools Minister Stephen Byers went further, saying that the zones would constitute 'a fundamental change to the education *status quo* and a real threat to those vested interests which have for too long held back our school system' (reported in *The Guardian*, 24 June 1998).

As the number of Education Action Zones escalates (with around seventy zones expected to be fully operational or ready to start by September 2000), it still remains to be seen how active and interfering private companies will be in the day-to-day running of the participating schools. If the critics' genuine forebodings prove to be justified, the government's controversial project, carrying as it does a clear implication that local authorities do not have 'a God-given right' to run schools, could represent, in Richard Hatcher's words (1998, p.9), 'a historic break from the social-democratic tradition of schools as a publicly-run service'.

A second strategy for dealing with 'under-performing schools', many of them situated in 'areas of disadvantage', has been the government's 'Fresh Start' policy. This was outlined briefly in New Labour's election manifesto in the section headed 'Zero Tolerance of Under-performance'. Here it was argued that every school in the country had 'the capacity to succeed'. It was the duty of all local education authorities to *ensure* and *demonstrate* that every school *was* improving. For those 'failing schools' unable or unwilling to improve, ministers would order a 'fresh start', whereby the school would be closed and then 'started afresh on the same site'. Where 'good schools' and 'bad' schools co-existed side by side, LEAs would be authorised to allow one school to take over the other 'to set the under-performing school on a new path' (Labour Party 1997, p.7).

The 1997 White Paper featured the 'Fresh Start' policy in the chapter called 'Standards and Accountability'. It stipulated that where drastic measures were clearly necessary, a local education authority would be required to close the school and then 're-open it on the same or a different site with a new name and new management. But, in the words of the White Paper:

> The change would have to be more than superficial. It would need professional leadership of the highest calibre and would need to be seen by everyone as a clean break and as an attempt to create a new and ambitious sense of purpose. The Government now intends to remove some of the legal and administrative barriers and to take powers to force an LEA to close a failing school where that is the best course.
>
> (DfEE 1997, p.30)

By the beginning of March 2000, there were in fact only ten secondary schools in the 'Fresh Start' programme; it was at this point that David Blunkett announced new and ambitious plans for 'obliging' local education authorities to close their 'under-performing' schools and then reopen them with a new name and a new and 'inspirational' headteacher. In a speech to a National Union of Teachers conference on secondary education held on 1 March, the Education and Employment Secretary warned that poverty would no longer be made the excuse for failure and under-achievement.

> There are cynics out there who say that school performance is all about socio-economics and the areas that these schools are located in. In fact, no child is preordained by their class, gender, ethnic group or home life to fail. . . . Comprehensive education requires equal opportunities for all. . . . I can't bus children from one end of a city to another, but I can do something to spread what is working. I can bring in to schools which are clearly not succeeding people who have made it work elsewhere.
>
> (reported in *The Guardian*, 2 March 2000)

In Mr Blunkett's view, it was disgraceful that there were eighty-six secondary schools with fewer than 15 per cent of students gaining at least five good GCSE passes at Grade C or above and as many as 530 schools with a current pass rate below 25 per cent. Local authorities would now be asked to consider a fresh start for all secondary schools where fewer than 15 per cent of GCSE candidates managed five good (A to C) passes for three years in a row.

Mr Blunkett announced three targets to secure rapid improvement in the secondary sector:

1.   By 2003, all secondary schools must secure a pass rate of at least 15 per cent of students gaining five good GCSE passes.
2.   By 2004, there should be no secondary school with a pass rate below 20 per cent.
3.   By 2006, all secondary schools should get a pass rate of at least 25 per cent.
       (reported in *The Guardian*, 2 March 2000)

Reactions to this speech from union leaders, educationists and headteachers were less than enthusiastic. Doug McAvoy, General Secretary of the NUT, pointed out that 'constructive criticism' could be helpful, but that 'constant denigration' was 'discouraging, dispiriting, demoralising and plain bad judgement'. In the view of John Dunford, General Secretary of the Secondary Heads Association, the government's latest announcement would simply make it harder for secondary schools with low GCSE results to 'retain and recruit good staff'. In any case, the proportion of students with at least five A to C grades was 'the wrong measure to use'. It had the effect of inviting schools under intense pressure to concentrate resources on 'the small number of children at the grade C/D borderline'. According to Peter Mortimore, Director of London University's Institute of Education: 'All the work of school improvement professionals shows that schools *can* make a difference; but they cannot completely overcome the effects of disadvantage'. Similarly, Ian Woodhead, the headteacher of a comprehensive school in Sheffield, conceded that poverty was not 'an excuse for failure'; but it was still a factor that left some students with 'a bigger mountain to climb' (quoted in *The Guardian*, 2 March 2000).

It was unfortunate for Mr Blunkett that by the middle of March, his 'Fresh Start' policy for reviving 'failing schools' had been rocked by three resignations within just five days of 'superheads' appointed to 'rescue' students from indiscipline and under-achievement.

Then in the same hectic month (it was also in March that the result of the Ripon ballot was announced), the Education and Employment Secretary unveiled yet another initiative for dealing with the cycle of inner city deprivation and failure to add to beacon schools, specialist colleges, education action zones and the 'Fresh Start' policy. In an address to the Social Market Foundation delivered on 15 March, Mr Blunkett announced plans for failing secondary schools to be offered in their entirety to businesses, churches, voluntary bodies and philanthropists, to be run in partnership with the government but without the involvement of local education authorities. These new schools would be known as 'city academies' and would be modelled on the city technology colleges founded by the Conservatives in the late 1980s. They would be given the freedom to change the length of the school day and the pattern of terms and holidays. They would have scope to adjust the National Curriculum to make space for subject specialisms. They would also be allowed to pay special bonuses to attract and retain the best staff. It was anticipated that the first of these new academics would be opened in September 2001.

Anticipating ideological criticism in an article that appeared in *The Daily Telegraph* on the day of the announcement, Mr Blunkett said:

> Our policy has always been: what matters is what works best to raise standards. In the end it is the education of our young people that must come first. . . . The Government is looking for a full range of alternative models to the idea of the all-purpose neighbourhood comprehensive. . . . The Government intends to run all the models in parallel. . . . What will survive is what works.

Nigel de Gruchy, General Secretary of the National Association of Schoolmasters/ Union of Women Teachers, saw things in more simplistic terms. In his view, Mr Blunkett's announcement was 'the final nail in the coffin of the traditional comprehensive system, hailed by Labour politicians of the 1960s and 1970s as the answer to so many of our educational and social problems' (quoted in *The Guardian*, 16 March 2000).

FURTHER CHANGES TO THE NATIONAL CURRICULUM

It would seem fair to argue that where the National Curriculum is concerned, New Labour has been happy to continue the process of dismantling initiated by the Conservatives in the first half of the 1990s.

In January 1998, the government announced that primary school children would no longer be required to stick to the detailed national syllabuses in geography, history, design and technology, art, music and PE. Then in February, a document from the QCA (Qualifications and Curriculum Authority) revealed that the Secretary of State had decided to open up major opportunities for the wider use of 'work-related learning' at Key Stage 4, both *within* and *beyond* the National Curriculum. Using powers available to him under Section 363 of the 1996 Education Act, David Blunkett proposed to allow schools to set aside the programmes of study for 14- to 16-year-olds in up to two National Curriculum subjects, excluding English, mathematics, information technology and physical education – 'subject to criteria designed to guarantee pupils' entitlement to breadth, balance and progression'. As we saw in Chapter 5, one of the outcomes of the Dearing review was to allow older students to follow a well-constructed vocational course as an acceptable alternative to a total diet of GCSE subjects.

Among all the curriculum changes that have been introduced over the past ten or so years, only Key Stage 3 has remained relatively free from government interference. But even this may not be true for very much longer: for example, David Blunkett said in an interview with Andrew Rawnsley on the BBC Radio 4 *Westminster Hour* programme (16 April 2000) that he would like to see 'greater flexibility' in the curriculum for the early years of secondary schooling, with a greater emphasis on vocational studies. At the same time, there could be new national tests for 12-year-old students, with classroom teachers increasingly being judged (and perhaps even paid) according to their students' performance in such tests (to be discussed more fully in Chapter 7).

On top of all this, teachers had to prepare for the launch of the new National Curriculum for 2000, which, while promising to cut content in a number of subject areas, also raised fears about overloading, particularly at the primary level. The National Union of Teachers, for example, has argued for the establishment of a new primary curriculum group to prevent literacy and numeracy dominating the timetable. The union has opposed the compulsory introduction of citizenship lessons as a separate subject for secondary students from 2002, arguing that legislation already in place requires schools to teach citizenship and democracy. There has also been concern about the new personal, social and health education framework for 5- to 16-year-olds, with debate focusing on the desirability or otherwise of including explicit references to different family patterns and lifestyles. This will be a subject for discussion in Chapter 8.

SUGGESTED ACTIVITIES

1. Consider, with colleagues, the possible advantages and disadvantages of the closer involvement of business interests in state education.

    To what extent does the new educational discourse of 'partnership' represent and embody worthwhile educational and democratic aims (including the improvement of educational provision for students in greatest need), and to what extent can it be dismissed as mere rhetoric disguising 'back-door privatisation', new forms of social control and continuing inequality of educational opportunity?

2.   What do you see as the central arguments in favour of and against the setting
      of students? What would your own arguments be, and what evidence could
      you draw upon to support these arguments?

          How far is it possible to reconcile setting or streaming with your own
      values related to state education and the comprehensive ideal? On balance,
      do you think setting is likely to help, hinder or make little difference to the
      academic and social development of students identified as low achievers?

3.   Discuss with colleagues which elements of education policy and reform from
      1997 onwards you feel most and least sympathetic towards – and why. Which
      policies and reforms do you think will last, and which do you think will,
      sooner or later, have to be abandoned?

SUGGESTED READING

Chitty, C. and Dunford, J. (eds) (1999) *State Schools: New Labour and the
Conservative Legacy*. In this wide-ranging book, a team of ten authors, largely
comprising headteachers and former heads, analyses the education agenda of the
Labour government, looking in particular at the willingness of ministers to
continue with the policies of the preceding administration.

DfEE (1997) *Excellence in Schools*. Published in July 1997, just sixty-seven days after
the election of the Blair administration, this White Paper is an essential document
for understanding the education agenda of New Labour.

7 Teachers' Conditions of Service and Professional Responsibilities: recent developments

This chapter is largely concerned with the 1998 DfEE document Teaching: High Status, High Standards: Requirements for Courses of Initial Teacher Training, *popularly known as Circular 4/98, which set out the criteria for what was, in effect, the first ever national curriculum for initial teacher training (ITT). Special attention is paid to Section D of the Circular, which, among other things, required that intending teachers should have a working knowledge and understanding of their professional duties as set out in the current* School Teachers' Pay and Conditions *document. It is argued that four recent developments have served to undermine any semblance of unified pay and conditions of service arrangements: (1) the creation of education action zones; (2) the introduction of beacon schools; (3) the creation of a new category of advanced skills teacher; and (4) the proposed introduction of performance-related pay.*

INTRODUCTION

So far we have concentrated on curriculum and school organisation. But what about teaching itself?

CIRCULAR 4/98

Circular 4/98 (DfEE 1998a) set out the criteria that had to be met by all courses of initial teacher training (ITT); and the standards itemised in Annex A of the document replaced the more general 'competencies' set out in earlier circulars. Successful completion of a course or programme of initial teacher training, including employment-based provision, required the trainee to achieve *all* these standards. In other words, all courses had to involve the assessment of *all* trainees to ensure that *all* the standards specified were met. Only then would trainees be awarded qualified teacher status (QTS), which was a requirement for all those wishing to teach in a maintained primary or secondary school. The requirements set out in this 'national curriculum' for initial teacher training would, in the words of the Circular, 'equip all new teachers with the knowledge, understanding and skills needed to play their part in raising student performance across the education system' (p.3).

The standards to be met were set out in Annex A of the Circular under the following four main headings:

A.   KNOWLEDGE AND UNDERSTANDING
1.   Standards for secondary specialist subjects
2.   Standards for primary subjects
3.   Additional standards relating to early years (nursery and reception) for trainees on 3–8 and 3–11 courses.

B.   PLANNING, TEACHING AND CLASS MANAGEMENT
1.   Standards for primary English, mathematics and science
2.   Standards for primary and secondary specialist subjects
3.   Standards for secondary English, mathematics and science
4.   Standards for primary and secondary for all subjects:
     ●   planning
     ●   teaching and class management
5.   Additional standards relating to early years (nursery and reception) for trainees on 3–8 and 3–11 courses.

C.   MONITORING, ASSESSMENT, RECORDING, REPORTING AND ACCOUNTABILITY
     The standards in this section apply to all trainees seeking qualified teacher status.

D.   OTHER PROFESSIONAL REQUIREMENTS
     The standards in this section apply to all trainees seeking qualified teacher status.

It is with Section D of the Circular (see Appendix B) that much of this chapter is chiefly concerned. While looking at what can be seen as largely *practical* requirements for classroom teachers, there will inevitably be some overlap with the more *theoretical* issues discussed elsewhere in the book. In particular, issues of equality, social justice, racism and sexism will be addressed more fully in Chapter 8. The next section of this chapter will examine teachers' conditions of service as set out in the current (1999) *School Teachers' Pay and Conditions* document (DfEE 1999), issued under the School Teachers' Pay and Conditions Act of 1991.

TEACHERS' CONDITIONS OF SERVICE

The 1999 *School Teachers' Pay and Conditions* document, often referred to as 'the Blue Book', sets out teachers' working time, professional duties and conditions of service. It has its origins in the acrimonious national salaries and conditions of service dispute of 1986–7, which caused then Education Secretary Kenneth Baker to dismantle much of the existing machinery for determining teachers' pay and conditions of service. Before 1987, negotiations on pay and other conditions of employment took place in the Burnham Committee and the Council of Local Education Authorities (School Teacher) Committee (CLEA/ST). The Burnham Committee was abolished, as part of the repeal of the 1965 Remuneration of Teachers Act, under the terms of the Teachers' Pay and Conditions Act of 1987 (HMSO 1987), which required the Secretary of State to appoint 'an Interim Advisory Committee on School Teachers' Pay and Conditions to examine and report to him on such matters relating to the remuneration and other conditions of employment of school teachers in England and Wales as he may refer to them' (p.1). The *School Teachers' Pay and Conditions* document has been published annually by Her Majesty's Stationery Office since 1987; and its production is always preceded by a prolonged consultation exercise during which the various teacher unions are able to make either joint or separate representations to a review body set up as one of the provisions of the School Teachers' Pay and Conditions Act of 1991 (HMSO 1991).

> An Order providing for conditions of employment to be incorporated into all teachers' contracts also came into force in 1987. The Order set down a contractual requirement that teachers be available for work for 195 days in any school year, 190 days of which should be spent with students ('pupils' in the Order). The allocation of 'directed time' for the year for all teachers should amount to 1,265 hours.

The Order also set out a list of required 'professional duties', and this list, which constitutes Part XII of the current (1999) *School Teachers' Pay and Conditions* document, is reproduced in Appendix A. As will be seen, the list covers a wide range of issues, including teaching, related activities, assessments and reports, appraisal, review of further training and development and induction, educational methods, discipline, health and safety, staff meetings, cover for absent teachers, public examinations, management, administration and working time (DfEE 1999, pp.65–70).

Many teachers enter the profession believing, as do many members of the public, that there is in existence a *national* system of education with corresponding unified pay and conditions of service arrangements. Yet as NUT regional officer Jeff Nixon has recently pointed out, this is simply not the case.

> Much of what happen in schools is . . . subject to local interpretation. In addition, initiatives may occur, either at local or national level, which change certain aspects of the teacher's job or may simply emphasise one or a number of items in the conditions of service package at a particular time.
>
> (Nixon 1999, p.1)

Nixon cites as an example of this the administration in different schools of in-service education and training days (INSET) – the so-called 'Baker Days', named after Kenneth Baker, who was Education Secretary from 1986 to 1989. The legislation does *not* specify *where* or *when* the INSET days need to be taken – some secondary schools, with the agreement of the relevant staff, convert days designated as 'Baker Days' into days of school closure, always ensuring, of course, that the school still provides the statutory 190 days of education for all students.

There may also be local agreements that modify the national picture, and these may be 'better' or 'worse' than the conditions agreed nationally. On what might be seen as the 'positive' side, for example, some LEAs honour maternity leave and maternity pay agreements that are preferable to the national one. On the 'negative' side, there can be conditions of service in the aided or voluntary sector where the governing body is the teachers' effective employer, which cannot be said to be in teachers' interests. In Church schools, for example, it is possible to find a clause in the contract of employment that stipulates that the teacher should not engage in any activity that could bring the Church into disrepute.

Jeff Nixon argues that the picture becomes even more 'complicated' when one takes into account the fact that there have recently been at least four major 'threats' to any semblance of unified pay and conditions of service arrangements:

1.   the creation of Education Action Zones (EAZs);
2.   the introduction of the idea of beacon schools;
3.   the creation of the new category of advanced skills teachers;
4.   the proposed introduction of performance-related pay.

We will look at each of these in turn, although, in the first two cases, there has already been some discussion of the issues involved in Chapter 6.

Education Action Zones

In the July 1997 White Paper *Excellence in Schools* (DfEE 1997), Education Action Zones constituted an important feature of New Labour's programme for tackling school under-achievement, particularly in inner city areas. Then in December 1997, the School Standards and Framework Bill covered in some detail the proposal to facilitate the disapplication of the Teachers' Pay and Conditions Order in relation to teachers working at schools participating in the new zones. Furthermore, in a lecture delivered at the Social Market Foundation in London at the beginning of July 1998, the then Schools Minister Stephen Byers talked in terms of the zones representing a major challenge to the education *status quo*, with the introduction of such 'radical concepts' as 'performance-related pay for participating teachers' and 'agreed working on Saturdays and during school holidays' (reprinted in *The Independent*, 2 July 1998).

Beacon schools

The idea of beacon schools was introduced by the Labour government at the end of April 1998, when Stephen Byers announced plans for a £1.8 million network of up to 100 such schools. As we saw in Chapter 6, these would be 'centres of excellence' committed to sharing the 'secrets' of their success and building local partnerships to raise standards. The extra money for being awarded 'beacon school' status would amount to a maximum of £50,000 per school, designed primarily to cover the extra work arising from the liaison necessary with local schools. It was intended that schools and teachers be 'rewarded' for sharing their valuable expertise. The first group of beacon schools began work in the autumn of 1998 and were selected from the 159 secondary schools named in the Inspectors' Annual Report for 1996/7 as 'best performing schools'.

Advanced skills teachers

The advanced skills teacher grade was created in 1998 to provide 'a new career path' for 'excellent teachers' who wanted to remain classroom practitioners and were prepared to undergo a rigorous assessment against agreed national standards. The list of 'professional duties' of advanced skills teachers constitutes Part XI (p.64) of the current (1999) *School Teachers' Pay and Conditions* document. The AST grade was to be introduced initially in specialist secondary schools and in Education Action Zones. ASTs would spend most of their time in the classroom but would also have a new contractual duty to 'participate in the induction and mentoring of newly-qualified teachers' and 'advise other teachers on classroom organisation and teaching methods'. The pay scale for ASTs would extend up to around £40,000 per year, with progression subject to regular performance reviews. One hundred ASTs were to be in post by the end of 1998. The number was planned to expand to 5,000 by the end of the year 2000, reaching a total of 10,000 in the longer term.

Performance-related pay

The idea of performance-related pay was probably the most controversial proposal to be included in the 1998 DfEE Green Paper *Teachers – Meeting the Challenge of Change* (DfEE 1998b). In setting out the objectives of a new pay policy, the DfEE document attacked a school culture that allegedly rewarded experience and responsibility but *not* performance.

> Heads and teachers have been more reluctant than have comparable professional groups to distinguish the performance of some teachers from others, except through the award of responsibility points. The tradition, to which adherence remains powerful, is to treat all teachers as if their performance was similar, even though teachers themselves know that this is not the case. The effects have been to limit incentives for

teachers to improve their performance and to make teaching much less attractive to talented and ambitious people than it should be. . . . We are now determined to create the conditions for this culture to change. We want to recognise and reward good performance and establish routes for *real* career progression. We want to reward teachers who are effective and whose students make good progress because of the motivation and inspiration they provide. We want to reward teachers who take on tough classes and deal with difficult children, and those who take the able to new heights. We recognise that many people working in schools make a substantial time commitment to carry out their professional duties. We want to reward teachers who contribute, with their expertise and their professional commitment, to raising standards of achievement and to the wider life of the school.

(DfEE 1998b, pp.32–3)

As part of the process of introducing performance-related pay, a new importance would be attached to the statutory scheme of teacher appraisal, which had been introduced by Kenneth Clarke in 1991. According to the Green Paper, the artificial separation of pay and appraisal under the scheme introduced a decade ago explained in large part why it had been viewed as 'marginal' and why it had not really been taken seriously by either heads or teachers.

The introduction of some form of performance-related pay linked to teacher appraisal was given a warm welcome in October 1998 by Nigel de Gruchy, General Secretary of the National Association of Schoolmasters/Union of Women Teachers:

Appraisal or assessment should certainly form a large part of the promotion process. In the 1980s, the NASUWT accepted the need for a sensible and fair appraisal system, properly administered, to be constructed in order to identify and reward good practice without the teacher having to leave the classroom.

(quoted in DfEE 1998, p.34)

Other teachers and educationists, and particularly members of the National Union of Teachers, have adopted a very different attitude towards performance-related pay, arguing that it will do *nothing* to tackle the problems of low status, low morale and low self-esteem in the teaching profession. According to the critics, it presupposes a model of teacher appraisal that is intended to promote *individual* rather than *collective* advancement. It ignores the fact that teaching is essentially a *collaborative* exercise, with all the recent evidence emphasising the 'whole-school' philosophy of 'effective' schools. It is also likely to encourage some teachers to concentrate on those aspects of their work that can be measured relatively easily, regardless of whether or not these are really the most important. Indeed, it could be argued that any scheme of performance-related pay is likely to benefit those teachers who take examination classes in the secondary school, where 'performance' is more susceptible to easy if superficial assessment.

In the event, the government has not found it easy to introduce its new scheme, and it suffered a humiliating defeat at the hands of the NUT in July 2000 when the High Court ruled that it had acted illegally by by-passing Parliament over the proposed introduction of performance-related pay. In a damning judgement, Mr Justice Jackson ruled that David Blunkett had 'evaded scrutiny' by seeking to impose new 'performance standards' without the approval of MPs and of the School Teachers' Review Body. Nearly 200,000 classroom teachers had applied to pass a controversial new performance 'threshold' to gain a £2,000 pay rise from September 2000, but that assessment process had to be temporarily halted.

THE EXPANDING ROLE OF THE TEACHER

There is no doubt that the role of the teacher has expanded greatly over the last thirty years, and this is particularly true in the area that can be loosely described as pastoral care and the welfare of the child. Good teaching is about much more than simply the effective communication of a set body of knowledge. Circular 4/98 (see Appendix B) rightly requires that all those awarded qualified teacher status be aware of their professional responsibilities 'in relation to school policies and practices, including those concerned with pastoral and personal safety matters, including bullying' (DfEE 1998a, p.16).

No secondary school can regard itself as 'effective' unless it provides a safe and caring environment for all its students (a point to which we will return in the next chapter). The tackling of bullying in *all* its forms must be a fundamental part of the role of every teacher, although this is clearly not an area where any teacher should be expected to act alone: successful anti-bullying policies should reflect the shared aims of the whole school community. In the words of the Elton Report, commissioned in the late 1980s in response to widespread but largely exaggerated reports that physical attacks upon teachers were a growing feature of school life: 'the most effective schools seem to be those that have created a positive atmosphere based on a sense of community and shared values (Elton 1989, p.8).

It is also clear that teachers are key if sometimes reluctant players in the difficult area of child protection. The Children Act 1989 came into force in October 1991 and emphasised that the child's welfare is paramount. The school's first duty of care is to the child, *not* to the parent or the carer. Individual teachers can play an important role in the recognition and referral of suspected child abuse cases, but it is not one they are expected to shoulder on their own. DfEE Circular 10/95 *Protecting Children from Abuse: The Role of the Education Service* (DfEE 1995) states that all schools should have a designated child protection liaison teacher, and it is that teacher's role to act as a focal point for all concerns that teaching and non-teaching staff may have concerning a child in the school.

In the light of the above, the prospect of becoming a teacher may indeed seem a daunting one. The important point to remember is that very few secondary schools nowadays adopt a 'sink or swim' attitude towards their new recruits and that good comprehensive schools will have developed an elaborate structure for supporting teachers through all stages of their career.

SUGGESTED ACTIVITIES

1. Do you agree with the suggestion that teachers' roles have expanded perhaps considerably during the last fifteen years? If so, what is the nature of that expansion? Are there elements of teachers' work that suffer from the increased workload? If so, what are these? What compromises do teachers have to make to accommodate their increased roles?

   Identify any elements of the expanding role that you personally feel happy with and any that you would really rather do without. What strategies do teachers adopt to cope with their changing role and increased workload – and what kinds of professional development (existing or possible) would you identify as being most helpful in supporting teachers and supporting or developing skills?

2. On balance, do you think regular OFSTED inspections and the introduction of competences and standards for teachers have helped to 'professionalise' teaching and ensure greater consistency of standards?
   OR
   Do you feel they have done more to demoralise teachers and turn teaching into an increasingly technical activity?
   OR
   Are you able to identify in them some benefits for education and some disadvantages?

   It would be helpful to support the elaboration of your views with reference to your own experience, including your experience of how colleagues have responded to these matters.

3. Conduct an informal survey to find out how familiar teachers in your school are with:

   ● their conditions of service generally;
   ● their statutory rights;
   ● their statutory responsibilities.

   Does it appear to you that teachers are sufficiently or insufficiently informed about these aspects of their work? Are there any particular 'knowledge gaps'? If so, how should these be filled – and with what support? How effective are you personally at translating your responsibilities into professional practice? What kinds of professional development might best support this aspect of your work?

SUGGESTED READING

Cole, M. (ed.) (1999) *Professional Issues for Teachers and Student Teachers*. This wide-ranging and accessible collection of essays provides practical advice and all the information required to help student teachers to prepare for their professional life. It is particularly useful on the conditions of service for teachers and on teachers' legal liabilities and responsibilities.

Lawn, M. (1996) *Modern Times? Work, Professionalism and Citizenship in Teaching*. In this challenging and provocative book, Martin Lawn explores aspects of the culture and politics of teaching to understand the struggle by teachers and their employers, in and around work, to define and shape teachers for schools.

8 Issues of Equality and Social Justice: the role of the secondary school

This chapter examines a number of key issues about which all teachers need to be informed and that together represent a general broadening of secondary schools' responsibilities. The issues discussed include those of class, 'race', gender, sexuality and disability. It is argued that each of these has tended to be viewed in a discrete compartment, with little attempt made to relate them to one another and to the general political and social context of schooling. Particular attention is paid to the need to tackle racism in schools, the policing of sexuality and the so-called 'failing boys' phenomenon. Since it is the task of all schools to ensure the well-being of their students, there can be no justification for tolerating practices that are biased or discriminating. It is argued that the time is long overdue for equal opportunities policies to occupy a major role in daily school life.

INTRODUCTION

Over the past two decades, a burgeoning literature has been generated by the 'race', gender and (to a lesser extent) sexuality debates in education, but it has to be said that much of this literature has been narrowly conceived, ahistorical and even apolitical in the sense that each of the debates has been viewed in its separate compartment, with little attempt made to relate the associated 'issues' or 'problems' to the broader social and political contexts out of which they grew. In particular, we have been in danger of abandoning the notion of class, which was so evident in the educational literature of the 1950s and 1960s.

THE POST-WAR PREOCCUPATION WITH CLASS

Looking back to the post-war period in Britain, we can see that much of the debate about education policy and social justice centred on issues of class: in academic and political circles, the sociology of education was the sociology of *access*. Writing in a paper published in 1962, the leading educational sociologist Jean Floud singled out 'the social distribution of educational opportunity' as the main focus of British educational sociology (Floud 1962, p.530).

As we saw in Chapter 2, prominent among the reasons for the mounting appeal of comprehensive secondary schooling in the 1950s and 1960s was the evidence provided by sociologists that in the existing divided system, grammar schools were largely middle-class institutions, while the children of working-class families invariably found themselves consigned to second-class secondary modern schools.

The post-war grammar schools were seen by many as the 'custodians' of middle-class values, and in their influential study *Education and the Working Class*, first published in 1962 and based on research undertaken in Huddersfield, Brian Jackson and Dennis Marsden showed that even when children from working-class backgrounds actually gained entry to a local grammar school, they found it an uncomfortable and disorienting experience. In the words of Jackson and Marsden:

> The grammar schools are a glory to the English middle classes, and to the first stages of state education. Their achievement is an honourable one. They are rich in middle-class values. Often good values, and good attitudes: but not *the only ones*, and not in our time always the best. Every custom, every turn of phrase, every movement of judgement, informs the working-class parent and the working-class child that the grammar schools do not 'belong' to them.
>
> (Jackson and Marsden 1962, p.237)

As the movement to promote comprehensive education gathered momentum in the 1960s, the reform was seen as having profound *social* implications. Not only would hitherto deprived working-class children now have access to a decent, well-resourced education, but the concept of 'equality of opportunity' could also be widened to apply to the situation in the wider world *outside* the school walls. Among many academics who attached themselves to the Labour Party, it was genuinely believed that capitalist society could be transformed without major upheaval and that the new comprehensive schools would be a significant step on the road to achieving greater social equality. Writing in 1965, for example, leading sociologist A.H. Halsey could begin a *New Society* article with the ringing declaration:

> Some people, and I am one, want to use education as an instrument in pursuit of an egalitarian society. We tend to favour comprehensive schools, to be against the public schools, and to support the expansion of higher education.
>
> (Halsey 1965, p.13)

Provided economic growth could be guaranteed (and this was one of the taken-for-granted assumptions of the 1960s), it was seen by many reformers as axiomatic that equality of educational opportunity would lead to the creation of a more classless society. As education journalist Peter Wilby observed in a *New Statesman* article published in 1977, education reform was viewed as a non-threatening and unproblematic way of achieving 'desirable' social objectives:

> The pursuit of educational equality was an attempt to achieve social change by proxy. More and better education was more politically palatable and less socially disruptive than direct measures of tackling inequality. So was economic growth. Even the most complacently privileged could hardly object to children attending better schools and to the nation producing more wealth. Equality of educational opportunity had an altogether more agreeable ring to it than any other form of equality, such as equality of income or equality of property. With its overtones of self-improvement, it could even appeal to the more conservative elements in society. Its beauty was that, while many must gain, it did not imply that any must lose. Ugly words such as redistribution and expropriation did not apply to education – or at least nobody thought they applied. Education was a cornucopia so prolific of good things that nobody would need any longer to ask awkward questions about who got what.
>
> (Wilby 1977, p.358)

Anthony Crosland, the Labour Education Secretary responsible for Circular 10/65, appeared to share the popular 1960s view that educational reform could have far-reaching *social* objectives. The main thesis of his influential book *The Future of Socialism*, which had been published in 1956, was that *class* had now replaced *capitalism* as the principal dragon to be slain, and that class hatred was buttressed by Britain's elitist education system. The book appeared to accept the theory that the comprehensive reform could be a critical tool in the process of improving British society without recourse to violent change.

Yet, on closer examination, it seems clear that Crosland was chiefly anxious to ally himself with the 'reformist' and Fabian elements within the Labour Party, which saw the comprehensive reform as having the more limited social objective of creating a more cohesive and harmonious society. In *The Future of Socialism*, he went on to argue that comprehensive schools would enable children coming from widely different social backgrounds to meet and respect one another – thereby playing a leading role in the task of combating class hatred. According to Crosland:

> the object of having comprehensive schools is . . . to avoid the extreme social division caused by physical segregation into schools of widely divergent status and the extreme social resentment caused by failure to

This concept of the 'social mix', while completely ignoring the basic realities of British capitalist society, gained a tremendous hold on the Labour Party's imagination in the 1960s. With its keen anticipation of the steady amelioration of social class differences through students' experience of 'social mixing' in a common secondary school, it possessed obvious appeal for those so-called radicals more committed to forms of 'social engineering' than to revolutionary change.

win a grammar-school place, when this is thought to be the only
avenue to a 'middle-class' occupation.

(Crosland 1956, p.272)

The concept found expression in Circular 10/65, which, as we saw in Chapter
2, laid down the intended pattern of comprehensive reorganisation after the Labour
victory in the 1964 general election. In the words of the DES Circular:

> a comprehensive school aims to establish a school community in which
> pupils over the whole ability range and with differing interests and
> backgrounds can be encouraged to mix with each other, gaining
> stimulus from the contacts and learning tolerance and understanding in
> the process. . . . The Secretary of State therefore urges authorities to
> ensure, when determining catchment areas, that the new schools are as
> socially and intellectually comprehensive as is practicable.

(DES 1965, p.8)

One of the definitions of a comprehensive school, used as a basis for the research
project sponsored by the Department of Education and Science and initiated by
the National Foundation for Educational Research (NFER) in 1966, was that of
a secondary school that collects students 'representing a cross-section of society in
one school, so that good academic and social standards, an integrated school society
and a gradual contribution to an integrated community beyond the school may be
developed out of this amalgam of varying abilities and social environments' (Monks
1968, p.xi).

At the same time, a pamphlet on streaming, written by two prominent Fabians
of the 1960s, Michael Young and Michael Armstrong, and published by *Where*
magazine in the autumn of 1965, saw the comprehensive reform as having *two*
linked purposes:

> These are to end selection, at any rate at the early ages at which it has
> been practised in England and Wales, and thereby to raise the standard
> of education of the great majority of children, and to bring about more
> social unity between people of different abilities, in different
> occupations and in different social classes.

(Young and Armstrong 1965, p.3)

This preoccupation with social objectives and the pursuit of an ill-defined
'classlessness' had the unintended effect of setting up convenient targets for the
opponents of comprehensive schooling to aim at. It was possible to argue, as did
R. R. Pedley, headteacher of St Dunstan's College, writing in the first Black Paper,
Fight for Education, published in March 1969, that supporters of the comprehensive
project were using schools 'directly as tools to achieve *social* and *political* objectives'.
It was easy for him to ridicule that 'Utopia of equality' where 'the Duke lies down
with the docker and the Marquis and the milkman are as one'. Indeed, in Pedley's
view, it was obvious that class divisions were actually *perpetuated* and *strengthened*

inside the comprehensive school: '4A doesn't mix with 4P, and the cabinet minister's son (or daughter) shows no particular eagerness to bring the bus conductor's child home to tea' (Pedley 1969, p.47). When Julienne Ford's researches in the late 1960s (Ford 1969) led her to support the view that the new comprehensive schools did not necessarily break down class barriers, this was promptly hailed by the editors of *Black Paper Three*, published in 1970, as a major condemnation of the whole reform (Cox and Dyson 1970).

So, from the above examples, we can see that throughout the 1950s and 1960s – among both radicals and reactionaries – the debate about educational opportunity was conducted largely in terms of social class. Of those issues that were to assume extraordinary significance in succeeding decades – principally those of 'race', gender and sexuality – only some aspects of *gender* discrimination received any meaningful attention from academic researchers; and such attention was very much in its infancy.

In an appendix to their 1962 study *Education and the Working Class* (referred to above), Brian Jackson and Dennis Marsden argued that much more research was urgently needed into 'the social nature and consequences of education' in a number of key areas, including that of gender inequality:

> Just as further research needs to concentrate on the educational
> deprivations felt by the working class, so it also ought to attend closely
> to the deprivations felt by women. Of course the two are (to a limited
> extent) related – but it is generally true to say that we have one
> educational system for women and another for men.
>
> (Jackson and Marsden 1962, p.251)

Jackson and Marsden went on to give a specific example of gender discrimination affecting girls in Huddersfield, arguing that such inequity could not be a localised phenomenon:

> Between 1955 and 1960, Huddersfield maintained its very prominent
> place in English education by winning 100 State scholarships to
> universities from its four grammar schools. Of these 83 were awarded to
> boys and only 17 to girls. . . . It seems likely that this kind of detail can
> be repeated again and again, both locally and nationally. . . . Is this a
> satisfactory situation? Is it not time we had fuller knowledge?
>
> (*ibid.*, p.252)

Then, in an address given at the Annual Conference for the Advancement of State Education in 1965, Brian Simon argued that the sharp inequalities in education in England and Wales were due to *three* main factors: differences in social class, in sex (or gender) and in geographical location. Where the advantages (or disadvantages) reinforced each other, real differences became enormous. At their maximum, according to statistics, the opportunity to reach full-time higher education for a middle-class boy living in Cardiganshire was roughly 160 times greater than that for a working-class girl living in West Ham in London (Simon 1965, p.1).

Yet, as late as 1977, Paul Willis's *Learning to Labour*, a brilliant account of how, in the words of the book's subtitle, 'working-class kids get working-class jobs', was in fact a study of a particular group of working-class *boys* as they proceeded through their last two years at school and into the early months of work. The school in question was a boys–only, non-selective secondary modern school in a town forming part of a huge industrial conurbation in the Midlands, and while the study was basically an ethnography of the school, its main focus was on the oppositional working-class cultural forms within it.

Despite a continuing interest in the under-achievement of working-class boys and the formation of 'deliquescent sub-cultures' (see, for example, Hargreaves 1967; Willis 1977; Robins and Cohen 1978), it was in fact in the early 1970s that the sociology of education saw a significant shift from a primary focus on social class to an exploration of the differentiated educational experiences of girls and of Asian and African–Caribbean students.

The new concerns were given a marked boost by the passing of the Sex Discrimination Act (1975) and the Race Relations Act (1976), which have been described as giving a special impetus to those who wished to remove 'some of the more formal obstacles to social justice' (Arnot and Weiner 1987, p.12). Equally importantly, a number of radical local education authorities were strategically significant in developing meaningful equal opportunities policies and programmes in schools. It was now seen to be one of the functions of schools – and of secondary schools in particular – to combat discrimination in all its forms.

At the risk of perpetuating the very 'compartmentalisation' complained of at the beginning of this chapter, we will now move on to examine some of the various equal opportunities issues that have concerned teachers and educationists over the past twenty-five years.

THE HISTORY OF RACISM AND THE CURRENT DEBATE ABOUT THE ROLE OF EDUCATION IN SECURING ITS ERADICATION

It will have been noted that so far in this chapter, the term 'race' has always been placed in quotation marks. The reason for this is that the term is problematic to say the least.

Many have argued persuasively (see, for example, Wright 1992; Gaine 1995; Basini 1996; Gaine and George 1999) that the term 'race' is 'socially constructed', arising out of the 'pseudo-scientific' doctrines of the nineteenth century, which were chiefly concerned to promote the idea that the 'white' races were generally superior. In fact, 'race' is not a viable biological concept and lacks scientific validity as a way of categorising people. According to Gaine and George (1999, p.5), 'a useful working definition is "a group of people who may share some physical characteristic to which special importance is attached"'. According to this viewpoint, the important facet of 'race' is not the skin colour, facial features or type of hair people have but the *social significance* that is placed upon these.

Before looking in some detail at the anti-racist movement in education and at the need to construct an anti-racist pedagogy, it will be useful to say something about the socio-historical background to current debates.

In the early period of post-war reconstruction, Britain, like many of its European counterparts, was in urgent need of labour – too many jobs were seeking too few workers. This labour shortage and 'the opportunities for advancement' were widely publicised in the Caribbean; and many responded to the call to 'come home' to 'the motherland' to assist in the worthy task of developing an advanced industrialised economy. In reality, however, the only deal that was on offer in the 1950s operated to 'deskill' black immigrants, to keep their wages down and to segregate them in the dirty, ill-paid jobs that 'indigenous' white workers did not want. Alongside the exploitation and segregation at work, there was a popular underlying and often blatant call by the white British public for the black immigrants to 'go home'. So, as Godfrey Brandt has pointed out (Brandt 1986, p.11), what was evident in the 1950s and 1960s was 'a duality of response to Black workers' – an *official* call to 'come home' and a *popular* cry of 'go home'. Within this contradiction, there was a shifting meaning of the word 'home'. For many immigrants, home meant 'the motherland', but it could also mean the colony from which the black person had recently come.

The period from the early 1950s to the late 1980s has often been divided into certain distinct phases characterised by the pre-eminent response of the state and of the British ruling class to the 'problem' posed by large-scale immigration, first from the West Indies and later from the Indian subcontinent. These phases are normally referred to as:

- assimilationist
- integrationist
- multiculturalist.

They found expression not just in the power relations between white and black people in society at large but also, more specifically, in the way West Indian and Asian children were treated in the education system.

The focus of the assimilationist phase was largely cultural. There was a 'culture deficit' ideology in operation that seemed to imply that if black people simply abandoned their deficient and inadequate cultures and became 'assimilated' into British society, they would in all but colour become white and therefore 'acceptable'.

This was followed by the integrationist phase, when it was accepted that black, Asian and other minority ethnic groups could not simply get lost in the social fabric and 'disappear', but when it was also considered to be the responsibility of the various immigrant communities to make an effort to integrate. The key concept may have been 'cultural tolerance', but the main concern of governments, both Labour and Conservative, was the maintenance and protection of the existing social order.

If the multicultural movement had a 'bible' or 'manifesto', this was the Swann Report, *Education for All*, published in March 1985. This was the Final Report of the committee set up in March 1979 by Labour Secretary of State Shirley Williams to inquire into 'the education of children from ethnic minority groups'. Although it made a number of references to racism and anti-racism, it seemed to endorse the primacy of culture as a key explanation of social/racial relations.

The report argued strongly that 'a broadly-based "multicultural" approach to the Curriculum' should be adopted by *all* schools, both 'those with ethnic minority pupils' and 'all-white schools'. It did not believe that education should seek to 'iron out the differences between cultures', or attempt to 'draw everyone into the dominant culture', but, rather, should 'draw upon the experiences of the many cultures that make up our society and thus broaden the cultural horizons of every child'. In both primary and secondary schools, headteachers and teachers, and 'especially those from ethnic minority groups', were seen as having a vital role to play in encouraging 'a multicultural approach throughout compulsory education' (DES 1985c, p.xx).

In the first chapter, on 'The Nature of Society', the report contained a powerful affirmation of 'cultural pluralism' as the desired goal for society in Britain:

> We consider that a multiracial society such as ours would, in fact, function most effectively and harmoniously on the basis of pluralism, which enables, expects and encourages members of all ethnic groups, both minority and majority, to participate fully in shaping the society as a whole within a framework of commonly accepted values, practices and procedures, whilst also allowing and, where necessary, helping the various ethnic minority communities to maintain their distinct ethnic identities within this common framework.
>
> (*ibid.*, p.5)

It went on to conclude the section on 'The Concept of Pluralism' with the following definition of 'a genuinely pluralist society':

> We would . . . regard a democratic pluralist society as seeking to achieve a balance between, on the one hand, the maintenance and active support of the essential elements of the cultures and lifestyles of all the ethnic groups within it, and, on the other, the acceptance by all groups of a set of shared values distinctive of the society as a whole. This, then, is our view of a genuinely pluralist society, as both socially cohesive and culturally diverse.
>
> (*ibid.*, p.6)

The policy of multiculturalism advocated by the Swann Report had a large number of positive and progressive features, but its implementation in many primary and secondary schools could be criticised for being largely 'tokenistic'.

> It was precisely this dissatisfaction with the basic limitations of the multicultural approach that led a number of schools to embrace the more powerful and pro-active focus known as anti-racism – a set of agreed strategies designed to combat racism both in the curriculum and in all the broader aspects of school life. In a wider context, this new approach did not accept the existing power relations between black and white people in Britain and was determined to challenge oppression in all its forms.

It was in the 1980s that the *identification* and *eradication* of racist practices became a live issue for a number of pioneering schools and local education authorities. Yet there was to be little or no support from central government; and it would have to be admitted that in matters relating to the elimination of racism at all levels in education and society, the Conservative administrations of 1979 to 1997, under both Margaret Thatcher and John Major, did not have a record of which to be proud. Back in 1979, there was in fact little government enthusiasm for implementing the key provisions of the 1976 Race Relations Act, which had made it unlawful to discriminate against anyone on the grounds of race and had placed a special duty on LEAs to eliminate unlawful discrimination.

While still Leader of the Opposition at the end of January 1978, and without any prior consultation with her colleagues and advisers, Mrs Thatcher had gone on television to deliver a powerfully sympathetic statement about 'the legitimate fears of White Britons' that they were being 'swamped by people with a different culture'. She pointed out that there would probably be four million blacks in the country by the end of the century and assured her audience that 'we Conservatives are not in politics to ignore White Briton's worries; we are in politics to deal with them' (quoted in Young 1989, p.111). Then later, in her triumphalist address to the 1987 Conservative Party Conference (already referred to in Chapter 1), she took great delight in denouncing those 'extremist teachers' who conducted lessons in 'anti-racist mathematics' and encouraged children to believe that they had 'an inalienable right to be gay'.

Throughout the 1980s, Conservative MPs and right-wing pressure groups subjected a number of left-wing local education authorities, mainly situated in London, to mockery and abuse for having the temerity to take issues of 'race', gender and sexuality seriously. The Hillgate Group, for example, argued that schoolchildren had to be 'rescued' from 'indoctrination in the fashionable causes of the Radical Left: "anti-racism", "anti-sexism", "peace education" (which usually means CND propaganda) and even "anti-heterosexism" (meaning the preaching of homosexuality, combined with an attack on the belief that heterosexuality is normal)'. To this end, all schools should be 'released from the control of local government', thereby 'depriving the politicised local education authorities of their standing ability to corrupt the minds and souls of the young' (Hillgate Group 1986, pp.4,13,18).

Despite the presence in the school system of over half a million students perceived as racially or ethnically different from the white 'norm', there was no mention in the 1988 Education Reform Act of race, ethnicity or even multicultural education. Where competition was the prevailing ideological ethic, the very notion of equality could easily be discredited. Indeed, the complacency and indifference of the Tory leadership were highlighted in the keynote speech delivered by John Major to the 1992 Conservative Party Conference, where the Prime Minister emphasised his respect for traditional values and poured scorn on the idea that schools should concern themselves with issues of equal opportunity:

> When it comes to education, my critics say I'm 'old-fashioned'. Old-fashioned? Reading and writing? Spelling and sums? Great literature – and standard English grammar? Old-fashioned? Tests and tables? British history? A proper grounding in science? Discipline and self-respect? Old-fashioned? Well, if I'm old-fashioned, so be it. So are the vast majority of Britain's parents. . . . Because I'm old-fashioned, I want reform of teacher training. Let us return to basic subject teaching, not courses in the theory of education. . . . Our primary teachers should learn how to teach children to read, not waste their time on the politics of gender, race and class.
>
> (Quoted in Chitty and Simon 1993, p.144)

Within a short time, MPs of all parties were to be taken aback by the public disquiet over the obvious shortcomings in the police investigation into the murder of Stephen Lawrence. The 18-year-old son of parents of Jamaican origin, Stephen suffered an appalling death at the hands of five violent racists near his home in Eltham in south London on 22 April 1993. He was stabbed to a depth of about five inches on both sides of the front of his body, with both stab wounds severing axillary arteries, causing blood to literally pump out of his body until he finally collapsed. So great was the public outcry over both the crime and the incompetence of the investigating officers that even the *Daily Mail* was prepared to risk a libel action by printing the names of the five young men popularly thought to be the perpetrators of the assault. Three of the prime suspects were taken to trial in 1996 in a private prosecution, which failed because of the absence of any firm and sustainable evidence. Then after a full hearing in 1997, the inquest jury returned a unanimous verdict that 'Stephen Lawrence was unlawfully killed in a completely unprovoked racist attack by five white youths'.

At the end of July 1997, Labour Home Secretary Jack Straw asked Sir William Macpherson to chair an inquiry into 'the matters arising from the death of Stephen Lawrence'; and the Macpherson Report was published in February 1999 (HMSO 1999). This contained far-reaching implications both for the future investigation and prosecution of racially motivated crimes and for the role of a number of institutions in the eradication of racism. In the words of the report:

> Racism, institutional or otherwise, is not the prerogative of the Police Service. It is clear that other agencies, including, for example, those dealing with housing and education, also suffer from the disease. If racism is to be eradicated, there must be specific and co-ordinated

action both within the agencies themselves and by society at large, particularly through the education system, from pre-primary school upwards and onwards.

(para. 6.54, p.33)

The report concluded by making a number of important recommendations under the heading 'Prevention and the Role of Education':

- That consideration be given to amendment of the National Curriculum aimed at valuing cultural diversity and preventing racism, in order better to reflect the needs of a diverse society.
- That Local Education Authorities and School Governors have the duty to create and implement strategies in their schools to prevent and address racism. Such strategies should include:
  - that schools record all racist incidents;
  - that all recorded incidents are reported to the pupils' parents/ guardians, School Governors and LEAs;
  - that the number of racist incidents are published annually, on a school-by-school basis; and
  - that the numbers and self-defined ethnic identity of 'excluded' pupils are published annually on a school-by-school basis.
- That OFSTED inspections include examination of the implementation of such strategies.

(*ibid.*, paras 67, 68, 69, pp.334–5)

The role of OFSTED in monitoring the implementation of anti-racist strategies in schools, referred to above, has recently come under critical scrutiny in a hard-hitting report prepared by Professor Audrey Osler and Dr Marlene Morrison from the University of Leicester for the Commission for Racial Equality. This CRE report, *Inspecting Schools for Race Equality: OFSTED's Strengths and Weaknesses*, published in July 2000 (CRE 2000), highlighted a lack of understanding or commitment on the part of OFSTED's inspectors to examining race equality practice during school inspections.

In particular, the report argued that OFSTED was failing to act on that key recommendation in the Macpherson Report, that it should take a lead role in preventing racism through education; and that OFSTED's inspectors were failing to implement the requirement to inspect race equality outcomes contained in both the old and new versions of OFSTED's own *Framework for Inspection*.

As part of the research, a text search on 10,623 reports published between 1997 and 1999 revealed the use of the terms 'racial equality' or 'race equality' in only 0.25 per cent of inspection reports. Nearly 80 per cent of the 10,623 reports contained the word 'bullying'. Over 17 per cent mentioned the word 'harassment'.

Yet only 208 of the reports contained any reference to 'racial harassment'. The word 'racism' was mentioned in only 603 reports. It was true that the new inspection framework that came into operation in January 2000 had a number of welcome features that could potentially contribute to greater race equality in schools. For example, it adopted the term 'educational inclusion' to cover a range of equality issues, including race equality. Yet the inspectors interviewed were not convinced that the OFSTED leadership recognised race equality as an essential component of quality in education. They looked to its leadership to support them actively in developing this aspect of educational and social inclusion, yet they felt that race equality had yet to become a central part of 'the corporate culture and discourse within OFSTED'.

It is essential for *all* secondary schools, including those with all-white catchment areas, to adopt a number of positive strategies that will both tackle racism in all its various forms and, at the same time, promote the academic progress and well-being of *all* students, including where applicable those from Asian, black and other minority ethnic communities. Recent studies make clear (see, for example, Gaine 1995; Dadzier 2000) that work in the classroom can be effective only if it is part of a whole-school strategy to convey the consistent message that anti-racism, with its attendant values of respect for diversity and fair treatment for all, is embedded in the life and work of the school. Clear policies, explicit codes of conduct, effective grievance procedures and consistent staff responses will create the right context for this work by reinforcing the message that racism is totally unacceptable and will be actively opposed. More specifically, all textbooks and worksheets used by the school – and particularly those for geography and history – should be carefully scrutinised for racist references and images. No opportunity should be lost throughout the curriculum to highlight the contributions made over the centuries by people from a wide variety of cultures to the sum of human knowledge and enquiry. On a personal level, it should be a fairly simple matter to monitor all exclusions from the school, both temporary and permanent, to ensure that no one group is over-represented in the figures. At the same time, it is important to know if certain groups of students are over-represented in the 'bottom' sets or streams of the school and to ascertain why this should be so. On the question of bullying, which can take many forms and involve a number of complicated factors, it is important to know if this is primarily a manifestation of racial harassment. No school that says it cares about equal opportunities can afford to let well-intended policies gather dust on the shelves while some groups of students are terrified to come to school for fear of being subjected to verbal and/or physical abuse.

GENDER AND THE 'FAILING BOYS' PHENOMENON

In 1954, a front-page story appeared in *The Hunts Post*, the county paper for Huntingdonshire, under the headline 'Girls Brainier than Boys'. Too many girls had been 'passing' the 11-plus, and the education authority, ignoring the formal protests of teachers, had decided to limited their numbers. 'As a result,' the paper wrote, 'some boys will be admitted to the grammar school, although their educational performance may be inferior to that of some of the girls who are excluded' (quoted in Grant 1994, p.37). While acknowledging the truth of the story, the scholarship sub-committee announced that it was aware that 'no useful purpose would be served by allowing the admittance of boys who were clearly incapable of taking a grammar-school course' (*ibid.*).

All the evidence suggests (see, for example, Chitty 1989, p.33; Plummer 2000, p.15) that this was not an isolated incident. For many years, most English local education authorities operated a quota system similar to those used by American Ivy League universities to limit the admission of Jewish and black students to their courses. It seems clear that many girls who had 'passed' the 11-plus were sent to secondary modern schools, while boys with lower marks were seen to be marching off in the autumn term in their smart grammar school blazers.

If quotas had not been imposed in mixed grammar schools, two-thirds of the classrooms would have been occupied by girls. Throughout primary school and in the early years of secondary education, girls performed better than did boys in *most*, if not *all*, academic subjects.

The accepted theory held that girls 'matured' earlier than did boys, but that in the later years of the secondary school, the boys would inevitably catch up. This case seemed to be proved by GCE O-level results at 16, where, on the whole, girls did not reach the standard expected of them, particularly in maths and some areas of science. At the same time, gender stereotyping was clearly reflected in the national entries for the O-level examination.

> As late as 1980, girls accounted for only 23 per cent of the entries for physics, 5 per cent for technical drawing and 4 per cent for design and technology, while constituting 74 per cent of the entries for sociology, 64 per cent for biology and 60 per cent for French (see Mortimore *et al.* 1986, p.30). For all those who really cared about equal opportunities, it was essential that older girls be encouraged to opt for, and then do well in, those subjects previously held to be the preserve of boys.

This, then, was a major issue of equity and social justice in the 1960s and 1970s; but in recent decades, the gender debate has shifted perceptibly, from concern about the educational opportunities and job prospects on offer for girls to a preoccupation with 'under-achieving' and 'failing' boys. Indeed, the current obsession with boys' 'under-achievement' has acquired something of the status of a 'moral panic'. Some of the blame for this must be attached to the BBC Television *Panorama* programme 'The Future is Female', broadcast on 24 October 1994, which used a lot of dubious statistics and anecdotal evidence to create the distinct impression that girls were indeed out-performing boys at all stages of the schooling process and were then moving on to occupy some of the most influential and lucrative posts that society had to offer. Concern about 'under-achieving' boys was also reflected in a statement by Chief Inspector of Schools Chris Woodhead to the effect that 'the failure of boys, and, in particular of white working-class boys, is one of the most disturbing problems we face within the whole education system (quoted in *The Times Educational Supplement*, 5 March 1996).

It is true that the view that girls are 'successful' while boys are 'failing' has been reinforced by some recent statistics on girls' academic achievements in all-female settings. Arnot *et al.* (1996), using data from 1994 of the percentage of students gaining five or more A to C grades at GCSE in seven specified categories of school (LEA comprehensive; LEA secondary modern; grant-maintained comprehensive, grant-maintained selective; independent selective; independent with no fixed admissions policy; voluntary-aided comprehensive), found that all-girls schools obtained higher ratings than did all-boys schools in all seven categories and were the highest-performing schools in six categories. Similarly, the 1994 survey of comprehensive education, referred to in Chapter 6 (Benn and Chitty 1996), found that girls' comprehensive schools obtained a higher percentage of 'good' GCSE results than did either boys' or mixed comprehensives, the figures being 39.3 per cent for mixed schools, 33.8 per cent for boys' schools and 40.7 per cent for girls' schools (*ibid.*, p.287).

Yet a closer examination of the evidence shows that the overall picture is far more complex than many would have us believe. For example (1998), Murphy and Elwood have shown that in many schools, girls' success in gaining grade C passes in GCSE mathematics has not, generally, enabled them to move on to A levels, because of the way the banding or setting of students is gendered. Girls are more likely than are boys to be placed in the second band or set for GCSE mathematics, where the expected grade is a C. This might enable the girls to gain a grade C pass at best, while only those in the 'top' band will be allowed to choose mathematics at A level and then move on to a range of mathematical and scientific courses in tertiary education.

At the same time, it is true that the alleged 'under-achievement' of boys at school is a strongly *classed* phenomenon. In her recent book *Failing Working-Class Girls* (2000), Gillian Plummer bemoans the fact that 'the greatest national concern at the present time is the under-achievement of boys – class and race differences in performance being virtually ignored'. In her view:

> The educational failure of working-class girls is hidden. First, by interpreting statistics recording the substantial rise in achievements of middle-class girls to represent 'all girls'. Second, by the persistence of serious concerns about the deviant behaviour and particularly poor performance of many working-class boys. In ignoring the educational failure of working-class girls, we ignore the many problems that underlie their failure and which manifest themselves in harmful behaviour patterns: self-exclusion, withdrawal, depression, anorexia and early pregnancies.
>
> (*ibid.*, p.vii)

Accepting all these caveats, there are a number of reasons why many working-class boys find it so difficult to carve out a role for themselves in modern society. Some of these were discussed in a Radio Four series with the apt title 'Men in Crisis', broadcast in July and August 2000, in which, according to *The Radio Times* (22–28 July 2000), Professor Anthony Clare was taking a 'personal look' at 'whether certain classes of men are now making themselves the *redundant* gender'. A number of academic researchers have argued that the decline of large manufacturing industries has brought about the 'emasculation' of traditional working-class men, while the growth in service industries and increased female employment have meant a marked change in working-class community lifestyles. These developments have strongly affected the nature of working-class men's and women's personal relationships both in the home and in the workplace. They also seem to affect the aspirations of both boys and girls as they move through the school system.

It is also true that for many boys, as they construct 'acceptable' versions of masculinity in the early years of secondary school, to be seen to be 'pleasing the teacher' and 'working hard' is to risk being labelled a 'sissy' or a 'poof' by other students in the class. Both Máirtín Mac an Ghaill (1994) and Tony Sewell (1997) have shown how different groups of boys learn to be men in schools while policing their own and others' sexualities. At the same time, schools themselves have their own mechanisms for actively producing, through both the 'official' and the 'hidden' curriculum, a set of normative masculinities to which young boys are encouraged to aspire.

So the issue of boys' 'under-achievement' is a highly complex one that does not lend itself to easy explanations or solutions and will not be eradicated by the 'quick fixes' so beloved of government ministers and OFSTED inspectors. It seems clear that some boys are experiencing an 'identity crisis', but we must also never forget that their relative 'lack of success' in academic terms is a strongly classed and racialised phenomenon. It is still true that men outnumber women in positions of power in British society and that there is a stark gender disparity in the sharing of the burden of unpaid work.

THE POLICING OF SEXUALITY

Much of the current debate about the provision of sex education and the discussion of sexuality in schools seems to focus on the arguments for and against the retention of Section 28 of the 1988 Local Government Act. It might therefore be useful to begin this section on 'the policing of sexuality' with a few paragraphs reminding ourselves of the provenance of this notorious clause.

The timing of Section 28 was in fact highly significant in the story of the Thatcher government's approach to the provision of 'acceptable' and 'appropriate' sex education in state primary and secondary schools. It can be argued that education reflects the dominant politics of a society's institutions and that sex education reflects the *sexual* politics of those institutions. In the late 1980s, as indeed is still the case today, sex education in schools was intended to both *construct* and *confirm* the categories of 'normal' and 'deviant', which could then be regulated, monitored and controlled.

It was in 1986 that the government found the pretext it needed to launch a major assault on so-called progressive sex education policies. This came in the form of a whipped-up controversy over the alleged use by teachers of a picture book from Denmark called *Jenny Lives with Eric and Martin* (Bösche and Mackay 1983). This had been published in Copenhagen without any fuss in 1981 and first appeared in the United Kingdom in an English translation in December 1983. It attempted to present a positive image of a young homosexual couple bringing up a 5-year-old girl, the daughter of Martin.

The 'crisis' over this well-intentioned little book came in the early summer of 1986 in the run-up to the first local elections since the abolition of the GLC (Greater London Council). A story splashed over the front page of *The Islington Gazette* at the beginning of May was taken up by sections of the tabloid press, with front-page headlines like 'VILE BOOK IN SCHOOL' (*Sun*, 6 May) and SCANDAL OF GAY PORN BOOK READ IN SCHOOLS' (*Today*, 7 May). All this conveniently ignored the fact that the book had been 'discovered' in a London Teachers' Centre (not, as was widely reported, in a London primary school) and that, moreover, the ILEA (Inner London Education Authority) had specifically warned of the difficulties that might be involved in using it with young students. As a result of the controversy, the ILEA set up a new panel, chaired by its chief inspector, to look at all classroom material that could prove contentious. 'It is not that we feel we have to go on the defensive; it is more that we are sensitive to all criticisms', said David Mallen, then Director of Education for Schools. 'Our concern is still to combat prejudice against all young people who are or may feel they are homosexual' (reported in *The Times Educational Supplement*, 23 May 1986).

Writing in early 2000 in *The Guardian*, the Danish author of *Jenny Lives with Eric and Martin*, Susanne Bösche, said that she had been devastated to find herself 'embroiled in a British political issue', with one of her children's books becoming 'a weapon in a war over the teaching of sexuality in schools':

> It was absolutely shocking to see the book vilified as homosexual propaganda in the British press back in 1986, and I am shocked to find the same thing happening (to a lesser degree) again now with all the fuss over Section 28. I feel angry that my intentions in writing this little book – namely to give children a little more knowledge about the world – have been twisted by grown-up people who choose to use it as a weapon in a political battle. . . . For what it's worth, I don't personally think that homosexuality . . . should be aggressively promoted in schools, but I do think it should be talked about in an informative unsensational way. And one way of doing that is by making books like mine available to children in schools and libraries – as is done in Denmark – and by letting teachers and parents be prepared to answer questions without unnecessary drama.
>
> (*The Guardian*, 31 January 2000)

At the time of this controversy over the 'availability' of *Jenny Lives with Eric and Martin*, a new Education Bill was in the process of passing through Parliament; and in the House of Lords a number of Conservative peers demanded urgent action on the provision of sex education in schools, claiming that the kind of teaching that condoned homosexuality as 'a valid alternative' to heterosexuality was not only undermining 'traditional family life' and encouraging divorce but was also linked to the increase in rapes, attacks on children and sexual crime in general. The fear engendered by the spread of HIV/AIDS was used to justify a Christian–heterosexual approach to morality and an attack on 'homosexual lifestyles'. Baroness Cox, a prominent member of the Hillgate Group, commented during the Lords debate: 'I cannot imagine how on earth in this age of AIDS, we can be contemplating promoting gay issues in the curriculum. I think that it beggars all description' (quoted in Jeffery-Poulter 1991, p.208).

Education Secretary Kenneth Baker succumbed to the mounting pressure from the Right, and a new clause was introduced into the Bill (Clause 46 in the resulting 1986 Education (No. 2) Act) requiring that:

> The local education authority by whom any county, voluntary or special school is maintained, and the governing body and head teacher of the school, shall take such steps as are reasonably practicable to secure that where sex education is given to any registered students at the school, it is given in such a manner as to encourage those students to have due regard to moral considerations and the value of family life.

It was Section 18 of the 1986 Education (No. 2) Act that removed responsibility for school sex education from local education authorities and placed it for the first time in the hands of school governors – a pretty transparent attempt to provide sex education with supposedly 'conservative' gatekeepers. School governors were now required to consider whether or not a programme of sex education should be included in the school curriculum, and, if they decided it should, to produce a detailed written statement on the form and content of that programme. This policy statement was then to be made available to parents. Although, at this stage, parents were not given the legal right to withdraw their children from sex education lessons, governors were given the discretionary power to allow students to be withdrawn if their parents had religious objections.

The new framework for the provision of sex education in schools was then elaborated upon in DES Circular 11/87, *Sex Education at School*, published on 25 September 1987 (DES 1987b). According to the Introduction to this Circular, 'appropriate and responsible sex education is an important element in the work of schools in preparing students for adult life; it calls for careful and sensitive treatment'. Yet, as a number of commentators have pointed out (see, for example, Baker 1988; Davies 1988), what was *intended* to be an authoritative statement of the government's position in the light of recent 'controversies' was in fact notable for its lack of clarity and its built-in contradictions. There is, for example, a marked difference between the beginning and the end of Section 19. The opening has clearly been influenced by the liberal perspective of Her Majesty's Inspectorate. It calls for facts 'to be presented in an objective and balanced manner, *so as to enable students to comprehend the range of sexual attitudes and behaviour in present day society*' (my italics). The final sentence of the section, which states that 'students should be helped to appreciate the benefits of stable married and family life and the responsibilities of parenthood', is there to appease the government's right–wing moralist faction. How teachers are expected to be 'objective and balanced' and at the same time 'encourage their students to appreciate something' is left unexplained. What *is* true is that the dominant tone of the Circular is narrow and homophobic. Section 22 states unequivocally:

> There is no place in any school in any circumstances for teaching which advocates homosexual behaviour, which presents it as the 'norm', or which encourages homosexual experimentation by school students. Indeed, encouraging or procuring homosexual acts by students who are under the age of consent is a criminal offence.
>
> (DES 1987b, p.4)

> The determination of the Thatcher government to pander to the forces of moral authoritarianism was then further emphasised by the inclusion of what was to become Section or Clause 28 in the 1988 Local Government Act. This amended the 1986 Local Government Act by laying down that a local authority shall not:
>
> 1. intentionally promote homosexuality or publish material with the intention of promoting homosexuality;
> 2. promote the teaching in any maintained school of the acceptability of homosexuality as a pretended family relationship.

As many commentators have argued, Section 28 was a key cultural and symbolic event in the recent history of sexual politics. Yet, despite the hostility and anxiety it aroused among caring and committed teachers, it is important to emphasise that its effect on the teaching of sex education in schools should have been negligible. What Conservative MP Dame Jill Knight and the other sponsors of the measure had overlooked was the fact that the 1986 Education Act had already removed sex education in schools from the control of local authorities – an important oversight, which the government itself was forced to concede in a rarely cited Department of the Environment Circular published in May 1988:

> Responsibility for school sex education continues to rest with school governing bodies, by virtue of Section 18 of the Education (No. 2) Act of 1986. Section 28 of the 1988 Local Government Act does not affect the activities of school governors, nor of teachers. It will not prevent the objective discussion of homosexuality in the classroom, nor the counselling of students concerned about their sexuality.
>
> (DoE 1988, p.5)

Nevertheless, the symbolic power of Section 28 was to prove immense, just as its sponsors had intended. By creating a climate of paranoia and fear around the provision of sex education in schools, it played a major role in undermining the confidence and professionalism of teachers. As Rachel Thomson observed in 1993:

> The phrase 'the promotion of homosexuality' had the insidious effect of constructing teachers as the potential 'corrupters' of young people and of frightening teachers from saying what they thought was sensible and right out of fear of losing their jobs.
>
> (Thomson 1993, p.225)

The emerging crisis of HIV/AIDS also made it easy for the moral lobby to insist that school sex education should be seized upon as an ideal opportunity to promote a prescriptive model of sexual and personal morality.

As part of a concerted effort in the early 1990s to further appease the moral Right, the Major government decided to alter the statutory position on sex education in schools by means of a last-minute amendment to the wide-ranging 1993 Education Act and, at the same time, replace Circular 11/87 with a new document in which there would no longer be any reference to students being encouraged to 'comprehend the range of sexual attitudes and behaviour in present-day society'.

As a result of the amendment to the 1993 Act, which became Section 241:

1.   Consideration of AIDS, HIV, sexually transmitted diseases and aspects of human sexual behaviour other than the purely biological could not form part of the National Curriculum Science.

2.   Governors of maintained secondary schools were now required to provide a programme of sex education to all registered students and no longer had the power, granted to them by the 1986 Education (No. 2) Act, of deciding whether or not sex education should form part of the school curriculum (although they were still required to develop a policy explaining *how* and *where* sex education would be taught, and to make that policy available to all parents).

3.   Most controversially, parents were now given the right to withdraw their children from *all* or *part* of the sex education programme laid on by the school. Parents were not required to give any reasons for their decision; once a request for withdrawal had been made, that request had to be granted until the parents revoked it.

In DfE Circular 5/94, *Education Act 1993: Sex Education in Schools*, published on 6 May 1994 (DfE 1994), a key passage in Section 19 of the 1987 Circular appeared in a truncated form that no longer allowed for the recognition of a range of sexual 'lifestyles':

> The Secretary of State believes that schools' programmes of sex education should . . . aim to present facts in an objective, balanced and sensitive manner, set within a clear framework of values and an awareness of the law on sexual behaviour. Students should accordingly

be encouraged to appreciate the value of stable family life, marriage and the responsibilities of parenthood.

(*ibid.*, p.6)

In May 1997, a Labour government was elected with a clear commitment both to repeal Section 28 and to make the regulation of sexual conduct fairer and more equitable by reviewing the thorny issue of the homosexual age of consent. Neither has proved easy to achieve.

Homosexual activity in private between consenting males over the age of 21 had been decriminalised by the Sexual Offences Act of July 1967 (see Jeffery-Poulter 1991, p.81). Then, in February 1994, Parliament had voted in favour of lowering the homosexual age of consent from 21 to 18 – a compromise between 21 and 16 that did little to appease those leading the campaign for equalising the age of consent.

On 22 June 1998, the House of Commons, now comprising a huge number of Labour MPs, voted in favour of lowering the homosexual age of consent from 18 to 16 by 336 votes to 129, a majority of 207; but this was overturned a month later in the House of Lords by 290 votes to 122, a majority of 168. On 25 January 1999, the Commons voted for a second time in favour of equalising the age of consent, this time by 313 votes to 130, a majority of 183; but once again this was overturned in the Lords: by 222 votes to 146, a majority of 76. Finally, in February 2000, the Commons voted for a third and final time to equalise the age of consent, by 263 votes to 102, a majority of 161. This was included by Jack Straw as part of the government's commendable record on human rights in a speech given by the Home Secretary to an equality dinner in London organised by the mainstream gay lobby, Stonewall, at the end of March 2001 (reported in *The Guardian*, 30 March 2001).

On the issue of Section 28, the government suffered a major defeat in the House of Lords on 7 February 2000, when peers voted in favour of a wrecking amendment by Baroness Young, a former Conservative Leader of the Lords, to retain the Section by 210 votes to 165, a majority of 45. Most Conservative peers, some cross-benchers and a few Labour rebels voted to keep the measure on the statute book. Baroness Young's campaign also had the backing of a number of prominent church leaders, including Archbishop of Canterbury Dr George Carey, and Cardinal Thomas Winning, leader of Scotland's Roman Catholics. Chief Rabbi Dr Jonathan Sacks and leading Muslims, including Labour peer Lord Ahmed, also opposed repeal.

It needs to be emphasised that the debate about Section 28 has never really been concerned with 'promoting' one kind of sexuality over another – at least from the reformers' point of view. As I have argued elsewhere:

> The idea that certain gay and lesbian teachers are seriously concerned to 'promote' homosexuality over and above any other sexual orientation has always been a myth perpetuated by Conservative ministers and a number of irresponsible right-wing newspapers. What many teachers *would* like to feel free to 'promote' is the *acceptability* not the *superiority* of the homosexual lifestyle (though the use of this term is itself

problematic, since it implies something 'chosen', like a fashion accessory).

(Chitty 2000a, p.3)

The issues at stake were neatly summarised in a finely crafted *Observer* editorial at the end of January 2000:

> Teachers have no wish to be in the business of 'promoting' any kind of sexuality, or family structure, over another. Section 28 was never about 'promotion' in this sense – it was all about stopping teachers from even talking about same-sex relationships as real, and serious, parts of the world for which children were being prepared. The main reason for ditching Section 28 is to allow children to be taught about the real world, a world in which moral values such as commitment, fidelity, care and responsibility are more important than ever, but are not attached exclusively to the marriage contract.
>
> (*The Observer*, 30 January 2000)

In July 2000, the Department for Education and Employment published *Sex and Relationship Education Guidance* (DfEE 2000), a new framework for the provision of sex and relationship education in schools designed to replace Circular 5/94 and to take account of the revised National Curriculum, published in September 1999. In many ways, it was a more 'liberal' and 'progressive' document than some of the advance publicity had led teachers to expect; and much of it has been welcomed by 'School's out! National', the organisation of lesbian, gay, bisexual and trans-gender teachers (STA 2000, p.14). It argues that school students should be taught about 'the nature and importance of marriage for family life and bringing up children', but it also recognises that 'there are strong and mutually supportive relationships outside marriage'. Students need therefore 'to be given accurate information and to be helped to develop skills to enable them to understand difference and respect themselves and others – and for the purpose also of preventing and removing prejudice' (*ibid.*, p.4). The section on 'Sexual Identity and Sexual Orientation' contains the following unequivocal statement:

> It is up to all schools to make sure that the needs of all students are met in their sex education programmes. Young people, whatever their developing sexuality, need to feel that sex and relationship education is relevant to them and sensitive to their needs. The Secretary of State for Education and Employment is clear that teachers should be able to deal honestly and sensitively with sexual orientation, answer appropriate questions and offer support.
>
> (DfEE 2000, pp.12–13)

Somewhat paradoxically, in the same month that this DfEE *Guidance* was published (July 2000), the Bill that would have repealed Section 28 was defeated for a second time in the House of Lords, by 270 votes to 228, a majority of 42.

CLASS AND HIGHER EDUCATION

One of the major themes of this chapter has been that a concern (and a *justifiable* concern) with issues of 'race', gender and sexuality should not divert us from the need to address the continuing importance of *social class* in all matters pertaining to equality, social justice and discrimination – and particularly in the field of educational opportunity. Many ministers and political commentators are wary of discussing this sensitive issue, because they prefer to subscribe to the myth that as 'post-modern' Britain has become steadily more 'meritocratic', so class has ceased to exercise the influence it once wielded. There was, it will be remembered, near hysteria among certain opposition politicians and in sections of the national press when Chancellor of the Exchequer Gordon Brown dared to use a speech to a TUC audience in London at the end of May 2000 to launch an outspoken attack on 'old school tie' elitism at Oxford and Cambridge in the wake of the much-publicised case of Laura Spence, the Tyneside comprehensive-school sixth-former rejected by Magdalen College, Oxford (see, for example, the report in *The Guardian*, 26 May 2000). Gordon Brown could have usefully broadened his attack to tackle the issues of selection and discrimination at all levels of education – particularly in the secondary sector – but he was clearly right to draw attention to the whole question of access to higher education in this country.

A report prepared by the Sutton Trust, *Entry to Leading Universities* (Sutton Trust 2000), details of which were released to the press in April 2000, showed that 'thousands of bright youngsters from the state sector' who possessed 'the necessary grades' were not gaining access to 'our leading universities'. The survey covered thirteen universities in Britain: Oxford, Cambridge, Birmingham, Bristol, Durham, Edinburgh, Nottingham, St Andrews, Warwick, York, Imperial College (London), the London School of Economics and University College, London. The source for the detailed statistics used by the trust was the Higher Education Funding Council (HEFC), which also publishes 'benchmark statistics' showing what the numbers of students should be based on entry qualifications and the subjects taught at the various institutions.

The research showed that while accounting for only 7 per cent of the secondary school population, students from the independent sector constituted 39 per cent of the entry to the 'top' universities. In fact, the probability of winning a place at one of the thirteen universities studied was approximately twenty-five times greater for those from a private school than for those who came from 'a lower social class' or who lived in 'a poor area'. At Oxford and Cambridge, around half of the intake each year came from independent schools, while only 10 per cent came from the three lowest socio-economic groups, accounting for 50 per cent of the population. The trust argued that the marked imbalance of entry to the top thirteen universities was due to *two* main factors: a low proportion of applications from 'suitably qualified less affluent students' and 'inadequacies in the universities' admissions systems'.

SPECIAL ARRANGEMENTS FOR STUDENTS

We cannot leave issues of education and social justice without reference to students designated as having special educational needs (SEN).

The Warnock Report published in 1978 (DES 1978) estimated that around 20 per cent of children might at some time in their schooling have 'special educational needs' (rather than the 2 per cent covered by the existing 'official' definition of 'special education'). Given this wider concept of 'special education', it was obvious that most of the provision would occur in ordinary schools and that careful planning was therefore required to ensure that the needs of *all* children were being met.

Three years later, the 1981 Education Act decreed that, wherever possible, children with special educational needs of whatever kind should be entitled to receive their education within a mainstream school. Each LEA would be required to maintain a 'statement' in the case of those children whose 'needs' were such as to necessitate separate educational provision. Yet, despite widespread official support for the concept of 'integration', research carried out in the 1980s showed that the percentage of students being educated in a segregated setting was actually being reduced only minimally – with the figure even rising in some parts of the country. And this despite the fact that the experience of 'disabled' children being educated in mainstream schools was that they did better, both *educationally* and *socially*, as long as the school was able to respond in a *positive* way to their 'special needs'. Able-bodied children and classroom teachers also reported that it was a genuinely positive and rewarding experience for them (see Rieser and Mason 1990, pp.147–8).

Micheline Mason argued in 1990 that the widely used phrase 'special educational needs' actually came into being as an attempt to 'demedicalise' the labelling of children with disabilities: in other words, to replace offensive terms such as 'retarded', 'subnormal', 'crippled' and 'maladjusted' with what was hoped to be less negative labelling based on real educational need. Disabled people, she said, welcomed the spirit in which this was done; but she suggested that it tended to overlook the *political* dimension. In her words:

> We do *not* consider ourselves to be *special*. As 'disabled' people, we consider disability to be *a norm* within every society, borne out by the statistics, and we want our needs to be taken into account as *normal human needs*. It seems to us questionable that 20 per cent of young people can have 'special needs'. It seems ridiculous that 45 per cent of young people within inner-city areas can have 'special needs'. Surely the real question that needs to be asked is: how does the education system fail to answer the needs of 45 per cent of its users?
>
> (Mason 1990, p.88)

Of the 1,413 comprehensive schools that responded to the relevant question in the 1994 survey of comprehensive education, 1,382 (or nearly 98 per cent) indicated that they had students with special educational needs *with* statements. In answer to a second question, 1,384 out of 1,404 responding schools (98.6 per cent) indicated that they had students with special educational needs but *without* statements. Only just over 30 per cent of schools (440 out of 1,398 responding) felt that their resources were adequate to meet these students' needs, and this was an area where schools reported considerable anxiety about the way in which the Warnock recommendations had been interpreted (Benn and Chitty 1996, p.243).

Clearly, the term 'special educational needs' covers a broad spectrum of 'conditions', from visual impairment to 'exceptional attainment'. Most teachers welcome the idea of integrating as many students as possible into mainstream schooling but fear the consequences if this is done 'on the cheap'.

CONCLUSION

In a keynote speech in Birmingham on 2 May 1999, intended to mark the 300th anniversary of the founding of the Sikh religion, Prime Minister Tony Blair spoke eloquently of the need to build 'the tolerant multiracial Britain the vast majority of us want to see'. Against the background of a number of recent nail-bomb atrocities that had brought bloodshed and chaos to various 'marginalised' communities in London, in Brixton, Brick Lane and Soho, he argued powerfully that an attack on any section of the community amounted to an attack on Britain as a whole:

> When one section of our community is under attack, we defend it in the name of all the community. When bombs attack the Black and Asian community in Britain, they attack the whole of Britain. . . . When the gay community is attacked and innocent people are murdered, all the good people of Britain, whatever their race, their lifestyle, their class, unite in revulsion and determination to bring the evil people to justice.

In the light of these fine sentiments, it is sad to report that for the majority of comprehensives, equal opportunities policies could not be said to occupy a major role in the life of the school. The 1994 Benn/Chitty survey found that policies for monitoring gender inequality were more popular and widespread than any relating to social class, race, sexuality or disability, although it is true that many of the participating comprehensives seemed to be unclear as to whether it was teenage boys or girls who needed their active encouragement and support. Many schools argued that there was neither time nor money to pursue policies designed to equalise opportunity (Benn and Chitty 1996, pp.245–6). Not quite the solid commitment to equity and fairness that one would have liked to applaud.

SUGGESTED ACTIVITIES

1. How familiar are you with any specific policies your school and (where relevant) your local education authority has on issues of race, class, gender and sexuality? To what extent do such policies influence or support your own

classroom practice? Do you agree that class prejudice – as manifested, for example, in curriculum design and materials or in common assessment criteria – remains an issue for teachers in the UK, or is class no longer a useful concept?

2.   It has often been suggested – and has been implicitly argued in this chapter – that schools and teachers find it particularly difficult to develop policies and good practice related to issues of sexuality, and that they have not been helped in this by the attitudes and policies of central government, or indeed by much of the press or by still-prevalent homophobic attitudes on the parts of many students.

How far do you agree that issues of sexuality are often marginalised or avoided in schools, and how might (a) you as an individual, (b) your school as a whole begin to tackle this issue?

3.   What is your understanding of 'special educational needs' and 'statementing'? Is it appropriate in your view to use the term 'special educational needs', or is this, as is sometimes cynically suggested, a way of marginalising and undervaluing certain students or of attracting higher funds or of 'massaging' a school's test and examination results?

If some students *are* to be identified as having special needs, do you believe that, given current levels of funding, appropriate and adequate provision is being made? What alternative approaches or forms of provision might you suggest?

SUGGESTED READING

Epstein, D., Elwood, J., Hey, V. and Maw, J. (eds) (1998) *Failing Boys? Issues in Gender and Achievement.* This important book challenges the widespread perception that *all* boys are under-achieving at school. It makes use of recent research studies to illuminate the nature of the 'moral panic' currently surrounding the issue 'failing' boys.

Gaine, C. and George, R. (1999) *Gender, 'Race' and Class in Schooling: A New Introduction.* In this excellent introduction for teachers and students, Chris Gaine and Rosalyn George provide an overview of recent research in three key areas of significant social inequality.

Hill, D. and Cole, M. (eds) (1999) *Promoting Equality in Secondary Schools.* This wide-ranging collection of fourteen essays is aimed at all those teachers and students who wish to tackle the inequalities of social class, 'race', gender, sexuality, disability and special needs provision apparent in our schools.

Plummer, G. (2000) *Failing Working-Class Girls.* This book reports on research showing how women from working-class backgrounds still seldom achieve higher-level academic qualifications and the lifestyle to which they provide entry.

9 Conclusion: Issues for the Future – Contradictions and New Aspirations

This concluding chapter analyses New Labour's approach to education in the light of the policies pursued by Tony Blair's administration since May 1997. It is argued that much of the programme has been decidedly right-wing, showing a willingness to continue with much of the agenda bequeathed by eighteen years of Conservative rule. Above all, issues of equity and social justice have not figured prominently among the government's list of priorities, and there has been a failure to devise admissions policies for secondary schools that would be fair to all students regardless of 'race', class or gender.

WHAT IS THE BLAIR PROJECT?

A front-page article in *The Guardian* dated 5 August 2000 reported that scholars working on *The New Penguin English Dictionary* had taken an unprecedented two months to arrive at a meaningful definition of the term 'Blairism'. Apparently, the first sixteen words of the definition posed few difficulties: 'Blairism, *noun*: the policies associated with Tony Blair, British Labour Leader and Prime Minister from 1997 . . .'; but almost every word and phrase suggested for the rest of the sentence proved to be controversial and problematic. Early drafts included '. . . especially regarded as a highly modified or modernised form of traditional Socialist thinking intended to appeal to a wider electorate'; '. . . characterised by the absence of a fundamental underlying ideology and a close attention to prevailing public opinion'; and '. . . characterised by a modified and inclusive form of traditional Socialism'. But all were thought likely to cause offence. The final version of the second half of the sentence, consisting of just nine words that commanded widespread acceptance, had the essential virtues of being both bland and unexceptional: '. . . especially regarded as a modified form of traditional socialism'.

It seems clear that New Labour has deliberately been vague (or, rather, *all-encompassing*) about its overall philosophy in order to make a real success of what has been called 'big-tent politics'. For that reason, it is remarkably difficult to be precise about what Blairism actually stands for on a wide range of issues. We are led to believe that the Prime Minister's thinking owes much to the concept of 'the Third Way' propounded by Anthony Giddens (see, for example, Giddens 1998,

2000); but that concept has itself been criticised for lacking precision and real content. Those close to the Prime Minister would probably argue that it was that very 'lightness of ideological being' that helped New Labour to come to power with such a huge and unexpected majority in May 1997; but, four years later, a perceived lack of commitment to traditional Labour Party values can probably be blamed for widespread grass-roots disillusionment with the so-called Blair Project.

Professor David Marquand has argued that Tony Blair's marked disdain for party – and, on a deeper level, for the differences of ideology and interest that have sustained the concept of party in Britain and other European democracies – is almost palpable. According to Marquand:

> Blair dreams of a united and homogeneous people, undifferentiated by class or locality, with which he, as leader, can communicate directly, without benefit of intermediaries. In his vision of it, at least, New Labour's vocation is to mobilise the suburbs as well as the inner cities; rich as well as poor; old as well as young; Christians as well as unbelievers; hunters as well as animal-rights activists; believers in family values as well as opponents of Clause 28. Its warm embrace covers all men and women of goodwill, provided only that they are prepared to enlist in the relentless, never-ending crusade for modernisation which he and his colleagues have set in motion.
>
> (Marquand 2000, pp.73–4)

In the field of educational policy, this lack of ideological commitment leaves us with a programme that is multidimensional, difficult to pin down and essentially incoherent.

A few clues to New Labour's thinking on education were provided by the then Schools Minister Stephen Byers in a lecture entitled 'Towards the Third Way in Education' delivered at the Social Market Foundation in London at the beginning of July 1998. Here the Education Action Zones programme was singled out as being indicative of New Labour's crusade for modernisation:

> The so-called Third Way applies traditional values to a changed setting. . . . For example, the 25 Education Action Zones are intended to tackle endemic levels of low achievement and low expectations. . . . They contain many proposals that would have been regarded as impossible to achieve just 12 months ago – performance-related pay for teachers; ditching the National Curriculum to focus on key skills and work-related learning; master-classes on devolved budgets for governing bodies run by some of the world's leading financial consultants; provision to identify and stretch our most able students; agreed working on Saturdays and during school holidays.
>
> (reprinted in *The Independent*, 2 July 1998)

So the government's 'modernisation' programme would seem to require or involve greater flexibility on the part of teachers, a policy of drastically revising, if not abandoning altogether, the original concept of the National Curriculum, and a willingness to involve 'outside interests' in the running of state schools. Cynics might argue that the Third Way is a somewhat vague term used to disguise a clear continuity between Thatcherism and New Labour.

MODERNISING THE COMPREHENSIVE PRINCIPLE

As we saw in Chapter 6, the 1997 White Paper *Excellence in Schools* talked in terms of 'modernising' the comprehensive principle in order to ensure that all students, *whatever their talents*, would be able to develop their diverse abilities. Comprehensive schools would be required to provide 'a broad, flexible and motivating education' that recognised 'the different talents of all children' and delivered 'excellence for everyone' (DfEE 1997, p.38).

In the event, Prime Minister Tony Blair has often come perilously close to echoing John Major's ill-informed and demoralising comments about the shortcomings of the comprehensive system. Before taking office, he made a speech in Oxfordshire in June 1996 (referred to in Chapter 6) where he appeared to blame low standards in many comprehensive schools on the prevalence of mixed-ability teaching. The modernisation of the comprehensive principle required the grouping of all students according to ability.

More recently, addressing a group of modernising New Labour activists known as 'Progress' in early September 2000, the Prime Minister broadened the scope of his attack on 'misguided comprehensive practices'. These apparently included 'no setting, uniform provision for all and hostility to the whole notion of specialisation and centres of excellence within areas of the curriculum' – amounting, in effect, to the adoption of 'a one-size-fits-all' mentality. These had to be replaced by rigorous setting, in which students were to be streamed by subject; more 'person-alised provision' for 'high-flyers'; more specialist schools; and 'centres of excellence' in some specified subjects. According to Mr Blair:

> The term 'comprehensive' should cease meaning the same for all; and instead should mean a policy of equal opportunity for all to develop their intelligence to the full. . . . The Government expects every secondary school to do its best for high-ability students through first-rate teaching and facilities, rigorous setting and personalised provision. Modern comprehensives should be as dedicated as any private school or old grammar school to high achievement for the most able.
>
> (reported in *The Guardian*, 9 September 2000)

In line with one of the themes in this speech, the government later announced (26 September 2000) that the target for the number of specialist colleges to be in place over the next three years should be raised from 800 to 1,000. This was itself later raised to 1,500 by September 2006, meaning that nearly half of all maintained secondary schools would become specialist schools over a five-year period (see DfEE 2001).

All the observations quoted above have been made against the background of what can fairly be described as a comprehensive 'success story' (see Dunford 1999; Chitty 2000b; Simon 2000). As long ago as the early 1980s, top civil servants and officials at the then Department of Education and Science were expressing the view, in interviews conducted by Professor Stewart Ranson, that comprehensive schools were, if anything, proving *too* successful in enabling their students to reach unprecedentedly high levels of achievement – thereby inadvertently creating aspirations that a contracting labour market was unable to meet. To quote from one such official:

> There has to be a return to selection because we are beginning to create aspirations which increasingly society cannot match. In some ways, this points to the success of comprehensive education in contrast to the public mythology which has been created. When our young people drop off the education production line and cannot find work at all, or work which meets their abilities or expectations, then we are only creating frustration with perhaps disturbing social consequences. We have to select: to ration the educational opportunities to meet the job opportunities so that society can cope with the output of education.
> (Ranson 1984, p.241)

From substantial research on the effects of comprehensive reorganisation in Scotland, where official commitment to the comprehensive ideal has always been greater than in the rest of Britain, McPherson and Willms concluded at the end of the 1980s that:

> Since the mid–1970s, the reorganisation that was initiated in 1965 has contributed *both* to a rise in examination attainment *and* to a fall in the effect on attainment of social class. We call these two trends respectively 'improvement' and 'equalisation'. . . . It seems clear from the evidence that there have been similar, but weaker, trends in England and Wales.
> (McPherson and Willms 1988, p.39)

Then again, a meticulous review of the impact of comprehensive reorganisation in Britain led Glennerster and Low to conclude that:

> The main and really major improvements in school examination performance since the 1960s were achieved by the 'average–ability' students; and this was the chief contribution of the comprehensive schools. . . . It is a tribute to these schools that they produced both more qualified leavers and the structural changes politicians were demanding.
> (Glennerster and Low 1990, pp.61–2)

Admittedly, examination statistics provide us with a very narrow and unsatisfactory means of judging schools, but since they do carry a lot of weight with parents and politicians, it seems fair to balance the government's relentless demands for 'modernisation' and reform with an account of the achievements that a largely comprehensive secondary system has chalked up over the last thirty years or so. For example, there has been a spectacular increase in the percentage of Year 11 students achieving five or more GCSE passes at Grades A to C (or their equivalent) since the early 1960s. In 1962/3, the proportion was a mere 16 per cent, with the grammar schools accounting for most of this pass rate, but by 1993 the figure had risen to 41 per cent. Since the inception of GCSE performance tables, there has been a year-on-year improvement in the percentage of 16-year-old students attaining five or more of the higher grades: 42 in 1994, 43.5 in 1995, 44.5 in 1996, 45.1 in 1997, 46.3 in 1998, 47.9 in 1999 and 49.2 in 2000. A similar story can be told about GCE Advanced Level, where the percentage of 18-year-olds passing in at least two subjects has risen from 14 to 28 per cent over the past twenty years and where the overall pass rate has grown from under 70 to well over 80 per cent during the same period. As John Dunford, General Secretary of the Secondary Heads Association (SHA), has been at pains to emphasise: 'contrary to the impression created by the ritualistic annual denunciations of a minority of academics and politicians, there is, in fact, no evidence that the standard of Advanced Level examination has fallen' (Dunford 1999, p.28). So teachers can be proud of the achievements of their older students; and with an increase in the proportion of the population in some form of higher education from 7 per cent in the 1960s to 33 per cent today, it seems clear that comprehensive schools have successfully answered the challenge of providing our universities and colleges with a sufficient number of well-qualified and well-motivated students.

THE NEED FOR EXAMINATION REFORM

It can be argued that young people have to sit *far too many* examinations in their eleven years of compulsory schooling. A recent survey, commissioned by the Professional Association of Teachers and backed by the Secondary Heads Association and the Children's Society, found that by the age of 16, most youngsters will have taken sixty or more external tests and examinations (based on the number of individual papers in each subject) – with the figure rising to around seventy-five for those staying on into the sixth form. The report, titled *Tested to Destruction? A Survey of Examination Stress in Teenagers* and published in August 2000, found that examination stress was severely damaging teenagers' physical and emotional well-being. Based on detailed responses from more than 8,000 secondary school students in England and Wales, the report claimed that many teenagers were enduring a variety of stress-related illnesses, had difficulty sleeping and were developing eating disorders such as bulimia and anorexia (reported in *The Guardian*, 4 August 2000). Yet far from heeding the results of this survey, the government has recently announced (*The Sunday Telegraph*, 15 October 2000) that compulsory school tests are to be introduced for those 12-year-olds who failed to reach the required standard in the existing primary school tests taken at 11.

As I have argued elsewhere (Chitty 2000b), one examination that *could* be shelved in the immediate future, thereby relieving teenagers of a good deal of stress, is the

General Certificate of Secondary Education (GCSE). Although this was introduced as recently as the autumn of 1986, with the first papers being taken in the summer of 1988, there are strong arguments for claiming that it has already outlived its usefulness. For one thing, because the all-important performance tables concentrate to an alarming degree on the percentage of Year 11 students achieving the 'top' GCSE grades, schools appear to be focusing all their efforts on their 'average' students while neglecting those youngsters thought unable to contribute to the five A–C grades benchmark. As a result, the percentage of candidates awarded a C grade is rising more sharply than the proportion awarded As and Bs, while the gap between high-scoring and low-scoring students is steadily rising. What this means in reality is that the GCSE has become, like the O-level it superseded, an examination for the 'brightest' students. Very few employers or parents take much notice of the grades below C. Yet, looked at in a less positive light, fewer than half of all Year 11 students achieve five A–C grades; and about 40,000 young people leave school each year without any qualifications. Above all, if we are serious about moving towards a situation where 18 is the effective school-leaving age, there seems little point in continuing with a major school examination at 16. In the words of an editorial in *The Independent*:

> An academic exam at the end of compulsory schooling which fails to give half its students a proper qualification is worthless. An exam at 16 is the last thing we need at a time when we are trying to encourage everyone to stay longer in education and training to help both themselves and the economy. For students in America and in most of Europe, there is no important student exam at 16: the first big hurdle comes at 18. In this country, sadly, the idea of a school-leaving certificate at 16 persists among parents, employers and the general public. The end of the GCSE would, in fact, bolster the belief that, for the vast majority, secondary education ends at the age of 18.
>
> (*The Independent*, 26 August 1999)

THE PRIVATISING AGENDA

New Labour has clearly embraced the Conservatives' obsession with league tables, testing and teacher accountability. It has also, perhaps more surprisingly, carried forward the previous government's privatising agenda.

The Education Secretary seemed remarkably unperturbed when Surrey County Council took the decision in October 1998 to invite bids for the contract to run a 'failing' comprehensive school in Guildford; and in February 1999, it was announced that the 'contract' had been awarded to 3E's Ltd, the commercial wing of Kingshurst City Technology College in Solihull.

Then, in November 1999, it was announced that Cambridge Education Associates – a consultancy that is also the largest contractor for school inspections – was the preferred bidder to take over all (or nearly all) the functions of Islington Local Education Authority in North London, arguably the *first* major privatisation of an LEA. Hackney Local Education Authority was already in the process of having *some* of its services privatised, but Islington would be the first to have *most* – probably *all* – functions run by a private contractor. Announcing the decision to the media, Schools Minister Estelle Morris said that the DfEE and Islington were determined that this would mark 'a new beginning'. She went on to tell reporters that she expected services to be privatised in up to fifteen more local education authorities (reported in *The Independent*, 27 November 1999).

Yet there are many who worry that the government's new privatising measures will result in a general undermining of local democratic accountability. At its annual conference held in London in May 2000, the Socialist Educational Association (SEA) set about drafting a manifesto for the next general election based on the fundamental principle of democracy in education. The delegates supported the vision set out by chairperson Peter Holland of 'a comprehensive and community-based education system with public participation at school and LEA level and with both levels being given adequate powers and resources to fulfil their roles'. In a keynote speech, Labour MP Tony Benn, whose wife Caroline was a founder of the SEA, argued that the privatisation (partial or otherwise) of the public education service and the setting up of further quangos and bureaucracies would serve to alienate teachers and parents. By-passing the LEAs would create more inequalities, demoralise teachers and increase the anxieties of the general public – as had privatising measures in the National Health Service. The New Labour project had simply taken over the market ideology of the Conservatives, along with privatisation and selection by ability and aptitude. But, in Tony Benn's view, it was not clear that there was broad popular support for the government's divisive education agenda:

> Middle England is not that keen on selection and is increasingly insecure about its future in terms of jobs, children's future, health and retirement prospects. They are looking to the democratic process to protect them and to the education system to help reduce inequalities and privileges. Schools should be the places where people come to discuss their problems and where local councillors can talk to them.
>
> (reported in *Educational Journal*, June 2000, p.13)

TEACHER MORALE

Following up one of Tony Benn's main arguments in the speech quoted above, there is much evidence to support the view that many of New Labour's education policies have had the effect of demoralising and antagonising both teachers and parents. It was surely a mistake for former Minister of State Stephen Byers to 'name and shame' the eighteen 'worst performing schools' shortly after taking office. Then again, the phasing of the 1998 pay settlement – inexcusable during a teacher supply crisis – was an easily avoidable error that lost much teacher goodwill. Most important of all, the decision by Tony Blair to emphasise *before* the 1997 General Election that Chris Woodhead would enjoy his full support as Chief Inspector of

Schools in the event of a Labour victory created considerable alarm throughout the education world. It is arguable that Woodhead failed to provide the degree of independence that his role should have guaranteed, and the joy that greeted news of his departure on 2 November 2000 showed that he had certainly succeeded in incurring the wrath of the vast majority of teachers, educationists and chief education officers.

The Prime Minister's keynote speech at the Labour Party Conference held in Brighton in September 2000 made clear his strong belief that many shortcomings were still to be addressed in the nation's secondary schools; and this left the strong impression that, henceforth, teachers had to be wholehearted advocates of the government's modernising project. Indeed, secondary teachers could be forgiven for thinking that their professionalism and expertise have been consistently under attack since the mid-1970s. The idea that many of them have been wedded to harmful and discredited practices, like mixed-ability teaching and policies showing a distaste for excellence, has been extremely damaging for teacher morale and confidence.

WHAT FUTURE FOR SECONDARY EDUCATION?

The glaring contradictions and inconsistencies in government education policy raise a number of important questions, which need to be addressed in the immediate future:

- How will the (albeit delayed) introduction of 'performance-related pay' enhance teacher morale *on a broad front* and avoid a situation where competition and envy reign supreme in most school staff rooms?
- Will a narrow concentration on the acquisition of a number of basic skills (which seems a likely future scenario for the framework for Key Stage 3) be compatible with the provision of a broad 'entitlement curriculum' for all students?
- Is there still a case for a 'common examination' for 16-year-old students at a time when many teenagers are following vocational courses from the age of 14 onwards and there is the real promise of a new school-leaving age of 18?
- Is the government really committed to a *comprehensive* system of secondary education (albeit in co-existence with a flourishing and privileged independent sector); or is it seeking to destroy the system by following and accelerating the Conservative policy of 'selection by specialisation'?
- Above all, is there any pressure at the DfEE for the creation of new admissions policies for all secondary schools that will be fair to all students, irrespective of their class, gender or ethnic status?

Without answers to these fundamental questions, many teachers and educationalists will view the future with considerable alarm and trepidation.

SUGGESTED ACTIVITIES

1. Comprehensive schools are very often criticised in the press and by politicians as having 'failed' large numbers of students and having contributed to 'falling standards' – and it is easy to accept uncritically this common-sense view.

    What is your own informed view of the comprehensive system, however, at this particular point in its history? It might be helpful to focus on what you think comprehensive education has *achieved* in terms of the needs of all sectors of society, and of some of the failings and difficulties of the system it has replaced. (This activity is intended for primary as well as for secondary teachers.)

2. If you were given the task of sitting down and constructing, from scratch, an educational agenda for the new millennium, what would that agenda look like and what would it prioritise?

    In approaching this challenge, it might be helpful to start with broad educational aims, philosophies and objectives before focusing on specific issues such as curriculum content and design, pedagogy, forms and loci of assessment, equality of opportunity, and continuity.

    It is important, too, to dare to be fairly iconoclastic and not to start with any 'givens'. You might decide, for example, that you wanted to scrap the typical current arrangement of primary, secondary and tertiary education in favour of something radically different – or that instead of beginning by itemising the detail of what was to be covered in the national curriculum (if, indeed, you had one) you began by prioritising the development of learning or social, political and collaborative skills.

SUGGESTED READING

Docking, J. (ed.) (2000) *New Labour's Policies for Schools: Raising the Standard?* This collection of twelve essays reviews the policies pursued by the New Labour government to raise standards in schools. It provides the main facts about current national initiatives for schools and offers a useful framework for analysing these critically and informatively.

DfEE (2001) *Schools: Building on Success: Raising Standards, Promoting Diversity, Achieving Results*. This important Green Paper, published in February 2001, sets out the 'achievements' of the Labour government since 1997 and its plans for the years ahead. One of its main themes is the need to 'transform' secondary education by 'modernising' the comprehensive principle and creating a large number of specialist schools. There will also be a broadening of the range of specialisms available, with engineering, science and business and enterprise joining technology, languages, sport and the arts.

Appendix A

Source: *School Teachers' Pay and Conditions Document*, 1999, pp. 65–70

PART XII – Conditions of Employment of Teachers other than Head Teachers

Exercise of general professional duties

48.1   Subject to paragraph 30.5, 31.2, 31.3 and 48.2, a teacher who is not a head teacher shall carry out the professional duties of a teacher as circumstances may require:

48.1.1 if he is employed as a teacher in a school, under the reasonable direction of the head teacher of that school;

48.1.2 if he is employed by an authority on terms under which he is not assigned to any one school, under the reasonable direction of that authority and of the head teacher of any school in which he may for the time being be required to work as a teacher.

48.2   A teacher who has failed satisfactorily to complete an induction period and who is employed pursuant to regulation 16(5) of the Induction Regulations must only carry out such limited teaching duties as the Secretary of State determines pursuant to that regulation.

Exercise of particular duties

49.1   Subject to paragraph 30.5, 31.2, 31.3, and 48.2 a teacher employed as a teacher (other than a head teacher) in a school shall perform, in accordance with any directions which may reasonably be given to him by the head teacher from time to time, such particular duties as may reasonably be assigned to him.

49.2   A teacher employed by an authority on terms such as those described in paragraph 48.1.2 shall perform, in accordance with any direction which may reasonably be given to him from time to time by the authority or by the head teacher of any school in which he may for the time being be required to work as a teacher, such particular duties as may reasonably be assigned to him.

Professional duties

50.   Subject to paragraph 30.5, 31.2, 31.3, and 48.2 the following duties shall be deemed to be included in the professional duties which a teacher (other than a head teacher) may be required to perform:

50.1   **Teaching**:

In each case having regard to the curriculum for the school:

50.1.1   planning and preparing courses and lessons;

50.1.2   teaching, according to their educational needs, the pupils assigned to him, including the setting and marking of work to be carried out by the pupil in school and elsewhere;

50.1.3   assessing, recording and reporting on the development, progress and attainment of pupils;

50.2   **Other activities**:

50.2.1   promoting the general progress and well-being of individual pupils and of any class or group of pupils assigned to him;

50.2.2   providing guidance and advice to pupils on educational and social matters and on their further education and future careers, including information about sources of more expert advice on specific questions; making relevant records and reports;

50.2.3   making records of and reports on the personal and social needs of pupils;

50.2.4   communicating and consulting with the parents of pupils;

50.2.5   communicating and co-operating with persons or bodies outside the school; and

50.2.6   participating in meetings arranged for any of the purposes described above;

50.3   **Assessments and reports**:

providing or contributing to oral and written assessments, reports and references relating to individual pupils and groups of pupils;

50.4   **Appraisal**:

participating in arrangements made in accordance with the Education (School Teacher Appraisal) Regulations 1991 for the appraisal of his performance and that of other teachers;

50.5   **Review, induction, further training and development**:

50.5.1   reviewing from time to time his methods of teaching and programmes of work;

50.5.2   participating in arrangements for his further training and professional development as a teacher;

50.5.3   in the case of a teacher serving an induction period pursuant to the Induction Regulations, participating in arrangements for his supervision and training;

50.6   **Educational methods**:

advising and co-operating with the head teacher and other teachers (or any one or more of them) on the preparation and development of courses of study, teaching materials, teaching programmes, methods of teaching and assessment and pastoral arrangements;

50.7   **Discipline, health and safety**:

maintaining good order and discipline among the pupils and safe-guarding their health and safety both when they are authorised to be on the school premises and when they are engaged in authorised school activities elsewhere;

50.8   **Staff meetings**:

participating in meetings at the school which relate to the curriculum for the school or the administration or organisation of the school, including pastoral arrangements;

50.9   **Cover**:

50.9.1   subject to paragraph 50.9.2, supervising and so far as practicable teaching any pupils whose teacher is not available to teach them:

50.9.2   subject to the exceptions in paragraph 50.9.3, no teacher shall be required to provide such cover:

(a)   after the teacher who is absent or otherwise not available has been so for three or more consecutive working days; or

(b)   where the fact that the teacher would be absent or otherwise not available for a period exceeding three consecutive working days was known to the maintaining authority or, in the case of a school which has a delegated budget to the governing body, for two or more working days before the absence commenced;

50.9.3   the exceptions are:

(a)   he is a teacher employed wholly or mainly for the purpose of providing such cover ('a supply teacher'); or

(b)   the authority or the governing body (as the case may be) have exhausted all reasonable means of providing a supply teacher to provide cover without success; or

(c)   he is a full-time teacher at the school but has been assigned by the head teacher in the time-table to teach or carry out other specified duties (except cover) for less than 75 per cent of those hours in the week during which pupils are taught at the school;

50.10   **Public examinations**:

participating in arrangements for preparing pupils for public examinations and in assessing pupils for the purposes of such examinations; recording and reporting such assessments; and participating in arrangements for pupils' presentation for and supervision during such examinations;

50.11   **Management**:

50.11.1   contributing to the selection for appointment and professional development of other teachers and non-teaching staff, including the induction and assessment of new teachers and teachers serving induction periods pursuant to the Induction Regulations;

50.11.2   co-ordinating or managing the work of other teachers; and

50.11.3   taking such part as may be required of him in the review, development and management of activities relating to the curriculum, organisation and pastoral functions of the school;

50.12   **Administration**:

50.12.1   participating in administrative and organisational tasks related to such duties as are described above, including the management or supervision of persons providing support for the teachers in the school and the ordering and allocation of equipment and materials; and

50.12.2   attending assemblies, registering the attendance of pupils and supervising pupils, whether these duties are to be performed before, during or after school sessions.

Working time

51.1   The provisions of this paragraph shall not apply to deputy head teachers, advanced skills teachers or to teachers employed to teach part-time and are subject to paragraphs 30.5, 31.2 and 31.3.

51.2   A teacher employed full-time, other than in the circumstances described in paragraph 51.4, shall be available for work for 195 days in any school year, of which 190 days shall be days on which he may be required to teach pupils in addition to carrying out other duties; and those 195 days shall be specified by his employer or, if the employer so directs, by the head teacher.

51.3   Such a teacher shall be available to perform such duties at such times and such places as may be specified by the head teacher (or, where the teacher is not assigned to any one school, by his employer or the head teacher of any school in which he may for the time being be required to work as a teacher) for 1265 hours in any school year, those hours to be allocated reasonably throughout those days in the school year on which he is required to be available for work.

51.4   Paragraphs 51.2 and 51.3 do not apply to such a teacher employed wholly or mainly to teach or perform other duties in relation to pupils in a residential establishment.

51.5   Time spent in travelling to or from the place of work shall not count against the 1265 hours referred to in paragraph 51.3.

51.6   Such a teacher shall not be required under his contract as a teacher to undertake midday supervision, and shall be allowed a break of reasonable length either between school sessions or between the hours of 12 noon and 2.00pm.

51.7   Such a teacher shall, in addition to the requirements set out in paragraphs 51.2 and 51.3, work such additional hours as may be needed to enable him to discharge effectively his professional duties, including, in particular, the marking of pupils' work, the writing of reports on pupils and the preparation of lessons, teaching material and teaching programmes. The amount of time required for this purpose beyond the 1265 hours referred to in paragraph 51.3 and the times outside the 1265 specified hours at which duties shall be performed shall not be defined by the employer but shall depend upon the work needed to discharge the teacher's duties.

Appendix B

Source: Annex A, Section D.
of DfEE Circular 4/98, p.16

D. OTHER PROFESSIONAL REQUIREMENTS

Primary and secondary

For all courses, those to be awarded Qualified Teacher Status should, when assessed, demonstrate that they:

a. have a working knowledge and understanding of:

   i.   teachers' professional duties as set out in the current School Teachers' Pay and Conditions document, issued under the School Teachers' Pay and Conditions Act 1991;

   ii. teachers' legal liabilities and responsibilities relating to:

   - the Race Relations Act 1976;

   - the Sex Discrimination Act 1975;

   - Section 7 and Section 8 of the Health and Safety at Work etc. Act 1974;

   - teachers' common law duty to ensure that pupils are healthy and safe on school premises and when leading activities off the school site, such as educational visits, school outings or field trips;

   - what is reasonable for the purposes of safeguarding or promoting children's welfare (Section 3(5) of the Children Act 1989);

   - the role of the education service in protecting children from abuse (currently set out in DfEE Circular 10/95 and the Home Office, Department of Health, DfEE and Welsh Office Guidance '*Working Together: A guide to arrangements for inter-agency co-operation for the protection of children from abuse 1991*');

   - appropriate physical contact with pupils (currently set out in DfEE Circular 10/95);

- appropriate physical restraint of pupils (Section 4 of the Education Act 1997 and DfEE Circular 9/94);

- detention of pupils on disciplinary grounds (Section 5 of the Education Act 1997).

b. have established, during work in schools, effective working relationships with professional colleagues including, where applicable, associate staff;

c. set a good example to the pupils they teach, through their presentation and their personal and professional conduct;

d. are committed to ensuring that every pupil is given the opportunity to achieve their potential and meet the high expectations set for them;

e. understand the need to take responsibility for their own professional development and to keep up to date with research and developments in pedagogy and in the subjects they teach;

f. understand their professional responsibilities in relation to school policies and practices, including those concerned with pastoral and personal safety matters, including bullying;

g. recognise that learning takes place inside and outside the school context, and understand the need to liaise effectively with parents and other carers and with agencies with responsibility for pupils' education and welfare;

h. are aware of the role and purpose of school governing bodies.

References

Aldrich, R. (1988) 'The National Curriculum: an historical perspective', in Lawton, D. and Chitty, C. (eds) *The National Curriculum*, Bedford Way Paper 33, Institute of Education, University of London, pp. 21–33.

Arblaster, A. (1970) 'Education and ideology', in Rubinstein, D. and Stoneman, C. (eds) *Education for Democracy*, Harmondsworth, Penguin, pp. 49–55.

Arnott, M. and Weiner, G. (eds) (1987) *Gender and the Politics of Schooling*, London, Hutchinson/Open University Press.

Arnott, M., David, M. and Weiner, G. (1996) *Educational Reforms and Gender Equality in Schools*, Manchester, Equal Opportunities Commission.

Baker, K. (1993) *The Turbulent Years: My Life in Politics*, London, Faber and Faber.

Baker, N. (1988) 'Facts versus morals', *The Times Educational Supplement*, 22 April.

Basini, A. (1996) 'Race', in Docking, J. (ed.) *National School Policy: Major Issues in Education Policy for Schools in England and Wales, 1979 Onwards*, London, David Fulton, in association with Roehampton Institute, London, pp. 86–99.

Batteson, C.H. (1999) 'The 1944 Education Act reconsidered', *Educational Review*, Vol. 51, No. 1, February, pp. 5–15.

Benn, C. and Chitty, C. (1996) *Thirty Years On: Is Comprehensive Education Alive and Well or Struggling to Survive?* (1st edn), London, David Fulton.

Benn, C. and Chitty, C. (1997) *Thirty Years On: Is Comprehensive Education Alive and Well or Struggling to Survive?* (2nd edn), Harmondsworth, Penguin.

Benn, T. (1987) 'British politics 1945–87: a perspective', in Hennessy, P. and Seldon, A. (eds) *Ruling Performance: British Governments from Attlee to Thatcher*, Oxford, Basil Blackwell, pp. 301–8.

Blishen, E. (1957) 'The potentialities of secondary modern school pupils', in Simon, B. (ed.) *New Trends in English Education*, London, Macgibbon and Kee, pp. 74–82.

Bogdanor, V. (1979) 'Power and participation', *Oxford Review of Education*, Vol. 5, No. 2, pp. 157–68.

Bösche, S. and Mackay, L. (1983) *Jenny Lives with Eric and Martin*, London, Gay Men's Press.

Boyle, E. (1972) 'The politics of secondary school reorganisation: some reflections', *Journal of Educational Administration and History*, Vol. 4, No. 2, June, pp 28–38.

Brandt, G. (1986) *The Realisation of Anti-Racist Teaching*, Lewes, Falmer Press.

Broudy, H.S., Smith, B.O. and Burnett, J.R. (1964) *Democracy and Excellence in American Secondary Education*, Chicago, Rand McNally.

Bush, T. Coleman, M. and Glover, D. (1993) *Managing Autonomous Schools: The Grant-Maintained Experience*, London, Paul Chapman.

Butler, R.A. (1971) *The Art of the Possible*, London, Hamish Hamilton.

Campbell, I. (1992) 'Key Stage Four: an opportunity?' *Forum*, Vol. 34, No. 4, autumn, pp. 105–7.

Chitty, C. (1979) 'The common curriculum', *Forum*, Vol. 21, No. 2, spring, pp. 61–5.

Chitty, C. (1988) 'Two models of a national curriculum: origins and interpretation', in Lawton, D. and Chitty, C. (eds) *The National Curriculum*, Bedford Way Paper 33, Institute of Education, University of London, pp. 34–48.

Chitty, C. (1989) *Towards a New Education System: The Victory of the New Right?* Lewes, Falmer Press.

Chitty, C. (1992) 'Key Stage Four: the National Curriculum abandoned?' *Forum*, Vol. 34, No. 2, spring, pp. 38–40.

Chitty, C. (ed.) (1993a) *The National Curriculum: Is it Working?* Harlow, Longman.

Chitty, C. (1993b) 'Great Debate or great betrayal?' *Education Today and Tomorrow*, Vol. 44, No. 3, pp. 9–11.

Chitty, C. (1997a) 'Interview with Keith Joseph', in Ribbins, P. and Sherratt, B. (eds) *Radical Educational Policies and Conservative Secretaries of State*, London, Cassell, pp. 78–86.

Chitty, C. (1997b) 'Privatisation and marketisation', *Oxford Review of Education*, Vol. 23, No. 1, pp. 45–62.

Chitty, C. (1997c) 'The White Paper: missed opportunities' *Forum*, Vol. 39, No.3, autumn, pp. 71–2.

Chitty, C. (1998a) 'Education Action Zones: test-beds for privatisation?', *Forum*, Vol. 40, No. 3, autumn, pp. 79–81.

Chitty, C. (1988b) 'Secondary education in the Wilson years: the comprehensive school becomes national policy', *Revue Française de Civilisation Britannique*, Vol. 10, No. 1, pp. 131–41.

Chitty, C. (1999) *The Educational System Transformed* (2nd edn), Tisbury, Baseline Books.

Chitty, C. (2000a) 'Intolerance, ignorance, bigotry: the story of Section 28', *Forum*, Vol. 42, No. 1, spring, pp. 1–3.

Chitty, C. (2000b) 'Why the GCSE should be abolished', *Forum*, Vol. 42, No. 1, spring, pp. 28–31.

Chitty, C. and Dunford, J. (eds) (1999) *State Schools: New Labour and the Conservative Legacy*, London, Woburn Press.

Chitty, C. and Simon, B. (eds) (1993) *Education Answers Back: Critical Responses to Government Policy*, London, Lawrence & Wishart.

Cole, M. (ed.) (1999) *Professional Issues for Teachers and Student Teachers*, London, David Fulton.

Conservative Party (1979) *The Conservative Manifesto*, London, Conservative Central Office, April.

Corbett, A. (1969) 'The Tory educators', *New Society*, 22 May, pp. 785–7.

Cox, C.B. and Boyson, R. (eds) (1975) *Black Paper 1975: The Fight for Education*, London, Dent.

Cox, C.B., and Boyson, R. (eds) (1977) *Black Paper 1977*, London, Maurice Temple Smith.

Cox, C.B., and Dyson, A.E. (eds) (1969a) *Fight for Education: A Black Paper*, London, Critical Quarterly Society.

Cox, C.B., and Dyson, A.E. (eds) (1969b) *Black Paper Two: The Crisis in Education*, London, Critical Quarterly Society.

Cox, C.B. and Dyson, A.E. (eds) (1970) *Black Paper Three: Goodbye Mr Short*, London, Critical Quarterly Society.

CPS (Centre for Policy Studies) (1988) *Correct Core: Simple Curricula for English, Maths and Science*, London, Centre for Policy Studies, March.

CRE (Commission for Racial Equality) (2000) *Inspecting Schools for Race Equality: OFSTED's Strengths and Weaknesses*, London, CRE.

Crosland, C.A.R. (1956) *The Future of Socialism*, London, Jonathan Cape.

Dadzie, S. (2000) *Toolkit for Tackling Racism in Schools*, Stoke-on-Trent, Trentham Books.

Dale, R. (1983) 'Thatcherism and education', in Ahier, J. and Flude, M. (eds) *Contemporary Education Policy*, London, Croom Helm, pp. 223–55.

Davies, P. (1988) 'Sexuality: a new minefield in schools, *The Independent*, 26 May.

Dent, H.C. (1968) *The Education Act, 1944* (12th edn), London, University of London Press.

DES (Department of Education and Science) (1965) *The Organisation of Secondary Education* (Circular 10/65), London, HMSO.

DES (Department of Education and Science) (1967) *Children and their Primary Schools* (2 vols) (The Plowden Report), London, HMSO.

DES (Department of Education and Science) (1976) *School Education in England: Problems and Initiatives* (The Yellow Book), London, DES.

DES (Department of Education and Science) (1977a) *Education in Schools: A Consultative Document* (Cmnd 6869) (Green Paper), London, HMSO.

DES (Department of Education and Science) (1977b) *Curriculum 11–16* (HMI Red Book 1), London, HMSO, December.

DES (Department of Education and Science (1978) *Special Educational Needs* (The Warnock Report), London, HMSO.

DES (Department of Education and Science) (1979) *Aspects of Secondary Education in England: A Survey by HM Inspectors of Schools*, London, HMSO.

DES (Department of Education and Science) (1980) *A Framework for the School Curriculum*, London, HMSO.

DES (Department of Education and Science) (1981a) *The School Curriculum*, London, HMSO.

DES (Department of Education and Science) (1981b) *Curriculum 11–16: A Review of Progress* (HMI Red Book 2), London, HMSO.

DES (Department of Education and Science) (1983) *Curriculum 11–16: Towards a Statement of Entitlement: Curricular Reappraisal in Action* (HMI Red Book 3), London, HMSO.

DES (Department of Education and Science) (1985a) *The Curriculum from 5 to 16* (HMI Series: Curriculum Matters 2), London, HMSO.

DES (Department of Education and Science) (1985b) *Better Schools* (Cmnd 9469), London, HMSO.

DES (Department of Education and Science) (1985c) *Education for All* (The Swann Report) (Cmnd 9453), London, HMSO.

DES (Department of Education and Science) (1987a) *The National Curriculum 5 to 16: A Consultation Document*, London, DES.

DES (Department of Education and Science) (1987b) *Sex Education at School* (Circular 11/87), London, HMSO.

DES (Department of Education and Science) (1988a) *Education Reform Act: Grant-Maintained Schools* (Circular 10/88), London, HMSO.

DES (Department of Education and Science) (1988b) *National Curriculum Task Group on Assessment and Testing: A Report*, London, DES.

Dewey, J. (1916) *Democracy and Education*, New York, Macmillan.

DfE (Department for Education) (1992) *Choice and Diversity: A New Framework for Schools* (Cmnd 2021), London, HMSO.

DfE (Department for Education) (1994) *Education Act 1993: Sex Education in Schools* (Circular 5/94), London, HMSO.

DfEE (Department for Education and Employment) (1995) *Protecting Children from Abuse: The Role of the Education Service* (Circular 10/95), London, DfEE.

DfEE (Department for Education and Employment) (1996a) *Equipping Young People for Working Life*, London, DfEE.

DfEE (Department for Education and Employment) (1996b) *Admissions to Maintained Schools* (Circular 6/96), London, HMSO.

DfEE (Department for Education and Employment) (1996c) *Self-Government for Schools* (Cmnd 3315), London, HMSO.

DfEE (Department for Education and Employment) (1997) *Excellence in Schools* (Cmnd 3681), London, HMSO.

DfEE (Department for Education and Employment) (1998a) *Teaching: High Status, High Standards – Requirements for Courses of Initial Teacher Training* (Circular 4/98), London, DfEE.

DfEE (Department for Education and Employment) (1998b) *Teachers – Meeting the Challenge of Change* (Cmnd 4164), London, HMSO.

DfEE (Department for Education and Employment) (1999) *School Teachers' Pay and Conditions Document 1999* (The Blue Book), London, HMSO.

DfEE (Department for Education and Employment) (2000) *Sex and Relationship Education Guidance*, London, DfEE.

DfEE (Department for Education and Employment) (2001) *Schools: Building on Success: Raising Standards, Promoting Diversity, Achieving Results* (Cmnd 5050), London, HMSO.

DfEE/QCA (Department for Education and Employment/Qualifications and Curriculum Authority (1998) *Education for Citizenship and the Teaching of Democracy in Schools: Final Report of the Advisory Group on Citizenship*, London, DfEE.

DoE (Department of the Environment) (1988) *Local Government Act 1988* (Circular 12/88) London, DoE.

Docking, J. (ed.) (2000) *New Labour's Policies for Schools: Raising the Standard*, London, David Fulton.

Dunford, J. (1999) 'The comprehensive success story', *Forum*, Vol. 41, No. 1, spring, pp. 28–30.

Edwards, G. and Kelly, A.V. (eds) (1998) *Experience and Education: Towards an Alternative National Curriculum*, London, Paul Chapman.

Elliott, J. (1993) 'The relationship between "understanding" and "developing" teachers' thinking', in Elliott, J. (ed.) *Reconstructing Teacher Education*, London, Falmer Press.

Elton, Lord (1989) *Discipline in Schools – The Report of the Committee of Enquiry chaired by Lord Elton* (The Elton Report), London, HMSO.

Epstein, D., Elwood, J., Hey, V. and Maw, J. (eds) (1998) *Failing Boys? Issues in Gender and Achievement*, Buckingham, Open University Press.

Evans, K. (1985) *The Development and Structure of the English School System*, Sevenoaks, Hodder and Stoughton.

Fenwick, I.G.K. (1976) *The Comprehensive School 1944–1970: The Politics of Secondary School Reorganisation*, London, Methuen.

Finn, D. (1987) *Training Without Jobs: New Deals and Broken Promises*, London, Macmillan.

Floud, J. (1962) 'The sociology of education', in Welford, A.T. *et al.* (eds) *Society: Problems and Methods of Study*, London, Routledge & Kegan Paul.

Floud, J.E., Halsey, A.H. and Martin, F.M. (1956) *Social Class and Educational Opportunity*, London, Heineman.

Ford, J. (1969) *Social Class and the Comprehensive School*, London, Routledge & Kegan Paul.

Gaine, C. (1995) *Still No Problem Here*, Stoke-on-Trent, Trentham Books.

Gaine, C. and George, R. (1999) *Gender, 'Race' and Class in Schooling: A New Introduction*, London, Falmer Press.

Giddens, A. (1998) *The Third Way: The Renewal of Social Democracy*, Cambridge, Polity Press.

Giddens, A. (2000) *The Third Way and its Critics*, Cambridge, Polity Press.

Gipps, C. (1988) 'The TGAT Report: trick or treat?' *Forum*, Vol. 31, No. 1, autumn, pp. 4–7.

Glass, D.V. (Ed.) (1954) *Social Mobility in Britain*, London, Routledge.

Glennerster, H. and Low, W. (1990) 'Education and the Welfare State: does it add up?' in Hills, I. (ed.) *The State of Welfare: The Welfare State in Britain since 1974*, Oxford, Oxford University Press, pp. 28–87.

Graham, D. and Tytler, D. (1993) *A Lesson for Us All: The Making of the National Curriculum*, London, Routledge.

Grant, L. (1994) 'Inside story', *Guardian Weekend*, 22 October, pp. 37–46.

Griggs, C. (1985) *Private Education in Britain*, Lewes, Falmer Press.

Halsey, A.H. (1965) 'Education and equality', *New Society*, 17 June, pp. 13–15.

Hargreaves, D.H. (1967) *Social Relations in a Secondary School*, London, Routledge & Kegan Paul.

Hargreaves, D.H. (1982) *The Challenge for the Comprehensive School: Culture, Curriculum and Community*, London, Routledge & Kegan Paul.

Hatcher, R. (1998) 'Profiting from schools: business and education action zones', *Education and Social Justice*, Vol. 1, No. 1, autumn, pp. 9–16.

Hill, D. and Cole, M. (eds) (1999) *Promoting Equality in Secondary Schools*, London, Cassell.

Hillgate Group (1986) *Whose Schools? A Radical Manifesto*, London, The Hillgate Group.

Hillgate Group (1987) *The Reform of British Education: From Principles to Practice*, London, The Hillgate Group.

HMSO (Her Majesty's Stationery Office) (1987) *Teachers' Pay and Conditions Act 1987*, London, HMSO.

HMSO (Her Majesty's Stationery Office) (1991) *Teachers' Pay and Conditions Act 1991*, London, HMSO.

HMSO (Her Majesty's Stationery Office) (1999) *The Stephen Lawrence Inquiry: Report of an Inquiry by Sir William Macpherson of Cluny*, London, HMSO.

Holt, M. (1976) 'Non-streaming and the common curriculum', *Forum*, Vol. 18, No. 2, spring, pp. 55–7.

Holt, M. (1978) *The Common Curriculum: Its Structure and Style in the Comprehensive School*, London, Routledge & Kegan Paul.

Jackson, B. and Marsden, D. (1962) *Education and the Working Class*, London, Routledge and Kegan Paul.

Jarvis, F. (1993) Education and Mr. Major: *Correspondence between the Prime Minister and Fred Jarvis, with a Commentary and Postscript* by Fred Jarvis, London, Tufnell Press.

Jeffery-Poulter, S. (1991) *Peers, Queens and Commons: The Struggle for Gay Law Reform from 1950 to the Present*, London, Routledge.

Jones, K. (1989) *Right Turn: The Conservative Revolution in Education*, London, Hutchinson Radius.

Joseph, K. (1981) speech to the Conservative Party Conference.

Joseph, K. (1982) speech to the Institute of Directors (printed in full in a supplement to *The Director*, May, pp. 33–5).

Karabel, J. and Halsey, A.H. (1977) 'Educational research: a review and an interpretation' in Karabel, J. and Halsey, A.H. (eds) *Power and Ideology in Education*, New York, Oxford University Press, pp. 1–85.

Kerckhoff, A.C., Fogelman, K., Crook, D. and Reeder, D. (1996) *Going Comprehensive in England and Wales: A Study of Uneven Change*, London, Woburn Press.

Knight, C. (1990) *The Making of Tory Education Policy in Post-war Britain, 1950–1986*, Lewes, Falmer Press.

Kogan, M. (1971) *The Politics of Education: Edward Boyle and Anthony Crosland in Conversation with Maurice Kogan*, Harmondsworth, Penguin.

Labour Party (1995) *Diversity and Excellence: A New Partnership for Schools*, London, Labour Party.

Labour Party (1997) *Because Britain Deserves Better* (New Labour Election Manifesto), London, Labour Party.

Lawn, M. (1996) *Modern Times? Work, Professionalism and Citizenship in Teaching*, London, Falmer Press.

Lawton, D. (1969) 'The idea of an integrated curriculum', *University of London Institute of Education Bulletin*, new series, 19, autumn, pp. 5–12.

Lawton, D. (1973) *Social Change, Educational Theory and Curriculum Planning*, Sevenoaks, Hodder & Stoughton.

Lawton, D. (1980) *The Politics of the School Curriculum*, London, Routledge & Kegan Paul.

Lawton, D. (1983) *Curriculum Studies and Educational Planning*, Sevenoaks, Hodder & Stoughton.

Lawton, D. (1984) *The Tightening Grip: Growth of Central Control of the School Curriculum*, Bedford Way Paper 21, Institute of Education, University of London.

Lawton, D. (1993) 'Is there coherence and purpose in the National Curriculum?' in Chitty, C. and Simon, B. (eds) *Education Answers Back: Critical Responses to Government Policy*, London, Lawrence & Wishart, pp. 61–9.

Lawton, D. (1994) *The Tory Mind on Education, 1979–94*, London, Falmer Press.

Lawton, D. and Gordon, P. (1987) *HMI*, London, Routledge & Kegan Paul.

LSI (Local Schools Information) (1992) *Opting Out 1988–1992: An Analysis*, London, LSI.

Loughran, J. (1996) *Developing Reflective Practice: Learning about Teaching and Learning through Modelling*, London, Falmer Press.

Mac an Ghaill, M. (1994) *The Making of Men: Masculinities, Sexualities and Schooling*, Buckingham, Open University Press.

Major, J. (1991) 'Education – All Our Futures', speech to the Centre for Policy Studies (CPS) at the Café Royal in London, 3 July.

Mandelson, P. and Liddle, R. (1996) *The Blair Revolution: Can New Labour Deliver?* London, Faber and Faber.

Manzer, R.A. (1970) *Teachers and Politics: The Role of the National Union of Teachers in the Making of National Educational Policy in England and Wales since 1944*, Manchester, Manchester University Press.

Marquand, D. (1988) *The Unprincipled Society: New Demands and Old Politics*, London, Jonathan Cape.

Marquand, D. (2000) 'Revisiting the Blair paradox', *New Left Review*, second series, No. 3, May/June, pp. 73–9.

Mason, M. (1990) 'Special educational needs: just another label', in Rieser, R. and Mason, M. (eds) *Disability Equality in the Classroom: A Human Rights Issue*, London, ILEA, pp. 88–90.

Maw, J. (1985) 'Curriculum control and cultural norms: change and conflict in a British context', *The New Era*, Vol. 66, No. 4, pp. 95–8

McPherson, A. and Willms, J.D. (1988) 'Comprehensive schooling is better and fairer', *Forum*, Vol. 30, No. 2, spring, pp. 39–41.

Ministry of Education (1944) *Education Act 1944*, London, HMSO.

Ministry of Education (1951) *Education 1900–1950* (Cmnd 8244), London, HMSO.

Ministry of Education (1963) *Half Our Future* (The Newsom Report), London, HMSO.

Monks, T.G. (1968) *Comprehensive Education in England and Wales: A Survey of Schools and their Organisation*, National Foundation for Educational Research in England and Wales, Research Reports: Second Series, No. 6, Slough: NFER.

Moore, A. (2000) *Teaching and Learning: Pedagogy, Curriculum and Culture*, London, Routledge Falmer.

Moore, A. and Edwards, G. (2000) 'Compliance, resistance and pragmatism in pedagogic identities', paper presented at the annual conference of the American Educational Research Association, New Orleans, 24–28 April.

Mortimore, J., Mortimore, P. and Chitty, C. (1986) *Secondary School Examinations: 'The Helpful Servants, not the Dominating Master'*, Bedford Way Paper 18, Institute of Education, University of London.

Murphy, P. and Elwood, J. (1998) 'Gendered learning outside and inside school: influences on achievement', in Epstein, D., Elwood, J., Hey, V. and Maw, J. (eds) *Failing Boys? Issues in Gender and Achievement*, Buckingham, Open University Press, pp. 162–81.

NCC/SEAC (National Curriculum Council/School Examinations And Assessment Council) (1993) *The National Curriculum and its Assessment: An Interim Report*, York, NCC; London, SEAC.

Nixon, J. (1999) 'Conditions of service of schoolteachers', in Cole, M. (ed.) *Professional Issues for Teachers and Student Teachers*, London, David Fulton, pp. 1–21.

OFSTED/TTA (Office for Standards in Education/Teacher Training Agency) (1996) *Framework for the Assessment of Quality and Standards in Initial Teacher Training*, 1996/97, London, OFSTED.

Patten, J. (1992) 'Who's Afraid of the "S" Word?' *New Statesman and Society*, 17 July, pp. 20–1.

Pedley, R.R. (1969) 'Comprehensive disaster', in Cox, C.B. and Dyson, A.E. (eds) *Fight for Education: A Black Paper*, London, Critical Quarterly Society, pp. 45–8.

Plummer, G. (2000) *Failing Working-Class Girls*, Stoke-on-Trent, Trentham Books.

Raison, T. (1976) *The Act and the Partnership: An Essay on Education Administration in England*, Centre for Studies in Social Policy, London, Bedford Square Press.

Ranson, S. (1984) 'Towards a tertiary tripartism; new codes of social control and the 17+', in Broadfoot, P. (ed.) *Selection, Certification and Control: Social Issues in Educational Assessment*, Lewes, Falmer Press, pp. 221–44.

Rhodes-James, R. (1986) *Anthony Eden*, London, Weidenfeld & Nicolson.

Rieser, R. and Mason, M. (eds) (1990) *Disability Equality in the Classroom: A Human Rights Issue*, London, ILEA.

RISE (Research and Information on State Education Trust) (1998) *Specialisation Without Selection?* RISE Briefing Paper No. 1, London, RISE.

Robins, D. and Cohen, P. (1978) *Knuckle Sandwich: Growing Up in the Working-Class City*, Harmondsworth, Penguin.

Rubinstein, D. and Simon, B. (1973) *The Evolution of the Comprehensive School, 1926–1972*, London, Routledge & Kegan Paul.

Schon, D.A. (1983) *The Reflective Practitioner: How the Professionals Think in Action*, New York, Basic Books.

Schon, D.A. (1987) *Educating the Reflective Practitioner*, San Francisco, Jossey-Bass.

SCAA (School Curriculum and Assessment Authority) (1993) *The National Curriculum and its Assessment: Final Report*, London, SCAA.

Schools Council (1975) *The Whole Curriculum 13–16* (Working Paper No. 53), London, Evans/Methuen Educational.

Seldon, A. (1986) *The Riddle of the Voucher: An Inquiry into the Obstacles to Introducing Choice and Competition in State Schools*, London, Institute of Economic Affairs.

Seldon, A. (1997) *Major: A Political Life*, London, Weidenfeld & Nicolson.

Sewell, T. (1997) *Black Masculinities and Schooling: How Black Boys Survive Modern Schooling*, Stoke-on-Trent, Trentham Books.

Sexton, S. (1987) *Our Schools: A Radical Policy*, London, Institute of Economic Affairs.

Simon, B. (1965) *Inequalities in Education*, Chelmsford, CASE Publication.

Simon, B. (1985) *Does Education Matter?* London, Lawrence & Wishart.

Simon, B. (1991) *Education and the Social Order, 1940–1990*, London, Lawrence & Wishart.

Simon, B. (2000) 'Blair on education', *Forum*, Vol. 42, No. 3, autumn, pp. 91–3.

Smith, W.O.L. (1957) *Education: An Introductory Survey* (1st edn), Harmondsworth, Penguin.

STA (Socialist Teachers Alliance) (2000) *Members Bulletin*, London, STA, July.

Stuart, N. (1988) Interview for video on *Accountability* produced by LEAP (Local Education Authorities Project).

Sutton Trust (2000) *Entry to Leading Universities*, London, The Sutton Trust.

Taylor, A.J.P. (1965) *English History 1914–1945*, Oxford, Oxford University Press.

Taylor, W. (1963) *The Secondary Modern School*, London, Faber and Faber.

Thatcher, M. (1987) speech to the Conservative Party Conference.

Thomson, R. (1993) 'Unlikely alliances: the recent politics of sex education', in Bristow, J. and Wilson, A.R. (eds) *Activating Theory: Lesbian, Gay, Bisexual Politics*, London, Lawrence & Wishart, pp. 219–45.

Valli, L. (ed.) (1992) *Reflective Teacher Education*, New York, State University of New York Press.

Vernon, B.D. (1982) *Ellen Wilkinson, 1891–1947*, London, Croom Helm.

Watkins, P. (1993) 'The National Curriculum: an agenda for the nineties', in Chitty, C. and Simon, B. (eds) *Education Answers Back: Critical Responses to Government Policy*, London, Lawrence & Wishart, pp. 70–84.

West, E.G. (1965) *Education and the State: A Study in Political Economy* (1st edn), London, Institute of Economic Affairs.

White, J. (1973) *Towards a Compulsory Curriculum*, London, Routledge & Kegan Paul.

Wilby, P. (1977) 'Education and equality', *New Statesman*, 16 September, pp. 358–61.

Williams, R. (1958) *Culture and Society*, London, Chatto & Windus.

Williams, R. (1961) *The Long Revolution*, Harmondsworth, Penguin.

Willis, P. (1977) *Learning to Labour: How Working-Class Kids Get Working-Class Jobs*, Aldershot, Saxon House.

Wright, C. (1992) *Race Relations in the Primary School*, London, David Fulton.

Young, H. (1989) *One of Us: A Biography of Margaret Thatcher* (1st edn), London, Macmillan.

Young, M. and Armstrong, M. (1965) *The Flexible School. The Next Step for Comprehensives. Where*, Supplement No. 5, Cambridge, Advisory Centre for Education.

Index